Meditation Moments

ALSO BY MILLIE STAMM . . .

Be Still and Know

Meditation Moments

MILLIE STAMM

ZONDERVAN
PUBLISHING HOUSE OF THE ZONDERVAN CORPORATION
GRAND RAPIDS, MICHIGAN 49506

MEDITATION MOMENTS
Formerly published as
Meditation Moments for Women

Copyright © 1967 by Zondervan Publishing House, Grand Rapids, Michigan
Library of Congress Catalog Card Number 67-22690

Thirty-third printing 1981

Cloth: ISBN 0-310-32980-9
Paper: ISBN 0-310-32981-7

Printed in the United States of America

In addition to the King James Version, several other modern translations are used in this book, by permission of the publishers, and are identified where they appear:

The New Testament in Modern English, copyright © 1958 by J. B. Phillips, the Macmillan Company.

Living Letters and *Living Gospels,* copyright © 1962 and 1966 respectively, by Tyndale House Publishers.

The Amplified New Testament, copyright © 1958 by the Lockman Foundation. Used by permission of the Zondervan Publishing House.

The Amplified Old Testament, Volume 1. Genesis to Esther, copyright © 1964 by the Zondervan Publishing House.

The Amplified Old Testament, Volume 2. Job to Malachi, copyright © 1962 by the Zondervan Publishing House.

The Holy Bible, The Berkeley Version in Modern English, New Testament portion copyright © 1945 by Gerrit Verkuyl, assigned to Zondervan, 1958, and Old Testament portion copyright © 1959 by Zondervan Publishing House.

In memory of

my beloved companion

Clarke E. Stamm

whose gracious understanding helped make
it possible for this book to be written.

FOREWORD

It is a privilege for us to write the foreword for this first book written by our beloved Millie Stamm.

From the very first contact with Millie, we knew she was a person who "touched God" when she prayed. Always her home was a "haven" for us as we traversed this continent and times of prayer with her were times of refreshing.

During the years that Millie served as an Advisor for the Denver Council, she was also active in the Gideon Auxiliary. Serving first as International Chaplain and later as International President of the Auxiliary, Mrs. Stamm saw their prayer groups triple in number and the entire program take on new vitality because of the increased prayer interest.

Prayer has always been the most vital part of the ministry of the Christian Business and Professional Women's Councils and the Christian Women's Clubs, with weekly prayer groups established with each Council and Club. As the work expanded, we recognized the urgent need for someone to carry on this phase of it nationally.

Much time was spent seeking the Lord's direction. It would not be an easy task, that we knew, for here would be where the Enemy of our soul would concentrate his opposition. We would need a "stalwart in prayer" for this responsibility. Truly the Lord led us to ask Mrs. Stamm to carry out the program He had given us.

During these twelve years that Millie has prepared the devotional material used each week by our Councils and Clubs, the Lord has used the thoughts He gave her to touch the hearts of thousands of women across our land. Countless letters have come expressing the thought, "Your devotional was just what I needed today."

Now, as Mrs. Stamm has gathered these together in book form, it is our prayer that yet countless others will find the answer to the needs of their lives as these words point them to the Lord Jesus Christ, the Source of Life itself.

Helen Duff Baugh
Mary E. Clark

Stonecroft
July 31, 1967

PREFACE

As this book nears completion, my thoughts travel back over the months and years which have made this possible.

It was in 1943 that I first saw Mrs. Helen Duff Baugh and became actively associated with the Christian Business and Professional Women's Council which she founded. In these intervening years, as I worked with the Council in Denver and later with both Councils and Christian Women's Clubs throughout Colorado, my interest and concern have never waned. Rather, they have grown as I have seen God at work throughout every phase of this many-faceted ministry.

Mrs. Baugh, and later Miss Mary E. Clark who joined her, had always known the inestimable value of prayer in the work of the Lord. Consequently, in 1955 the Lord led them to talk with me about directing the prayer ministry of the Christian Business and Professional Women's Councils and Christian Women's Clubs nationally. Although I, too, recognized the importance of prayer, it was difficult for me to agree to assume the responsibility of writing devotional material every month. Writing was not my field!

After months of prayer, the Lord gave me the assurance that this was from Him, and I became the National Executive Secretary of MEDITATION MOMENTS, the prayer arm of the ministry.

As a busy housewife, the time for writing had to be fitted into what seemed then like an already-full schedule. My husband, Clarke, was vitally interested in the Council and Club ministry and graciously helped me in many, many ways in order that I might have time to prepare the monthly material needed, never complaining at the many hours spent in this way. Constantly I had to look to the Lord to provide the Scripture, the illustrations, the very words that He wanted written—and He always supplied.

During this past year — the very hardest year of my life in many ways — the material written over these twelve years has been compiled into this book. For many months during that time Clarke was desperately ill and on November 6, 1966, he went to be with the Lord he loved so well. What is written on these pages has spoken to my own heart and Jesus Christ has proven to be all that I need in every circumstance of life . . . . even at such a time as this.

I wish to acknowledge my thanks to Mrs. Ray Cheyney, Jr., Helen E. Nichols and Genevieve Kesby for their untiring help in typing the manuscript and to Mildred Cooper for her careful proof-reading.

As the long days of preparation have ended, I humbly offer this book to the Lord Jesus Christ, desiring only that He may be seen in its pages and that whatever is a blessing in it will bring glory to His Name.

MILDRED E. STAMM

STONECROFT
July 29, 1967

Meditation Moments

We see Jesus. Hebrews 2:9

Today a new year has been placed in our hands. It is like a book whose pages are fresh and unspotted. Nothing is recorded in it. Yet as soon as we receive it, the clock begins to tick off its minutes and the recording of a new year has begun.

Success may come this year. The deepest desires of our hearts may be realized. Heartaches and problems may fill some of the pages. This can be a year of defeat or a year of triumph, depending on the focus of our eyes. We can either look at the circumstances surrounding us or we can *see Jesus,* the author and finisher of our faith.

Some years ago I was staying at the Hotel Statler in Washington, D. C. One morning a great crowd was gathered about the entrance because President Eisenhower was coming to the hotel for breakfast. Although I had seen him before, I joined the crowd cagerly awaiting a glimpse of the famous statesman. At last the word spread, "He's coming! He's coming!" We stood on tiptoe, stretching as tall as possible to see him.

As I turned away, God reminded me that one day I will have the joy of seeing the Lord of lords and King of kings, Jesus Christ. "Thine eyes shall see the king in his beauty" (Isaiah 33:17). What a day it will be when we see Him face to face, the One who loved us and gave Himself for us!

Until then may we see Him with eyes of faith. May we search each page of God's Word for a fresh revelation of Himself. May we see Him in prayer. May we see Him in our circumstances. Then others will see Him in our lives.

Let our motto this year be: "We see *Jesus.*"

2

> *But thou, when thou prayest, enter into thy closet, and when thou hast shut thy door, pray to thy Father which is in secret; and thy Father which seeth in secret shall reward thee openly. Matthew 6:6*

When a native in Uganda accepted Christ, he was told to select a quiet spot in the bush for his daily devotions. As he went there daily, a path was worn in the grass. But the grass grew rapidly. If he missed a day, the grass grew a little, making the path less distinct. If he missed a second day, the grass grew higher. If he continued to miss his quiet time, the path completely disappeared. The spiritual condition of the natives was gauged by their prayer paths. Do we have distinct prayer paths into God's presence, or has the grass grown over them because we have neglected our quiet times?

It has been said of prayer, "The equipment for the inner life of prayer is simple. It consists of a quiet place, a quiet time and a quiet heart." These are not easily achieved. Perhaps it is difficult to find a place where we can have solitude and quiet. It may be that our schedules are so full that we have difficulty finding a time to be quiet. There may be so much tension, confusion and turmoil in our lives that it seems impossible to quiet our hearts in His presence.

Our quiet time with God is important. A dear Christian mother was left to rear a family of little ones. She knew she couldn't do this without God's help, so each day she went into her bedroom, her "quiet place," for a time of prayer. Her children were very small and she was afraid to leave them alone so she gave them toys with which to play while she prayed. Then she would say, "You must be quiet for awhile — Mommie is going to talk with Jesus." At first she left them alone for only a very few minutes. As they grew older, however, she lengthened her quiet time. What a rich heritage those children enjoyed as they grew up with the precious assurance that "Mommie talked with Jesus"!

For the Lord knoweth the way of righteousness.
Psalm 1:6

3

How often we have heard this: "I do not know what tomorrow holds but I know who holds tomorrow." He knows our way through this day, this month, this year. The word "way" in this verse means "trodden path." But Joshua 3:4 reads, "For ye have not passed this way heretofore." If we have not taken this way before, how can it be a trodden path for us?

One night we had a snowstorm. The next morning I watched our neighbor with her two small girls and two neighbor boys playing "Follow the Leader" in the snow. She went ahead of them as their leader, making a trodden path in the snow. As long as they followed in her path they had no trouble. But when they left the path, they stumbled and fell.

In our Christian lives we can follow our Leader, who is the Lord, "simply fixing our gaze upon Jesus, our *Prince Leader* in the faith" (Weymouth). The way ahead is unknown to us, for we have not taken it before. But as we follow our Leader who goes before us, it becomes a trodden path for us.

Today does your way ahead look dark? Are the clouds hanging low? Are there shadows surrounding you? Your Leader, Jesus Christ, knows your way ahead. Keep your eyes on Him and your unknown way will become a trodden path as you follow Him.

4   *Draw nigh to God, and he will draw nigh to you.*
     James 4:8a

Once we had an out-of-town guest to whom we showed points of interest in our city. Knowing of her interest in nursing, we took her past some of our fine hospitals. I noted that usually there was a sign which said "Hospital Zone" or "Quiet Zone," indicating that we should decrease our speed and proceed quietly in the vicinity of the hospital.

These signs reminded me that life, too, should have quiet zones. Our schedules become so full that we find ourselves rushing with the heavy traffic of the avenues and boulevards of daily living. It is important that we have a time of communion and fellowship with God. We need a quiet place where we can hear Him speak to us.

During the day the great clock bell of St. Paul's Cathedral cannot be heard even a few blocks away because of heavy traffic noise. But as the noise of the city subsides at night it can be heard throughout half of the metropolis. So in our lives. In the hustle and bustle of living it is difficult to hear God speaking to us. We need daily quiet times when we listen to Him and let Him speak to us.

One day a friend told of a little neighbor boy who was at their home when they were having daily devotions. Later the lad said to his mother, "They had their commotions." Sometimes our devotional times do indeed seem filled with commotion and it is difficult to hear God speak. We need to draw apart from the stress and strain of life to hear all He wants to share with us. "God speaks loud enough for the willing soul to hear."

My voice shalt thou hear in the morning, O Lord; in the morning will I direct my prayer unto thee, and will look up. Psalm 5:3

5

What a privilege to begin the day in the presence of God! It has been said, "The morning is one end of the thread on which the day's activities are strung and should be well-knotted with devotion." It makes a difference when we look into the face of God before going out to face people.

Here we read something about David's prayer life. Out of a heart of love and worship He directed his prayer to God at the beginning of the day. He *lifted* his *voice* to God in prayer. "Hearken unto the voice of my cry. . . . My voice shalt thou hear in the morning" (vss. 2, 3a). He began his day talking to God, confident that He would hear and answer.

Not only did the Psalmist lift his voice, but he *lifted his heart* also. "In the morning will I direct my prayer unto thee." In the original Hebrew the expression "direct my prayer" implies coming to God with a prepared heart, a heart quieted from the hustle and bustle of the day, ready to listen to Him. Often we rush into and out of His presence without that quiet preparation of heart which is essential to communion with Him. "In the morning I prepare [a prayer, a sacrifice] for You, and watch and wait [for You to speak to my heart]" (vs. 3, Amplified). *Lift* your *heart* with your *voice* to God.

David's eyes followed the direction of his voice and heart: "and will *look up.*" We may lift our voices to God but keep our eyes focused on our problems, our needs, our weaknesses and disappointments. When we *lift* our *eyes*, we see Him. "And when they had lifted up their eyes, they saw no man, save *Jesus only*" (Matthew 17:8).

6

Ask, and it shall be given you; seek, and ye shall find; knock, and it shall be opened unto you; for every one that asketh receiveth; and he that seeketh findeth; and to him that knocketh it shall be opened. Matthew 7:7

When my sister was small, we nicknamed her "Gimme." She was constantly saying, "Gimme this" or "Gimme that." The Bible reveals that God wants us to be "Gimme," or "asking," children. He says, "Ask, and it shall be given you." How simple! In the home there is an "ask and receive" relationship. There is also an "ask and receive" relationship between God and His children.

We are told, "Seek, and ye shall find." Seek the Lord, who is our approach to God. "No man cometh unto the Father, but by me" (John 14:6). Seek His conditions for prayer. "And whatsoever ye shall *ask in my name,* that will I do, that the Father may be glorified in the Son. If ye shall *ask any thing in my name,* I will do it" (John 14:13, 14). We are also told, "Knock, and it shall be opened unto you." As we knock at God's limitless storehouse, the door will open and our needs will be supplied.

No need is too great or too small for Him to supply. He is limited only from the human side. "Ye have not, because ye ask not" (James 4:2). He may not answer in our way or time but in His. Perhaps we have lessons of trust or patience to learn before He can answer.

A man received a letter from a friend giving him certain information. Since a reply was not necessary, his friend wrote at the bottom of the letter, "No answer expected." Do we ever by our attitude add this to our prayers? Or do we ask, seek and knock, "expecting to receive, find and have opened to us the rich resources of heaven?

I am debtor both to the Greeks, and to the Bar-   **7**
barians; both to the wise, and to the unwise. Romans
1:14

A young couple, with several little children, were very dear friends of our family. In fact, they thought of my mother as their mother. They moved away for a time. However, during a period of reverses they returned. They had no place to go and were in desperate financial need. Although my mother had a small home and very little money, she took them in and supplied their needs until they found work and were established. They began to prosper materially and helped my mother in numerous ways as much as possible. "We can never do enough for you to repay you for what you have done for us," they said gratefully.

This was Paul's feeling toward the One who had paid the debt for his sin. Because the Lord Jesus Christ had died for him, Paul felt that he owed a debt to mankind. In deep appreciation to Christ for what He had done for him, he felt a tremendous obligation to take the Gospel to the world of that day. He considered all, irrespective of class, position or education, his creditors.

This is the true missionary spirit and one that should be manifest today. Many people think that the world owes them something, but Paul felt that he owed the world his life.

We, too, are debtors to the world. Someone has said, "The debt we owe God for our salvation is payable to man." We owe the world our lives — lives dedicated to sharing the Gospel with humanity.

8   *A certain woman named Martha received him into her house. And she had a sister called Mary, which also sat at Jesus' feet, and heard his word. Luke 10:38, 39*

Mary and Martha were entertaining Jesus. Martha was concerned about making Him comfortable. She wanted Him to be relaxed and refreshed, which was a wholesome desire. Her difficulty was that she "was cumbered about much serving" (vs. 40). She was so involved with the preparation for His comfort that she missed the joy of sitting at His feet and listening to Him as Mary did.

If the sisters knew beforehand that He was coming, I am sure Mary did her part in preparing for His visit. But as soon as He arrived, she wanted to spend her time with Jesus, listening to Him. Even though our Lord appreciated Martha's concern, would He not have preferred that she take time to hear His teaching?

Mary responded to His visit by taking the *needful position.* Jesus said, "One thing is needful." She took time to sit at His feet and hear His word. In these days of tension and turmoil one thing is needful for us, too — we must have quiet times alone with Him as we hear His Word for us.

Jesus not only said that she had taken the needful position but that she had chosen the *necessary part:* "Mary hath chosen that good part." She put first things first. She didn't miss the best by being satisfied with the good. Furthermore, this good part was a *never-ending possession:* "which shall not be taken away."

Service for the Lord is important but it must not keep us from spending time alone with Him. Martha's mistake was not that she desired to serve Him but that she was cumbered with service. Perhaps we become cumbered because we fail to spend time listening to His Word. May we not become so busy doing for Him that we miss being with Him.

For this cause we also . . . do not cease to pray for you. Colossians 1:9a

9

Paul was a great man of prayer. In this portion of Scripture we hear Paul open his heart in prayer for the Colossian Christians. He prayed that they "might walk worthy of the Lord" (vs. 10a). This does not refer merely to a behavior that one can take off and put on at will, but the apostle is speaking of life as a whole. To walk worthy means to walk in a way that will honor Christ. Phillips says, "We also pray that your outward lives, which men see, may bring credit to your Master's name."

A life worthy of the Lord is completely satisfying to Him: "So that you may lead lives worthy of the Lord to His full satisfaction" (Williams). This implies more than merely obeying His commands; it means contemplating His desires and doing all that will please Him, "as the servants of Christ, doing the will of God from the heart" (Ephesians 6:6).

The secret of walking worthy of the Lord, of completely satisfying Him, is found in Colossians 1:9. Paul prayed, "That ye might be filled with the knowledge of his will" (vs. 9b). God's will and our walk should not be separated.

The result of a walk worthy of the Lord, one walked in the knowledge of His will, is a walk "fruitful in every good work" (vs. 10b). Not only should our lives be fruitful in our Christian service but in our everyday activities — at work, before our families and in our neighborhoods. A little girl once said, "My mistress knows I'm converted." "How does she know?" the child was asked. "Because I sweep under the mats now," was the reply.

A worthy walk not only produces fruit but increases the knowledge of God Himself (vs. 10c). Is your knowledge of God increasing? Is He becoming a dearer Friend to you? May this be your prayer today, "That I may know him" (Philippians 3:10a).

10

As the hart pants and longs for the water brooks, so I pant and long for You, O God. My inner self thirsts for God, for the living God. When shall I come and behold the face of God? Psalm 42:1, 2, Amplified

I once took a strenuous mountain hike. Persistently my companions and I climbed one mountain and struggled to the top of another. Five hours later we returned from our unforgettable adventure. Although we were indescribably weary, our one desire was for water to quench our intense thirst. I still remember how refreshed we were as we drank the cool mountain water.

In the above verse we read of one whose innermost being longed intensely for God. The Psalmist uses the illustration of a deer which craves water to quench its thirst when it is pursued by the hunter.

As the hart pants for the water brooks, possibly after a long chase by the hunter, so the human soul, pursued by sorrow, heartache and fear, cries out for God Himself. His desire was not for pleasure, people or position, but for God Himself. Augustine said, "Thou hast made us for Thyself, O God, and our hearts are restless till they rest in Thee."

God promises that the thirsty soul will be satisfied. He who hungers and thirsts after righteousness "shall be filled" (Matthew 5:6). God Himself is the One Who satisfies. "He satisfieth the longing soul" (Psalm 107:9). This satisfaction is not in what He gives us, not in what He does for us, but in Himself.

This cry of David's was answered years later when God came to earth in the person of His Son, Jesus Christ. One day Jesus came to the Temple during the time of the Feast of Tabernacles. "In the last day, that great day of the feast, Jesus stood and cried, saying, If any man thirst, let him come unto me, and drink" (John 7:37). "And the Spirit and the bride say, Come. And let him that heareth say, Come. And let him that is athirst come. And whosoever will, let him take the water of life freely" (Revelation 22:17).

Certainly I will be with thee. Exodus 3:12

Moses had been commissioned by God to deliver Israel out of Egypt. Conscious of his lack of ability, he began to give God reasons why he shouldn't assume this place of leadership. He lacked confidence. "Who am I?" he asked.

The question really did not concern who he was or was not, but who God *is*. When God calls, not only does He provide the ability needed, but He promises His presence as well. He immediately answered Moses, saying, "Certainly I will be with thee." The Hebrew word for "certainly" means "without a doubt." "Without a doubt I will be with you. I — God — will be with you."

When Moses became the leader, he learned the strength to be found in having God's presence with him. When burdens became heavy, he turned to God for strength. When the people murmured and complained, he was comforted by the One who understood and sympathized. One day when his heart was broken, he cried out to God, "If thy presence go not with me, carry us not up hence." He knew he could not face the future without the assurance of God's presence with him.

Today God speaks the same reassuring words to us: "Certainly I will be with *thee*." What has He asked you to do for Him today? Where has He asked you to go for Him? Go forth reassured, for He has promised you, "Without a doubt I will be with you."

12   *Commit your way to the Lord — roll and repose [each care of] your road on Him; trust, lean on, rely on and be confident also in Him, and He will bring it to pass. Psalm 37:5, Amplified*

Do you face insurmountable problems? Does there seem to be no solution? God says, "Commit and trust and I will bring it to pass." This is a conditional promise. He will work in our behalf *if* we commit and trust.

The word "commit" has several meanings: "to entrust"; "to hand over to someone else"; "to let go so another can take over." Once I heard this illustration of committal. When we mail a letter, we have confidence that the Post Office Department will deliver it to the person to whom it is addressed. However, the letter cannot be delivered until we "let go" and drop it into the mailbox.

What need do you have? What problem? There is not one too great or too small to bring to God. He is saying, "Hand it over to Me; trust Me with it." Drop it into God's Mailbox, take your hands off completely and let Him work.

A literal translation can read, "Roll upon Jehovah thy way; trust upon Him; and He worketh." When our burdens seem too heavy to lift, we can roll them on Him. Then He *works;* the meaning is not "will work" but "is working now." Someone has said, "*Relinquish* and *rest;* then leave the *results* with Him."

A pilot, lost in the clouds and fog, was not experienced in instrument landing. The station tower promised to bring him in on radar. He began to receive his instructions when suddenly he remembered a tall pole which was in the flight path. Frantically he called the tower. The command came back, "You obey the *instructions:* we will take care of the *obstructions.*"

We may be in a fog. The clouds of trouble may be heavy above us. We may be looking only at the obstacles before us. God says, "You are to obey My instructions [commit and trust]; I will take care of the obstructions [and bring it to pass]."

Men ought always to pray, and not to faint. Luke 18:1

13

God emphasizes the importance of prayer. Needs are supplied, problems solved, the impossible accomplished through prayer. Therefore we *ought* to pray. We may not feel like it, but we ought to pray. We may be discouraged, but we ought to pray.

We are *always* to pray — not merely when we have a need or only at some set time, but always. The line to heaven is always open. We are sometimes prone to make our own plans or decisions before we pray, but we should pray about everything first.

Not only are we to pray, but we are not to faint. Perhaps we have been praying about something for a long time and do not see the answer. We may think God hasn't heard or doesn't care. However, we are not to faint. I once witnessed the joy of one who had just received word that her brother had become a Christian. With tears running down her cheeks, she said, as she related her inspiring experience, "I have prayed for him for forty years." Rubinstein, the famous composer and pianist, once said, "If I fail to practice one day, I notice it; if two days, my friends notice it; if three days, my public notices it."

"They ought always to pray and not to turn coward — faint, lose heart and give up" (Amplified).

14   *Be still, and know that I am God.* Psalm 46:10

How many times a day do you say, "Be still"? If you don't do so audibly, at least you want to. You may say it to your children innumerable times a day. Perhaps you long to say it to a girl in your office or to a neighbor who seems to talk constantly.

Sometimes God may want to say to us, "Be still." But you may say, "I do try to be quiet in His presence and what happens? The phone rings, or the children in the neighborhood all congregate outside and begin to scream, or the neighbors' stereo is so loud I can't think."

It is difficult to put aside the voices of the world and become quiet enough to hear Him. It is even hard to quiet our thoughts. Sometimes it seems impossible to do so. The world says, "Be busy; be active; be industrious." But God says, *"Be still."* This means much more than cessation of activities. We must become so quiet of heart and spirit that we can sense His presence.

One of the great benefits of being still is getting to know God. "Be still, and *know that I am God.*" A. B. Simpson said, "There is in the deepest center of the believer's soul a chamber of peace where God dwells and where, if we will only enter in and hush every other sound, we can hear His still voice." We need to become conscious of His presence. Someone has said, "God speaks loud enough for the willing soul to hear."

There was a time when Beethoven was almost at the point of despair. He discovered he was becoming deaf. As his loss of hearing increased, he became anxious and despondent but gradually he accepted the affliction and resigned himself to it. It was during those days when he was deaf to all sound that he wrote his grandest music.

But as we were allowed of God to be put in trust   *15*
with the gospel, even so we speak; not as pleasing
men, but God, which trieth our hearts. I Thessalon-
ians 2:4

A colporteur in India was telling a group of natives about the Book he had which told of One who loved them, One who had died for them that they might have eternal life. One of the natives finally asked, "How long ago did He do that for us?" "Nearly two thousand years ago," was the reply. "Who has been hiding the Book from us all that time?" was their accusing question.

Paul was a "messenger with a Message," the Gospel of Jesus Christ. This is the message God wants to communicate from His great heart of love to a needy world: "For I delivered unto you first of all that which I also received, how that Christ died for our sins according to the scriptures; and that he was buried, and that he rose again the third day according to the scriptures" (I Corinthians 15:3, 4). The Gospel was a trust which God had given to Paul and he knew that one day he would have to give an accounting to God of what he had done with it.

How many people there are today who have never heard the Gospel! We, too, have been entrusted with it to share with others. We, too, will have to give an accounting to God of what we have done with it. Can anyone say to you and me today, "Who has been hiding the Book from us?" Am I hiding it from anyone by not sharing it? Are you?

16 *But when he saw the multitudes, he was moved with compassion on them, because they fainted, and were scattered abroad, as sheep having no shepherd. Matthew 9:36*

Do you like crowds? Or do you avoid them? Some people are thrilled by multitudes.

When Jesus was on earth, crowds followed Him wherever He went. Some were curious, but many were people with needs which they believed He could meet. Jesus did not view these crowds as an indication of the success of His ministry. He saw them as individuals with needs. He was moved with compassion for them.

These crowds also were representative of the multitudes down through the ages who would have needs. Knowing that laborers would be needed to continue His work, He said, "Pray the Lord of the harvest to force out and thrust laborers into His harvest" (Amplified).

What is our reaction to the crowds about us today? How do we view them? Merely as people, or as people with spiritual needs? Often I have to wait in an airport or train station. Since I am interested in people, I enjoy watching them. As I sit waiting for my plane or train, I wonder where these crowds of men and women are going, what goals they are seeking in life, and what unseen heartaches they may be enduring. My heart is always moved by the realization that, even though I may not know what it is, each has a need of some kind.

I realize, however, that it is not sufficient for me merely to know that the crowds around me have needs, or even to be moved by their distress. They must know the One who can meet all of their needs. They need to know Jesus Christ as their personal Saviour. Therefore I have a responsibility — *"Pray ye"* (vs. 38). This is a personal instruction from the Lord. It is to me. I must not shift it to someone else. After I pray, God may use me to answer my own prayer for the multitudes about me. The harvest is plenteous. It is waiting for us. *"Pray ye."*

Philip saith unto him, Come and see. John 1:46

Philip had met the Saviour. When Jesus found him and said, "Follow me," Philip responded. His life was then filled with a new joy which he couldn't keep to himself, for the next recorded fact about him is that "he findeth Nathanael, and saith unto him, we have found *Him*." When Nathanael questioned him about this new joy of his, Philip didn't deliver a lengthy theological discourse. He simply said, "Come and see." His contact with Christ had been so real and so wonderful, and such joy and peace filled his heart, that he wanted others to meet Jesus, too. Since he knew a personal contact was most effective, he asked Nathanael to come and see *Him*.

We, too, have this privilege — the opportunity to "come and see" Him. He can fill our vision. "We see Jesus" (Hebrews 2:9). We can see Him as the One who loved us and gave Himself for us. We can see Him as the Lily of the Valley, the Rose of Sharon, the Bright and Morning Star. The closer we draw to Him, the more completely our vision will be filled with Him. The closer we are to Him, the dearer He will be to us. The dearer He becomes to us, the greater will be our desire to do what Philip did — tell others to come and see *Him*.

A traveler viewed Thorwaldsen's statue *Christus Consolator*. As he looked at it, he expressed disappointment. A little girl overheard him and said, "You must go up close, kneel down, and look up into His face."

18   *He that goeth forth and weepeth, bearing precious seed, shall doubtless come again with rejoicing, bringing his sheaves with him.* Psalm 126:6

We are living in a confused world where only a small percentage of the population have a vital personal relationship with Jesus Christ. The world truly is a field to be sown with the Word of God.

We are to *possess* this field for God — "He that goeth forth." The seed — the Word of God — is to be sown. In order to reap, we must sow. If we are to sow, we must go forth. The farmer doesn't stay in his back yard to sow his seed; he goes out to the field and scatters the seed.

We are to go forth "bearing precious seed" to *plant*. If no seed is sown, there will be no harvest. The amount of the harvest depends upon the amount of the sowing. "He which soweth sparingly shall reap also sparingly; and he which soweth bountifully shall reap also bountifully" (II Corinthians 9:6).

As we go forth, sowing the seed, we are to *pray* — "and weepeth." It has been said, "Seed doesn't grow very well in dry ground." Tears come from a heart of compassion and love. Our Saviour had seeing eyes and a weeping heart. "And when he was come near, he beheld the city, and wept over it" (Luke 19:41). We need more than the mechanics of sowing; the seed needs the moisture of tears and the warm rays of love.

If we faithfully plant and pray, one day we will have the joy of standing before Him to *present* our sheaves, laying them at His feet. On the eve of the coronation of Queen Elizabeth, news was flashed around the world that a British climbing party had conquered Mt. Everest. Many attempts had been made, all ending in failure. But the climbers were undaunted. At last victory came. As their coronation gift of love and honor to the Queen, they presented their conquest of Mt. Everest. Will we have sheaves to lay at His feet — our love gifts to Him?

But my God — so great is His wealth of glory in Christ Jesus — will fully supply every need of yours. Philippians 4:19, Weymouth

What a wonderful promise this is for us! For Paul it was a personal possession. He could say, *"My God."* His relationship with the Lord Jesus Christ as his own Saviour was gloriously real. He said, "I know *whom* I have believed" (II Timothy 1:12). Can you, like Paul, say, *"My God,"* knowing you have invited Him into your life as your Saviour?

God, our Banker, has promised to supply our needs. *"Shall supply"* indicates certainty and security. The text does not say "may supply" or "perhaps will supply," but *"shall."* With confidence we can bring our needs to Him, counting on His faithfulness. "Great is thy faithfulness" (Lamentations 3:23). God's supply also is limitless — He will supply *"all your needs,"* material and spiritual. Notice that the verse does not say "all your wants," but "all your *needs.*"

Our needs will be met *"according to His riches in glory."* The text doesn't say "according to what we deserve," or "according to what we earn," but "according to his riches." This is our heavenly deposit. His riches are limitless. They never run out and there is enough for every need. His riches are available to us *"in Christ."* God honors our requests because of His Son.

George Mueller, the founder of the Bristol Orphanage in England, was relating some of his experiences in providing food for the orphans each day. When he had finished, his friend replied, "You seem to live from hand to mouth." "Yes," replied Mueller. "It is my mouth, but God's hand."

20 *There is a friend that sticketh closer than a brother. Proverbs 18:24*

One of our most treasured possessions is a true friend. A friend always understands us; is one in whom we can confide; is loyal and true; knows all about us and still loves us; is one with whom we can always be ourselves; brings out the best in us; is one of whom we can say as did Paul, "I thank my God upon every remembrance of you" (Philippians 1:3).

However, a time may come when even our dearest friends don't seem to understand. There are some experiences we can't share even with those nearest and dearest to us. We need a friend with whom we *can* share our innermost thoughts, heartaches and problems; one who *does* understand and sympathize. We need a friend who will never let us down or disappoint us but who will always remain loyal and true. We need a friend who will always love us.

God has provided such a Friend for us. This "friend that sticketh closer than a brother" is none other than our Friend of friends, Jesus Christ. He is always available to us. We can share our joys with Him and know that He rejoices with us. We can cry out to Him in our sorrows and heartaches and feel the healing Balm of Gilead which He pours into broken hearts. He demonstrated His great love for us when He "gave himself" for us (Galatians 2:20).

The story is told of an old Lancashire woman who listened as several members of her church discussed her minister's success. They spoke of his gifts, his style, his manner. "Nay," she said, "I will tell you what the secret is. He is very thick with the Almighty." We, too, can have a close friendship with our dearest Friend, the Lord Jesus.

See then that ye walk circumspectly, not as fools, but as wise, redeeming the time, because the days are evil. Ephesians 5:15, 16

How often we say, "Oh, I just don't have enough time." Someone asks you to do something and you reply, "I'm sorry but I don't have time." In this day of modern efficiency, with all its labor-saving devices, surely we should have more free time, but I am sure each of us would say, "Not so."

As far as time is concerned, we are all on the same level. Each is allotted the same amount. The question is not how much time we have but how we use it. Time is valuable. It is important how we invest it. We must guard each moment, using it to bring the greatest profit. I once read this on a bulletin board: "God wants our precious time, not our spare time."

The Amplified New Testament reads, "Look carefully then how you walk! Live purposefully and worthily and accurately, not as the unwise and witless, but as the wise — sensible, intelligent people; making the very most of the time — buying up each opportunity — because the days are evil." We must redeem the time, buying up the opportunities as they come to us. Because time is valuable, because time allotted to us on earth is short, we should buy up opportunities with eternal value.

Are you making the best use of *your* time? Are you investing it in such a way that it will bring the greatest possible return? Too often we permit the world to dictate the management of our time whereas we should let God govern its use. Each day He entrusts us with twenty-four hours. At the close of the day what accounting can we give God as to our spending of these precious hours? Is He pleased with our investment? Will each day count for eternity?

22 *And this is the confidence — the assurance, the [privilege of] boldness — which we have in Him: [We are sure] that if we ask anything (make any request) according to His will (in agreement with His own plan) He listens to and hears us. And if (since) we [positively] know that He listens to us in whatever we ask, we also know [with settled and absolute knowledge] that we have [granted us as our present possessions] the requests made of Him. I John 5:14, 15, Amplified*

One of the reasons for the increase in the number of believers during the early days of the Church was their power in prayer. D. L. Moody said, "Every great movement of God can be traced to a 'kneeling figure'." God has given many promises to those who are willing to be "kneeling figures" interceding for a needy world.

In the above verses God assures us that we can have great confidence that our prayers will be heard and answered, for our confidence is in the right source — *in Him.* It is not in ourselves, nor in others, but in the One with whom *all things* are possible.

The scope of our prayer is "if we ask *anything*," conditioned by "*according* to His *will*." We don't need to plead or beg. If what we desire is according to His will, we can simply ask Him for it. God has given us His promise that He will listen to and hear us. Moreover, He assures us that not only will He listen but He will also grant the requests we make of Him.

It has been said that the great people in God's work are the "pray-ers." When we pray, God works. "What is the secret of your power?" a young student asked Mr. Spurgeon. "What work will I have to do to get the power you have?" Mr. Spurgeon answered quickly, "Kneework, young man! Kneework!"

That the trial of your faith, being much more precious **23**
than of gold that perisheth, though it be tried with
fire, might be found unto praise and honour and
glory at the appearing of Jesus Christ. I Peter 1:7

The automotive industry has proving grounds where cars are tested under every conceivable condition. Weaknesses and defects are discovered and corrected. God has a proving ground for His children where our faith is tested; where our weaknesses and defects are discovered so that they can be corrected. Do you ever wonder why trials enter your life? They are used as a proving ground to test and perfect your faith.

Trials are an inescapable reality in the lives of God's children. "Ye are in heaviness through manifold temptations." We are not promised that we will be kept *from* trials, but we are told to expect them. Precious jewels cannot be fashioned without the process of refining, cutting and polishing. This explains the reason for the trials in our lives: they are part of the refining process. Therefore afflictions are valuable to us, "much more precious than of gold that perisheth." It has been said, "A trial is an experiment made upon a person by affliction to prove the value and strength of his faith." When we are experiencing our trials, we don't often think of them as more precious than gold, do we? Yet God says they are.

Fire is a method used by God to test our faith. Our faith must stand this test of fire. Steel is iron plus fire. Faith plus fire becomes a tested and proved faith. Out of the testing of our faith come "praise and honour and glory at the appearing of Jesus Christ" and a deeper love for Him, "whom having not seen, ye love" (vs. 8).

24 *But be thou an example of the believers, in word, in conversation, in charity, in spirit, in faith, in purity. I Timothy 4:12*

Have you ever attended a flower show and admired a choice specimen which had won a "blue ribbon?" It was a "sample" of the exhibitor's ability to produce a prize-winning flower.

God wants to produce "samples, choice specimens" of Christianity. We are to be sample Christians in *"word"* — samples in our talk. Are we sweet and patient in what we say when things go wrong? What happens when the telephone keeps ringing? Or when the children become difficult? What do we say when the boss is cross or unreasonable? Is our talk pleasing to God? Would He choose us as sample Christians because of what we say?

We are told to be sample Christians in our *"manner of life,"* which is the meaning of the word "conversation." What of our habits, pleasures, friends, business, conduct, our entire manner of living? We must also be sample Christians in *"love."* How considerate are we of others? How concerned are we for their needs?

Furthermore, we are told to be sample Christians in *"spirit."* Do we exhibit the Spirit of Christ? Can people sense His presence in our lives? We must be sample Christians in *"faith."* We need to show our complete reliance on and trust in God in our lives. Someone has said, "Faith is the vision of the heart. It sees God in the dark as in the light." Scripture exhorts us to be sample Christians in *"purity."* Our thoughts, words and deeds must be pure.

An Ethiopian girl became a Christian. She could read a little English and was interested in an advertisement concerning vitamin B-1 tablets. Since the Ethiopians often assumed new names when they became Christians, she called herself "Vitamin." "Why do you call yourself 'Vitamin'?" the little girl was asked. She replied, "Because I want to *be one.*"

If God were to select His choice samples, whom would He choose? May each of us strive prayerfully to *"be one."*

And when he was come near, he beheld the city, and wept over it. Luke 19:41

25

What compassion Jesus had for Jerusalem! He knew of the destruction that was to come upon the city, and His heart was touched. Our Lord loved the people. He had come to be their Saviour, yet He knew their eyes were blind to His identity and that they would reject Him.

As He looked out over the city, His tender love for it moved Him to tears. "He wept (audibly) over it" (Amplified). He had "seeing eyes" — ("he beheld the city") — and a "weeping heart" — ("and wept over it"). His tears were real — the tears of God. What about our concern for a needy world? Do we have a compassion that brings us to tears?

Gypsy Smith told that when he was converted, he immediately became concerned about the conversion of his uncle. Among the gypsies, however, it was not considered proper for children to speak to their elders regarding such matters or to voice opinions, so the boy prayed patiently and waited for God to open the way. One day his uncle noticed a hole in the lad's trousers. "Rodney, how is it that you have worn the knees of your pants out so much faster than the rest of the trousers?" he asked. "Uncle," the boy replied, "I have worn them out praying that God would make you a Christian." Tears came to his uncle's eyes. He put his arm around the lad and soon was down on his knees asking the Saviour to come into his life.

Check your eyes and your heart today. Do you have "seeing eyes" and a "weeping heart" as you behold the people living in your "city"?

26 *All these things are against me. Genesis 42:36*

Have you ever said, "It seems that everything is against me"? Nearly everyone of us has made such a statement, or at least said words to that effect. Perhaps there is illness in your home; you may be experiencing reverses; your employer may be difficult; you may not like the place where you live. Finally you cry out in desperation, "All these things are against me!"

This was what Jacob did. He said, "Joseph is not, and Simeon is not. . . . All these things are against me." He was full of self-pity. He was looking at the seen, not the unseen. He was walking by sight, not by faith. He had his eyes on *things,* not on *God.* He saw the circumstances instead of God.

Paul had a different reaction to the circumstances of his life. He said, "None of these things move me" (Acts 20:24). He could not be moved, for his faith was anchored in Jesus Christ. He was not moved by things, for he had learned that "we are assured and know that [God being a partner in their labor], all things work together and are [fitting into a plan] for good to those who love God and are called according to [His] design and purpose" (Romans 8:28, Amplified).

"All these things are against me," or "None of these things move me" — which is our reaction? Do we say, "All these things are against me" or "All things work together for good"? Which "all" is controlling your life? If we believe that all things are working together for our good, then none of these things can move us.

Someone has said, "Those who leave everything in God's hand will eventually see God's hand in everything."

Pray without ceasing. I Thessalonians 5:17

As you read these words you may say, "I can't always be on my knees." No, you can't. But he who prays only on his knees doesn't pray enough. The praying of which the verse speaks is the fragrance of the heart that lives in the presence of the Holy Ghost and breathes His very life. We are not to pray once a day or twice a day only, but we are to live in the spirit of prayer all day long. Such prayer is more than asking — it is breathing the very life of God.

Someone may say, "I can't pray without ceasing, for I have to wash, iron, cook, and perform many other duties each day." However, we can have the spirit of prayer while we are engaged in our daily activities. Nehemiah prayed while he was serving the king as a cupbearer. One day the monarch asked him a question. "So I prayed to the God of heaven. And I said unto the king . . . ." the prophet tells us (Nehemiah 2:4, 5). Nehemiah lived in the spirit of prayer. Thus when he needed an answer from God he quickly prayed where he was and God gave him the answer.

In our state there is a creek that can be seen for a long way. Then it disappears underground. It is still there although it is not visible. Eventually it can be seen again and flows into a lake. Prayer is like this. Sometimes it is expressed in audible petitions. Occasionally there may not be outward evidence, but nevertheless it is still the powerful undercurrent influencing our thoughts. As we pray without ceasing there will be definite times when we pause to make our requests known unto God. Constantly, however, our lives will be lived in the spirit of prayer as we stay in constant touch with Him.

28 *One of his disciples said unto him, Lord, teach us to pray. Luke 11:1*

The disciples had been with Jesus when He prayed. After He had finished, one of them said, "Lord, teach us to pray." He did not merely want to learn *how* to pray, but to pray. As the disciples listened to Jesus, they recognized their own inadequacy in prayer. They wanted Christ to teach them to pray as He prayed.

"Whenever I mention any of my problems to our pastor," said a woman, "he asks, 'Have you prayed about it?' He is making me prayer-conscious." Jesus made His disciples prayer-conscious. They heard Him pray. They witnessed the results of His praying. They now wanted such a prayer life for themselves.

We, too, must be taught to pray as Christ prayed. This the Holy Spirit is willing to do. "So too the (Holy) Spirit comes to our aid and bears us up in our weakness; for we do not know what prayer to offer nor how to offer it worthily as we ought, but the Spirit Himself goes to meet our supplication and pleads in our behalf with unspeakable yearnings and groanings too deep for utterance" (Romans 8:26, Amplified).

Lord, teach us to pray. Teach us to be prayer-conscious not only with respect to our own needs, but teach us to so pray that our prayer lives will make others prayer-conscious. After hearing Jesus pray, the disciples wanted to pray as He did. Are there those who want to pray as we do after they have heard us pray?

There was once a missionary who had such a prayer life. One day a friend entered her room and found the missionary earnestly engaged in intercessory prayer for souls, as tears streamed down her face. She didn't even notice her visitor come into her room or leave. The missionary's inspiring example caused her friend to pray later, "Lord, teach me to pray as she prays."

I am the way, the truth, and the life: no man cometh **29**
unto the Father, but by me. John 14:6

Some time ago I was standing on a corner as I waited for a bus. A woman joined me just as it was approaching. To her great dismay, she discovered that she had left her coin purse at home and had no money. She knew that if she returned home for her purse, she would miss the bus and, since the next would not arrive until forty-five minutes later, she would be unable to keep her appointment. I asked her if she would let me pay her fare, to which she agreed. It was then her privilege to board the bus and ride to her destination because someone else had paid the fare for her.

This is an illustration of what God has done for us. There is only one price sufficient to purchase our fare to heaven: the death of Jesus Christ on the cross. He is the only way to heaven. As my newly made friend was able to ride the bus because I had paid her fare for her, so we, too, can "board the bus" for heaven when we have accepted the fare provided for us by Jesus by inviting Him into our lives as our Saviour.

Today there are thousands all around us who have not received their "fare" to heaven. We have the privilege of pointing them to the One who has provided their fare for them. "And He said to them, Go into all the world and preach and publish openly the good news (the Gospel) to every creature (of the whole human race)" (Mark 16:15, Amplified).

30
    *Peace I leave with you; My [own] peace I now give
    and bequeath to you. Not as the world gives do
    I give to you. Do not let your heart be troubled,
    neither let it be afraid — stop allowing yourselves to
    be agitated and disturbed; and do not permit your-
    selves to be fearful and intimidated and cowardly
    and unsettled. John 14:27, Amplified*

Jesus gave wonderful promises and bequeathed precious gifts to His disciples before He returned to heaven. One of the gifts He left is His peace.

As we read today's newspapers and listen to the newscasts, we say, "There seems to be anything but peace today." Yet Jesus promised to leave His peace. He could do this, for *"He is our peace"* (Ephesians 2:14). Today, when our hearts are filled with fear and tension, we can hear Jesus say, "Let not your heart be troubled. Remember I give you *My peace* which can quiet your heart in these days of turmoil. I am the peace which can fill your heart and calm your fears."

Are you upset by problems in your life? Does there seem to be no solution? "Is *any thing* too hard for the Lord?" (Genesis 18:14). In the midst of our troubles, He says, "Let not your heart be troubled. I give you My peace — I *am* your peace." Yes, today — in all your burdens and heartaches — this peace is for *you*. Peace is not the absence of feeling, but assurance in God who brings inward peace.

A missionary was translating God's Word into the language of a jungle tribe. A native who was helping him couldn't give him a word for "peace." One day he hurried in, saying, "I know now how to let my people know that Jesus gives peace inside." "What is the word?" asked the missionary. "Oh, I don't know a word to use, but they will understand if you say, 'Jesus will make your heart sit down.'"

And Enoch walked with God. Genesis 5:24

For before his translation he had this testimony, that he pleased God. Hebrews 11:5

Enoch was a man who walked with God and pleased Him. It wasn't easy to live such a life in those days of great wickedness on the earth. But in the midst of such conditions he lived a godly life. He was an ordinary man, a family man. He faced the problems and needs of a home. However, he could face them confidently for God was his partner. His was a steadfast walk of faith.

Walking with God is more than merely living piously on Sunday. It means maintaining a consistent and godly walk on Monday when we are washing clothes or on Tuesday when we are working in the office. It has been said, "It is the godly walk set to the common and ordinary round of duties that really counts." Sometimes our walking needs to catch up with our talking.

Brother Lawrence was a raw farm hand, awkward and uneducated, working in a monastery where he washed dishes and assisted the cook. One day while he was washing dishes, the thought came to him, *God is everywhere! God is here!* This thought gripped him so forcibly that ever afterwards he practiced the presence of God, realizing that God was constantly with him. The result was that he was so transformed and refined that he became the talk of the monks and of the neighborhood. Men came great distances to interview this man who walked with God.

Fill in your own name. "I . . . walk with God. And I . . . have this testimony that I . . . please God."

1   *I being in the way, the Lord led me.* Genesis 24:27b

Eliezer, Abraham's trusted servant, learned from experience that God leads in a wonderful way. Abraham wanted a wife for Isaac, his son. The great responsibility of returning to Abraham's homeland to find one was entrusted to Eliezer. How would he know the right girl? He trusted God to lead him to her. God would lead him to the right place at the right time to find the right girl.

In Genesis 24 we read about his trip and how God led him definitely to Rebekah. There could be no question in his mind regarding God's choice. As he recounted God's leading, he said, "I being in the way [of obedience and faith] the Lord led me to the house of my master's kinsmen" (Amplified).

To experience God's leading, we must be in God's way. God's way is through His Son, who said, "I am *the way,* the truth, and the life: no man cometh unto the Father, but by me" (John 14:16). Eliezer was successful in his mission because he *committed himself* to God and God's way. He said, "I being in *the way."* He was also successful because he *committed his need* to God. He had asked God to lead him to the right girl. Later he could say, "The Lord led me to the house of my master's kinsmen." There he found Rebekah, God's choice for Isaac.

Do you need God's leading in solving some problem today? Commit yourself to Him — "I being in the way." Commit your need to Him — "the Lord led me." As He led Eliezer, so will He lead you. He will time every circumstance perfectly, not a minute too early or too late. Then you, too, can say, "The Lord led *me."*

Sir, we would see Jesus. John 12:21b

A missionary visited one of the islands of the South Pacific. When he told the natives about Jesus, one of them remarked, "Oh, He used to live here." The missionary, surprised, began to inquire regarding his meaning. He learned that a few years earlier a missionary had spent some time in the area. Although he hadn't known the language of the natives, he had helped them in every possible way, and his life had radiated the presence of the One with whom he lived in close fellowship. Now as the natives heard about Jesus, they concluded that He must have been the kind friend who had lived with them a few years earlier.

Have you ever seen a picture of people you knew, yet didn't recognize? When you were told who they were, you may have remarked, "I wouldn't have recognized them; the picture doesn't resemble them." Or perhaps you said, "Oh, yes, I know who they are; the picture looks exactly like them." God's Word tells us that we are to be conformed to the image of God. Are we so like our Lord that people recognize Him in our lives? Do they see Jesus in us?

It has been said, "To win some, we must be winsome." "Winsome holiness" has been defined as follows: "The *holy calm of God* mirrored in the face; the *holy quietness of God* manifested in the voice; the *holy graciousness of God* expressed in the manner; the *holy fragrance of God* emanating from the whole life." This kind of life will attract others to our lovely Lord. The world should be able to see Jesus in our lives. "Sir, we would see Jesus." "And when they had lifted up their eyes, they saw no man, save Jesus only" (Matthew 17:8). This is the secret of "winsome holiness."

3   *In that they received the word with all readiness of mind, and searched the scriptures daily, whether those things were so. Acts 17:11b*

How we enjoy receiving a letter from a friend! If it is from someone very special, we read it over and over. Why? Because of our affection for the one who wrote it. We want to know every word the sender has for us. One of my dearest treasures is the last letter I received from my mother. It was written the day before she passed away, but I did not receive it until the day after her death. Needless to say, I have read the precious message countless times.

If earthly letters can mean so much to us, how much more should we treasure God's precious letter! It is from One who loves us infinitely more than any earthly person loves us. Again and again in God's Word we find comfort, help and strength for the day: "Strengthen thou me according unto thy word" (Psalm 119:28b). It is our instruction book, giving us directions for each day: "Order my steps in thy word" (Psalm 119:133a). We can have sweet fellowship with the Lord through the Word: "And thy word was unto me the joy and rejoicing of mine heart" (Jeremiah 15:16b).

The text for this meditation tells us that the Bereans searched the Scriptures daily. It was God's letter to them and they wanted to know its message. We, too, should search the Scriptures for God's message to us so that we can receive His directions for our lives. "Man shall not live by bread alone, but by every word that proceedeth out of the mouth of God" (Matthew 4:4). Not only should we search His Word, but we should also meditate on it and appropriate it in our lives. Someone has said, "When one reads the Bible, not snapshots but time exposures should be the rule."

Some of our earthly mail goes to the dead-letter office. I wonder how many of God's messages do not reach us because we fail to call for them. Where are your messages going? Are you going to His Word to claim them, or are you letting them go to your "dead-letter office"?

Peter therefore was kept in prison: but prayer was **4**
made without ceasing of the church unto God for
him. Acts 12:5

R. A. Torrey said, "All that God is, and all that God has, is at the disposal of prayer. Prayer can do anything that God can do, and as God can do everything, prayer is omnipotent." Peter experienced the power of such prayer in his life. He was in prison. Since help was needed, a group of his friends gathered to pray for him. They knew the power of prayer.

They prayed "without ceasing." In the Greek this has the meaning of "stretch-out-ed-ly," indicating that every nerve and muscle is stretched out to God. Prayer is the soul stretched out to God in intense earnestness or desire. Is this true of our prayers? These concerned believers were in one accord in praying to God for Peter. They were definite and specific in their prayer for him. There is power in such definite and united prayer.

In the meantime, the angel of the Lord appeared to Peter in prison and told him to follow. Peter's chains fell away and he was free. "They came unto the iron gate that leadeth unto the city; which opened to them of his own accord."

Today there are many who are in prisons — not like that in which Peter was confined, but prisons of sin, hopelessness, despair, loneliness or discouragement. Through prayer there is power to release these prisoners. Deliverance can come as you pray without ceasing — earnestly and definitely — for them.

5

> And, behold, I am with thee, and will keep thee in
> all places whither thou goest, and will bring thee
> again into this land; for I will not leave thee, until
> I have done that which I have spoken to thee of.
> Genesis 28:15

Jacob had to leave home because of trouble with his brother. After traveling all day, he looked for a place to spend the night. "And he lighted upon a certain place, and tarried there all night, because the sun was set" (vs. 11). Very likely he was homesick. His future was insecure and uncertain. How alone he must have felt!

God came to him that night with a reassuring promise. He reminded Jacob of His presence: "I am with thee." What comfort for Jacob in that lonely place that night! God also guaranteed protection: "I . . . will keep thee in *all* places whither thou goest." He assured Jacob of His guidance, "I . . . will bring thee again into this land," and promised, "I will *not* leave thee." The God who made these promises to Jacob is our God also, and what He did for Jacob He will do for us.

God will meet us, as He met Jacob in a place of need. He has promised, "Lo, I am with you alway, even unto the end of the world" (Matthew 28:20b). He assures us, "I am with you at home, at work, in your field of Christian activity." No matter where you are or what you face, He has promised you His protection, His guidance and, best of all, His own presence.

When Jacob awoke, he said, "Surely the Lord is in *this* place; and I knew it not." Are you in a place of despair, loneliness and heartache, and have you failed to see Him there? Look for Him in "this" place, wherever you are. As you look for Him and find Him in "this" place, He will give you the promise of His abiding presence: "I am with you and I will watch over you wherever you go . . . for I shall not forsake you until I have done everything I have mentioned to you" (Berkeley).

Weeping may endure for a night, but joy cometh in the morning. Psalm 30:5

6

What blessed truths we learn from David's experiences with God as they are shared with us in the Psalms! The world was full of tears in his day as it is in ours. The Psalmist had been going through a serious time of testing. Friends had deserted him; difficulties were pressing around him. Although, in David's experience, weeping had endured for a night, in the midnight of his life he possessed the complete assurance that "joy cometh in the morning." God was very real and very personal to him. He knew he could trust God in the dark places, knowing that they had a purpose in his life. David learned that God uses the tears of the night to prepare for the joy of the morning.

Are you in the night of weeping, pain, disappointment, trials or burdens? God has assured us of the dawn of a new day. In the night of trial, be patient. In the midnight of life, God gives the assurance that "joy cometh in the morning."

There are lessons that only tears can teach us. They give clearer vision. They cleanse our eyes so that we can see our Saviour more clearly. Out of weeping comes joy — not the kind of joy the world knows, but the joy that comes from the assurance of God's presence. "God gives . . . the oil of joy for mourning, the garment of praise for the spirit of heaviness" (Isaiah 61:3). The tears of today turn to the songs of tomorrow.

7   *And now you have become living building-blocks of stone for God's use in building His house. I Peter 2:5, Living Letters*

On one of our visits to our nation's capital, we visited the Washington Cathedral. We were told that it had been under construction for a number of years and still was not completed. After touring the cathedral, we went behind the building. There we saw an interesting collection of stones of various shapes and sizes, each bearing a number. We learned that each had been cut into a certain size and shape to fit into a particular place. They were numbered so that the workmen would know where to place them.

God is building a spiritual house. Christ, the Living Stone, is the Foundation and Cornerstone. Christians are living stones placed in this building. These living stones are not all the same size or shape but are especially prepared for the place God has for them in His building. As I looked at the stones to be placed in the great cathedral, I could see that they had been cut and chiseled in preparation for their particular place. We, too, must be prepared for the place God has for us. This may require cutting and chiseling. Of course, we may rebel against this, but the day will come when we will see its value.

During the depression a man lost his job, his wife, and his home, but he tenaciously held onto his faith — which was all he had left. One day he stopped to watch several men doing stone-work on a huge church. One of them was chiseling a triangular piece of stone. "What are you going to do with that?" asked the man. The workman replied, "See that little opening up there near the spire? Well, I am shaping this down here so that it will fit in up there." Tears filled the eyes of the man as he walked away. God had spoken to him through the workman to explain the ordeal through which he was passing. It was as if the Divine Workman Himself had said, "I am shaping you down here so that you will fit in up there."

Thou hast put gladness in my heart, more than in
the time that their corn and their wine increased.
Psalm 4:7

8

David had been going through deep waters. At a time when friends and family had deserted him, he could have become despondent. But, no! He writes of the gladness he had in his heart.

Too often we assume that joy and gladness come from prosperity. It is not difficult to be glad when everything is going our way and we have all we need. But this is not the gladness about which David was writing. The source of this joy was in God — "*Thou* hast put gladness in my heart." It is a gladness that results from an inner peace of heart.

The "corn and wine" increase of material things does not put this kind of gladness in our hearts. David didn't mean that he had no material blessings. He didn't mean that one cannot have gladness of heart if he has possessions. But he did mean that the Lord was far more precious and wonderful to him than anything he owned. God gave him a "more than" gladness in the midst of troubles and trials. This gladness was entirely independent of circumstances.

Do we have this kind of gladness — a gladness that does not depend on what we have or what we do? — a gladness that does not depend on friends, on where we live, on praise or on circumstances? This gladness comes from God Himself and it is for His own dear children.

9 *And he gave heed unto them, expecting to receive something of them. Acts 3:5*

Do you know people who seem to be able to do anything? They fit beautifully into any situation; they always seem to say just the right thing. Because of this ability, others turn to them for help, for comfort, for advice. Everyone seems to *expect* much of such capable people.

The text for this meditation speaks of a lame man who was daily carried to the Temple, where he asked alms. One day this hopeless cripple, observing Peter and John on their way to the Temple, saw in them a potential source of help. He *expected* to receive aid from them. The disciples were ready to help him, but not in the way he expected.

Because Peter and John were dedicated to the work of sharing Jesus Christ with others, they had *seeing eyes* for the needs of those around them. "Peter, fastening his eyes upon him with John, said, Look on us." They had *ready voices* to tell of Jesus. "Then Peter said, Silver and gold have I none; but such as I have give I thee: In the name of Jesus Christ of Nazareth rise up and walk." They had *stretched-out hands* ready to serve. "He took him by the right hand, and lifted him up."

Today there are those who are just as helpless spiritually as the lame man. Can they *expect* to receive something from us? If they cannot expect help from Christians, to whom can they look for aid? Peter and John could not give the lame beggar material help, but they gave him something far more precious — that which could meet his spiritual need. We, too, can help to meet the spiritual needs of those around us if he have seeing eyes, ready voices and stretched-out hands dedicated to Him.

Trust in the Lord with all thine heart; and lean not unto thine own understanding. In all thy ways acknowledge him, and he shall direct thy paths. Proverbs 3:5, 6

10

This Scripture verse tells us how we can be assured of divine guidance. Our trust is not to be in man, a creed or a code of ethics, but in the Lord. We can trust Him, for He keeps His Word. We are to trust Him with *all* our hearts — we are to have undivided hearts. "Lean on, trust and be confident in the Lord with all your heart and mind" (vs. 5a, Amplified). We are not to lean on our own understanding, for it is not a sufficient guide through the perplexities of this world. "Do not rely on your own insight or understanding" (vs. 5b, Amplified).

We are to acknowledge Him in *all* our ways. To acknowledge Him means to commit our way to Him, to put Him first in everything. We are to acknowledge Him in our ambitions, choices and decisions; in our homes; in our relationships with others; in our friendships. God has promised that if we keep our part, He will keep His — we are guaranteed His direction.

Three students visiting Switzerland were killed in a fall over a mountain precipice. They tried to make a dangerous ascent without a guide. Lacking the knowledge, skill and experience needed, they came to disaster. How foolish they were to undertake such a venture without an experienced guide! Yet sometimes we are equally foolish. We try to make life's journey without our Guide. We lean on our own wisdom or that of a friend. We try to direct our own ways and we come to disaster. Reliance on God brings guidance from Him. "In all your ways know, recognize and acknowledge Him, and He will direct and make straight and plain your paths" (vs. 6, Amplified).

11   *That in all things he might have the preeminence.*
        Colossians 1:18

This chapter reveals the pre-eminence and supremacy of the Lord. He is pre-eminent in His revelation of God. "[Now] He is the exact likeness of the unseen God — the visible representation of the invisible" (vs. 15, Amplified). God revealed Himself in Jesus Christ; what we know of God we know through Christ. Jesus said, "He that hath seen me hath seen the Father" (John 14:9).

He is pre-eminent in His relation to the universe — the natural creation. "For it was in Him that all things were created, in heaven and on earth, things seen and things unseen, whether thrones, dominions, rulers or authorities; all things were created and exist through Him (by His service, intervention) and in and for Him" (vs. 16, Amplified). All things were created in, through and for Him.

Not only did He create the universe, but He maintains it. "And He Himself existed before all things and in Him all things consist — cohere, are held together" (vs. 17, Amplified). His hand holds the stars in their courses, directs the planets in their orbits and controls the laws of the universe.

He is pre-eminent in His relation to His spiritual creation, of which He is the Head of the body. "He also is the Head of [His] body, the church." As the head controls every part of the body, so Christ, the Head, has authority over us as members of His body. He has a personal interest in each member of His body. A. B. Simpson has said, "He who bears the universe upon His shoulders, carries His loved ones on His heart and plans every incident of their lives and causes all to work together for their good."

As the Creator and Maintainer of the universe, is He not also able to direct our lives and fit everything into the plan He has for us? He who is pre-eminent in the natural creation desires to be pre-eminent in us, His spiritual creation.

But they that wait upon the Lord shall renew their strength; they shall mount up with wings as eagles; they shall run, and not be weary; and they shall walk, and not faint. Isaiah 40:31

12

Someone has said that three words characterize this age of speed — "hurry," "worry" and "bury." Often we rise in the morning so weary that we wonder how we can survive the day. After we have had our time with God in the Word and in prayer, we rise from our knees refreshed and renewed, assured that we have His strength, not ours, for the day. We have gone to the very source of strength, God Himself.

The condition for renewing our strength is waiting. We are to be waiting pilgrims, not weary ones. The Hebrew word for "wait" means "looking unto and expecting from": "looking unto God" — *prayer* — and "expecting from Him" — *trust*. "My soul, *wait* thou only upon God; for my *expectation* is from him" (Psalm 62:5). *Wait prayerfully — expect trustingly.*

As we wait on God, our strength is renewed. We have exchanged our finite weakness for His infinite strength. This is illustrated by the eagles who have power to rise high above the storm. We, too, as we face the storms of life, can mount up with wings as eagles. God has "wing power" for us, but these wings are only for those who *wait* on the Lord. If we meet this condition, we can rise above disappointments, sorrows, heartaches and problems.

Renew your strength today by waiting on the Lord. Then you can rise above the difficulties of your life. You can run and not grow weary; you can walk and not faint.

13   *And Moses said, I will now turn aside, and see this great sight, why the bush is not burnt. Exodus 3:3*

Have you ever started out for a drive and suddenly decided to turn off the main highway and take an intriguing side road, wondering what you might find? Suddenly you came to a spot of breath-taking beauty, perhaps a field of flowers, a shady nook or a beautiful mountain or ocean view. How delighted you were that you had taken time to turn aside!

Moses had a wonderful experience when he turned aside. While taking his flock to the backside of the desert, he saw a bush burning but not consumed. "Moses said, I will now *turn aside,* and see this great sight, why the bush is not burnt." For Moses this was not merely an ordinary day. Unexpectedly he received a visit from God. "And when the Lord saw that he turned aside to see, God called unto him out of the midst of the bush, and said, Moses, Moses. And he said, Here am I" (vs. 4). As he turned aside, he experienced the joy of being in God's presence and hearing God speak to him. God then revealed His plan for Moses.

God waits to reveal Himself to us as He did to Moses, but we must turn aside as Moses did and be alone with Him if we are to hear Him speak. Sometimes we become so entangled in the things of this life that we fail to turn aside, and thus we miss what God may want to share with us. If we turn aside, God will reveal to us new and precious things about Himself as we study His Word and pray. Moses said, "I will *now* turn aside." Why not take time today to turn aside and let God speak to you?

Whom having not seen, ye love; in whom, though now ye see him not, yet believing, we rejoice with joy unspeakable and full of glory. I Peter 1:8

14

Valentine's Day is a special time for showing our love to those who are dear to us, but every day is a special time for expressing our love to the Saviour. Peter writes of loving Him, the Saviour of mankind. Who can do other than love Christ when he has experienced the Lord's love in his life? "Who loved me, and gave himself for me" (Galatians 2:20). "We love him, because he first loved us" (I John 4:19).

Human love is centered in those we see, but supernatural, divine love is centered in One whom we have not seen. Yet when we believe on Him, the Holy Spirit makes Him so real and precious to us that our hearts respond by loving Him. He becomes dearer and sweeter to us as the days go by. Although we have not seen Him with the physical eye, we have felt His love, His comfort, His strength, His power. Although we do not see Him, we love Him with joy unspeakable and full of glory.

One day a wealthy woman came to an orphanage to take one of the little girls home as her own. After it had been decided that Jane was to be hers, she told the child about what she would give her — new clothes, a room of her own, a beautiful doll. After a moment's hesitation, Jane asked, "What am I to do for all this?" Her new mother replied, "Only love me and be my little child."

"Without having seen Him you love Him; though you do not [even] now see Him you believe in Him, and exult and thrill with inexpressible and glorious (triumphant, heavenly) joy." (I Peter 1:8, Amplified).

15   *Now the God of peace, that brought again from the dead our Lord Jesus . . . make you perfect in every good work to do his will, working in you that which is wellpleasing in his sight, through Jesus Christ; to whom be glory for ever and ever.* Hebrews 13:20, 21

Today world leaders are trying to bring peace to a world torn with conflict. Individuals are trying to find peace in their lives. The sad truth is that all these who seek peace through their own efforts are doomed to failure because they do not go to the source of peace. God is the only One who can give peace, for He is the source of peace — not the outer peace of circumstances but the inner peace of the heart.

The God of peace wants to make us "perfect in every good work to do his will." In the Greek this word means "to make an adjustment," such as setting a dislocated bone. God may see in your life something that is dislocated, out of touch with Him. An adjustment may be necessary to bring you to the place of doing His will. This may be painful for a short time, but it is necessary. He entrusts this operation to no one else but performs it Himself as gently and as tenderly as possible, watching over you lovingly. He adjusts us that he might work in us "that which is wellpleasing in his sight." Yielding to His touch upon our lives brings peace to our hearts.

A man was watching a potter. Thinking he could make a pot, he tried and failed. Then the potter said, "Let me help you." Sitting behind him, the potter put his arms, hands and fingers over the man's arms, hands and fingers. The wheel then began to spin. "Do not let your fingers resist mine," cautioned the potter. The vessel became beautiful as the man yielded himself to the potter. As we yield our lives to the skillful touch of the Master Potter, He will shape us into vessels "meet for the master's use" (II Timothy 2:21).

He will not suffer thy foot to be moved: he that keepeth thee will not slumber. Behold, he that keepeth Israel shall neither slumber nor sleep. Psalm 121:3, 4

16

In these days of world tension, what comfort and assurance we have in these verses! The Hebrew word for "slumber" means "to be drowsy." The Hebrew word for "sleep" means "to be off guard."

We may lose nights of sleep if there is illness in the home. When my mother was seriously ill, I was with her constantly, night and day, for three weeks, during which I had not more than an hour's sleep a night. Human love serves without ceasing. However, if we continue indefinitely without rest, our bodies will eventually be exhausted.

Not so with God. He never becomes drowsy and is never off guard. The Keeper of Israel neither slumbers nor sleeps. He never shuts His eyes to our needs. He assures us that He is never unaware of our problems. There is never a moment night or day when He does not see us.

One night a little girl was getting ready for bed. It was a moonlit night. "Mommy," said the little girl, "is the moon God's light?" "Yes," replied the mother. "It is God's light shining in the sky." "Will God turn off His light and go to sleep, too?" "No," the mother answered. "God's light is always burning; God doesn't go to sleep." "I'm so glad," answered the child. "While God is awake, I am not afraid."

17
He who dwells in the secret place of the Most High shall remain stable and fixed under the shadow of the Almighty (Whose power no foe can withstand). Psalm 91:1, Amplified

This is a favorite portion of Scripture. Someone has called it our "air-raid shelter." If we are in danger, it gives us a feeling of security. If we are sorrowing, its comfort fills our being. God has a secret place for us — a place of safety and quiet — a place near to His heart. No harm can come to us there, for we are safe in Him.

He who dwells in this secret place abides under the shadow of the Almighty. Have you ever traveled across the desert as the shadow of a cloud suddenly passed over you? What relief you experienced! Or perhaps you came to an oasis of trees beside a spring of water and you stopped for a few minutes to rest. How refreshing it was! Similarly, the shadow of our Almighty God refreshes our spiritual lives as it falls upon us. David had assurance and confidence because he could say, "*My* refuge, *my* fortress, *my* God." This is also the basis of our confidence in God. We must know Him personally so that each of us can say, "*My* God."

An insurance salesman was trying to sell a policy to a woman. She declared emphatically, "Mister, I have all that I need and more in a policy I have. It didn't cost me as much money as yours would." Curious, the salesman asked to see her policy. She opened her Bible and turned to Psalm 91. "This is all the insurance I need," she said. "I have social security — 'abide under the shadow of the Almighty' (vs. 1); insurance against damage — 'he is my refuge and my fortress' (vs. 2); health insurance — 'neither shall any plague come nigh thy dwelling' (vs. 10); collision insurance — 'lest thou dash thy foot against a stone' (vs. 12); accident insurance — 'thou shalt tread upon the lion and adder' (vs. 13); life insurance — 'with long life will I satisfy him, and shew him my salvation' (vs. 16)."

The Lord is the portion of mine inheritance.
Psalm 16:5a

18

This is a day of materialism — a day when "things" seem to be very important in our lives. While the world scrambles madly for material gain, the believer can say with the Psalmist, "The Lord is the portion of mine inheritance."

David is here speaking of the portion which belonged to the priesthood tribe of Levi. When the land of Canaan was distributed among the tribes of Israel, the tribe of Levi received no part of it. We read in Joshua 13:33, "But unto the tribe of Levi Moses gave not any inheritance: the Lord God of Israel was their inheritance, as he said unto them." They were to serve the Lord and be sustained by the supply of the Temple. The Lord Himself was their portion and would care for them. The word "portion" is defined as "allotment" or "share from an estate."

The portion of our inheritance — the Lord Jesus Christ — is available today for everyone who has a personal relationship with Him. Our portion of this inheritance includes His life, His strength, His peace, His joy — all that He is, is available to us. Thus each of us can say, "Thou art *my* portion, O Lord: I have said that I would keep thy words" (Psalm 119:57). It is an everlasting portion: "God is the strength of my heart, and *my portion for ever*" (Psalm 73:26b).

Someone has said, "Faith in Christ is the key that unlocks the cabinet of His promises and empties out their treasures into the soul."

19   *My sheep hear my voice, and I know them, and they follow me. John 10:27*

What a joy it is to hear a voice and recognize it as that of someone dear to us! It is sweet to see the look of recognition on a baby's face as it hears and recognizes its mother's voice.

Animals also have this faculty of recognition. Eastern shepherds sometimes keep several small flocks of sheep in one fold at night. In the morning every shepherd calls his own by name, and each sheep recognizes his own shepherd and immediately goes to him. God's sheep also recognize the voice of their Shepherd when He calls them. He sees their needs — their hunger and thirst — their scratches and wounds. He calls to them, and they hear His voice and respond to it.

He knows us, His own sheep. He knows all about us, where we are, and what our needs are. He knows and hears every individual cry and answers immediately. This truth is illustrated by the story of a man who was visiting a huge sheep ranch in Australia. It was shearing time. The owner of the farm took a little lamb from a pen and turned it loose in a large enclosure where there were several thousand sheep. He explained that he wanted it to join its mother. The visitor wondered how the lamb would find its mother among so many sheep. The tiny animal raised its head and made a weak sound. The mother heard the faint bleating of her little lamb and, recognizing it immediately, ran to it.

As the sheep follow, keeping their eyes on the Shepherd, He provides for and protects them. A drilling officer was training a company of new recruits. They were trying hard but making little progress. Finally the officer said, "Take your eyes off your feet and look. Then your feet will follow your eyes."

The Lord said that he would dwell in the thick   **20**
darkness. I Kings 8:12

We have made a number of visits to the Carlsbad Caverns and are always impressed by the unforgettable experience of being in total darkness when all the lights are extinguished far below the earth's surface. What a thrill to our hearts as the light gradually appears in the far distance and slowly grows brighter! We appreciate the light much more after we have spent time in the darkest darkness I have ever experienced.

How many of you prefer the darkness to the light? Not many, I'm sure. Yet the night is as important as the day. God created both. We are told that some plants grow faster at night than in the daytime. Are you going through a "dark place" in your life? Perhaps you need a period of "growing" which can take place only in the darkness. The Lord dwells not only in the darkness but even in the *thick* darkness. He is with you in your dark place.

The following story illustrates this truth. A man was taking a journey by train. In the same compartment were a mother and her little girl. The child was quietly playing with her toys as she sat beside her mother. Suddenly the train entered a tunnel and the compartment became dark — so dark that nothing could be seen. The man was surprised that the child was not at all frightened. When they emerged again into the light, he knew the secret. The little girl had put her arms around her mother's neck and was not afraid in the darkness.

"I will trust, and not be afraid" (Isaiah 12:2).

21 *Now faith is the assurance (the confirmation, the title-deed) of the things [we] hope for, being the proof of things [we] do not see and the conviction of their reality — faith perceiving as real fact what is not revealed to the senses. Hebrews 11:1, Amplified*

Someone has said, "Faith is to believe what we do not see — its reward is to see what we believe." Have you not sometimes wondered how much faith you really have?

In Matthew 21:21 and 22 we read, "If ye have *faith,* and *doubt not,* ye shall not only do this which is done to the fig tree, but also if ye shall say unto this mountain, Be thou removed, and be thou cast into the sea; it shall be done. And all things, whatsoever ye shall *ask* in prayer, *believing,* ye shall receive." The prayer of faith has the promise of an answer. Instead of saying "Amen" at the end of her prayer, a little girl said, "R. S. V. P." ("a reply is expected"). Ask in faith and doubt not. Ask in prayer, believing. This is the faith that triumphs over impossibilities.

Do you want to move mountains in your life? Exercise faith and doubt not. Ask and believe. Doubt sees the obstacles; faith sees the way. Reading of the faith of George Mueller, one exclaims, "Oh, if only I had faith like his!" When someone questioned the great Christian about it, he said, "My faith is the same kind of faith that all of God's children have had down through the ages." But he was willing to trust the faithfulness of God, and he exercised his faith in the Heavenly Father. The secret of his faith was that he studied the Word of God and believed its precious promises.

"When we work, *we* work; but when we pray, *God* works."

The effectual fervent prayer of a righteous man avail- **22**
eth much. James 5:16

Have you noticed the numerous "before and after" advertisements appearing in current publications? Women's magazines
feature striking pictures of rooms and houses before and after
they were redecorated or remodeled. This approach is also used
in advertising medicines and many other products.

Is this not an illustration which we can apply to prayer? Consider all the needs you have in your personal life, in your family,
in your church, with respect to your friends, at work. The problems, heartaches, difficulties — how great and numerous they are!
These are the "before" of prayer. What makes possible the wonderful "after" of prayer? "The earnest (heartfelt, continued)
prayer of a righteous man makes tremendous power available —
dynamic in its working" (Amplified). God's power is available
after prayer.

Consider what can be accomplished after we have prayed.
The possibilities are limitless. It is our privilege to intercede for
the needs of the world, for our country, for our loved ones and
friends, for our avenues of service. If we are to have specific
answers, we must make specific requests.

A little crippled girl was ill and knew she would never recover.
She was concerned because she had not been able to do more
for the Lord. Her pastor suggested that she make a prayer list
of those who needed Jesus Christ and that she pray for them by
name each day. Soon there was a great spiritual awakening in
the town. As the child heard about what was happening, she
prayed more earnestly. Some time later she went home to glory.
Under her pillow was the list of those for whom she had prayed.
All had come to Christ. The last had accepted the Saviour the
night before the little girl's death. Such is the power of definite,
specific, fervent prayer in the Spirit.

23 *For the eyes of the Lord are over the righteous, and his ears are open unto their prayers.* I Peter 3:12

Today people are burdened with trouble that they want to share with someone. They want a listening ear. It is a comfort to know that God has listening ears.

One day as I was wading in a mountain creek, I slipped on the rocks and fell face down in the water. The powerful current carried me downstream over the rocks, scratching my face and bruising me. I was helpless and recognized the need for immediate assistance. I didn't have time to explain how I fell or what had happened to me. I could only lift my face out of the rushing water and cry "Help!" Immediately aid came and I was lifted out of the creek. God's ears are open to our slightest cries as the ears of those about me were open to my cry of distress. Amy Carmichael calls these cries "little prayers."

Peter had learned from experience that God's ears are open to His children and that He hears their faintest calls for help. One day the disciples were on the Sea of Galilee during a severe windstorm. The waves were strong and the men were in desperate need of help. Jesus came walking to them on the sea. After the Master had identified Himself, Peter said, "Lord, if it be thou, bid me come unto thee on the water" (Matthew 14:28), and Jesus told him to come.

As long as Peter kept his eyes on the Lord, he was able to walk on the water, but when he "saw the wind boisterous," he began to sink. In the desperateness of his situation he cried, "Lord, save me." The ears of the Lord were open to his cry. Peter's prayer was not long. It was only three words: "Lord, save me." Immediately the Lord stretched forth His hand and caught him.

Are you in a desperate situation today? Do you need help? The ears of our loving Lord are open to you. He is only a "little prayer" — a "cry" — away.

He must increase, but I must decrease. John 3:30

Occasionally we hear it said of someone, "He is a great person." How do we determine this greatness? Position, wealth, education, talent — these are usually considered to be the essential ingredients in greatness.

John the Baptist was one whom the Lord called great. However, he had no desire that the people honor him as he went about ministering. His one purpose was to turn their eyes away from himself and to focus all their attention on the Saviour. John said, "*He* must increase, but I must decrease." This was the secret of his greatness. He wanted to be hidden from view so that the people might see Jesus Christ only.

Your life can be compared to a television screen. An object in a televised picture may occupy only a very small part of the screen and may appear to be a great distance from the viewer. Suddenly, however, a close-up picture, occupying the entire screen, may flash into view. This picture has "increased" over the first. What about the television screen of your life? How much of it does Christ occupy? — only a small corner, or the entire screen? Is He increasing daily in your life? It has been said, "The beginning of greatness is to be little; the increase of greatness is to be less; the perfection of greatness is to be nothing." May each of us say with John, "He must *increase,* but I must decrease."

25 *Joseph is a fruitful bough, even a fruitful bough by a well; whose branches run over the wall. Genesis 49:22*

Jesus spoke of the Vine-branch relationship in John 15, saying, "I am the vine, ye are the branches." In the Old Testament, Jacob spoke of his son Joseph as a bough. Boughs are the branches closest to the trunk; they are the strongest branches, not easily tossed by the wind. The outer branches may be stirred by the gentle breezes, but the boughs are not easily moved. Boughs are usually hidden from sight.

Can it be said of us, as of Joseph, that we are boughs? As boughs we live close to the heart of God. As boughs we are strong in the Lord, not easily tossed about by the winds of life. As boughs we are hidden from sight so that the world may see Christ in our lives.

Joseph was a fruitful bough by a well. His daily life bore fruit for God because he drank daily of the Water of Life. Water is necessary to keep plants fresh and green. If we fail to water them, they droop and become yellow and dry. To be fruit-bearing boughs, we too, need to be by a well, daily drinking of the Water of Life.

The branches from Joseph's bough ran over a wall. The walls in our lives keep us set apart for God, living close to Him. Thus the branches of our lives spread out as a blessing to others.

A woman was disappointed because she saw no blossoms on a rose bush which climbed her fence. One day her invalid neighbor called to her, saying, "Oh, how I am enjoying the roses on your bush! Just see how they are blooming on my side of the fence!"

It has been said, "God doesn't bless our overwork, but our overflow."

She hath done what she could. Mark 14:8a

Jesus was being entertained in the home of Simon the leper. A woman entered, bringing an alabaster box of ointment of spikenard, very precious. This she broke and poured the rare perfume on Jesus' head. To some in the room this seemed a waste as they believed the ointment should have been sold and the money given to the poor. But Jesus could see into Mary's heart filled with love for Him. Praising her desire to give Him that which was precious to her, He said, "She hath done what she could . . . . Wheresoever this gospel shall be preached throughout the whole world, this also that she hath done shall be spoken of for a memorial of her" (vss. 8, 9).

Mary did what she could. She used her money and time to purchase the ointment which she poured on Jesus' head. Perhaps there were others who could do more, but she did what she could because she loved Him. Nothing ever given to Christ is wasted. It was Mary's motive — not the value of her gift — that was important. For this she received the praise of the Saviour.

What about us? Are we really doing what we can? May we pour out our time, our talents, our very lives in love at His feet today, that He may say of us that we have done what we could.

27   *But they, supposing him to have been in the company, went a day's journey. Luke 2:44*

Mary and Joseph had taken Jesus to the Temple in Jerusalem. On the way home, after they had gone a day's journey, they missed Him — "*supposing Him* to have been in the company." To their dismay they discovered that He was not with them — He was lost.

Do we ever go a day's journey without Him, supposing that He is with us? Have we ever run ahead of Him or lagged behind? How often do we take Him for granted? Do we direct our daily lives as we want to, making our own decisions and choices and "supposing Him" to be in them? We choose our own pleasures, friends, habits, fields of service, and then we ask the Lord to bless them. We can become so involved in our own lives that we lose ourselves in *our* plans, and in so doing, lose *Him*.

As soon as Joseph and Mary missed Jesus, they returned to Jerusalem *seeking Him*. After three days they found Him. Where? In the place where they had left Him — in the Temple about His Father's business. Have you lost Him somewhere in your life? Have you crowded Him out of even a corner of it? Then seek Him where you left Him — He is waiting for you there.

Our search for Jesus takes us down the pathway of prayer which leads us back to Him. We then experience the sweetness of His presence in our lives and a moment-by-moment walk with Him. When we find *Him* we are completely *satisfied:* "For he satisfieth the longing soul, and filleth the hungry soul with goodness" (Psalm 107:9).

*For we are fellow workmen — joint promoters, labor-
ers together — with and for God. I Corinthians 3:9
Amplified*

There is a story told about a house which was badly in need
of paint. "I am going to paint the house," said a can of paint,
waiting, already mixed, in a shed. "No, I am going to paint it,"
the brush asserted, bristling with impatience. "You are, are you?"
sneered the ladder, lying against the wall. "How far would
either of you go without me?" "Or without me to pay the bill,"
arrogantly added the checkbook belonging to the owner of the
house, in a voice muffled by the pocket of the coat hanging on
a nail. Just then the painter, who had overheard the proud remarks, ventured to put in a word. "Perhaps I'd better take a
holiday," he said quietly. "I wonder if the house would be
painted by the time I got back."

Even the most efficient among us are only tools in the hands
of the Great Master Worker. As we work with Him and for
Him, He works in us and through us. In verses 6 and 7 Paul
says, "I have planted, Apollos watered; but God gave the increase.
So then neither is he that planteth any thing, neither he that
watereth; but God that giveth the increase."

One worker is not more valuable or important than another.
He that plants and He that waters have a unity of purpose.
There is no reason for rivalry. Each has his task; each has his
place. Perhaps it is our task to plant — or it may be to water.
There may be times when we plant and other times when we
water. But whatever our place may be, we are laboring with
and for God. Then God will give the increase.

29

It is of the Lord's mercies that we are not consumed, because his compassions fail not. They are new every morning; great is thy faithfulness. Lamentations 3:22, 23

Every year we celebrate special holidays such as Thanksgiving and Christmas. Other days are celebrated in honor of a person — such as Washington's Birthday. February 29th is very unique — it occurs only once every four years. It is not a special holiday. It is not named in honor of a person. Yet the day is important to those who celebrate their birthdays on this day.

How thankful we are that God's faithful love and care is not just for a special day. It is not given to us occasionally or once every four years. We receive it moment by moment, day after day.

In the above Scripture we are reminded of the faithfulness of God. He is compassionate and loving to His own children, ever mindful of them. Because of the steadfastness of His love, His mercies are renewed to us day by day. One meaning of the word "mercies" is "loving kindnesses." A little boy was asked "What is loving kindness?" He replied, "When my mother gives me a slice of bread and butter, that is kindness; but when she spreads jam on it too, that is loving kindness."

In His great faithfulness He renews His loving kindness to us each morning. How precious it is to awaken to face the stress and strain of a new day assured that His love and mercy are renewed to us for that day's needs.

God's Word assures us "But though He causes grief, yet will He be moved to compassion according to the multitude of His loving kindnesses and tender mercies. For He does not willingly and from His heart afflict or grieve the children of men." (Lamentations 3:32, 33).

Cast thy burden upon the Lord, and he shall sustain thee: he shall never suffer the righteous to be moved. Psalm 55:22

1

How often we see someone who looks as if he is carrying the weight of the world on his shoulders. Perhaps at some time someone has said to you, "You look as if you've lost your last friend." Have you ever felt that no one really cared and that you were carrying the burdens of the whole world? In these days of confusion and frustration, such a feeling is a frequent experience. Burdens become increasingly heavy; cares press upon us; problems arise in the home; difficult situations distress us at work; heartaches and sorrows overwhelm us. Are you feeling the weight of these burdens today? Are you facing insurmountable problems for which you have no solution?

God says, "Cast your burdens on *Me*." Often we take our burdens to everyone else before we take them to the Lord. A well-known Gospel song reminds us to take our burdens to the Lord and *leave* them there. When we take our burdens to Him, we are strengthened by His sustaining hand, we are comforted by Him, and we find that He is the One who can solve our problems and lighten our burdens.

Our experiences in life become steppingstones to bring us closer to Him if we let Him carry our burdens. A biologist relates that he was fascinated by an ant carrying a piece of straw which seemed to be a tremendous burden for the tiny insect. The ant came to a small hole which it could not cross. It stopped for a few seconds, and then, with amazing intelligence, used the piece of straw as a bridge over the hole. Learning from this wise little insect, we, too, can use our afflictions as steppingstones.

If we cast our burdens on Him, and slip our hands into His, our adversities are transformed into victories. Someone has said, "Out of the brass of trials God fashions trumpets of triumph."

2   *Speak, Lord; for thy servant heareth.* I Samuel 3:9

The hearing aid is a wonderful invention. It has restored the blessing of sound to many whose hearing has been impaired.

As Christians we are provided with spiritual "hearing aids" with which we can hear God speak to us. Samuel's spiritual hearing aid enabled him to hear God speak to him. He replied, "Speak, for thy servant is listening" (Berkeley). We must be quiet enough to hear our Heavenly Father's voice. God did not speak to Elijah in the wind, the earthquake or the fire, but in the "still small voice."

Today the confusing sound of other voices — the voices of pleasure, fame, business — makes it difficult to hear God's voice. These other voices must be tuned out if we are to hear God speak. Some people turn off their hearing aids if they don't want to hear what is being said. Christians can do this, too. They can "turn off" their spiritual hearing aids by indifference, lethargy, disobedience or busyness.

Go into your closet today and check your spiritual hearing aid. Is it in good working order, or has it been turned off? Are all the sounds of this world tuned out? Is it perfectly tuned in to God? If so, you can say, "I will hear what God the Lord will speak" (Psalm 85:8a).

[No, you] yourselves are our letter of recommenda-
tion (our credentials), written in your hearts, to be
(perceived, recognized,) known and read by every-
body. You show and make obvious that you are a
letter from Christ delivered by us, not written with
ink but with [the] Spirit of [the] living God, not on
tablets of stone but on tablets of human hearts. II
Corinthians 3:2, 3, Amplified

A pastor had been praying that a young man might become a Christian. One Sunday his prayer was answered, and the young man received Christ as his Saviour. The pastor asked him, "What was it in my sermon that caused you to receive Christ?" "Oh," replied the young man, "it wasn't anything in your sermon. It was my Aunt Mary's life." True indeed is this statement: "What you do speaks so loudly that I cannot hear what you say."

Genesis 27 tells us how Jacob tricked his brother Esau so that he received the special blessing which Isaac, his aged father, was to give to Esau. Rebekah, his mother, encouraged Jacob in this deception. He hurried out to get venison for his father. Then he put on Esau's clothes before he went in to see Jacob. He even put skins on his hands and neck, for Esau was hairy. Since Isaac couldn't see well, he was deceived by scheming Jacob. Scripture tells us, however, that he said, "The voice is Jacob's voice, but the hands are the hands of Esau." The hands and the voice didn't agree.

Does what we say agree with what we do? We are "living epistles," "walking letters," for Christ. Many people who don't read the Bible are reading the living epistles of our lives. How closely they watch us! It has been said, "More people read the Bible bound in shoe leather than the one bound in morocco." We may be the only Bible some people will ever read. We can say that there are five Gospels: "Matthew, Mark, Luke, John and the Gospel According to *You*."

4   *And He said to them, Come after Me [as disciples] —
letting Me be your Guide, follow Me — and I will
make you fishers of men!" Matthew 4:19, Amplified*

We often hear a person say that he has been called to a certain
task or vocation. When Jesus lived on earth, He called men to
Himself. One day He saw Peter and Andrew and said to them,
"Follow me, and I will make you fishers of men." He *gave* a call
to them as they were engaged in their daily occupation. They
were fishermen — not men of great religious training. They had
different personalities and capabilities. Peter was different from
Andrew. Andrew couldn't do what Peter could.

The important aspect of Christ's call to them was that they
were to follow *Him* — not a human leader or a particular occupation, but *Him*. What was their *response* to His call? It was
immediate — "And they straightway left their nets." It was complete — they "followed him."

Our Saviour's call still goes forth today. He calls us first to
Himself — "Come after *Me;* follow *Me*." Then He makes His
call more specific. Not only does He call us to be pastors and
missionaries, but also to be secretaries, nurses, bookkeepers, home-
makers. We are not all alike. Our talents and abilities vary.
But He will use each of us in the place of His choosing.

What is your response to His call? Is it immediate? Is it
complete? Follow Him and He will make you a fisher of men.

Where is God my maker, who giveth songs in the night? Job 35:10b

The story is told of a little piece of ebony which complained bitterly because its owner persistently whittled on it. Since he was making a flute out of the piece of ebony, he paid no attention to its complaining. "Without this whittling and cutting you would be only a stick. You may not like it, but wait. Little piece of ebony, I am changing you into a flute, and soon your sweet music will cheer and comfort many. This whittling and cutting is needed to make you a blessing," the owner said.

Perhaps you are rebellious because of the whittling and cutting you are experiencing in your life. God says, "Be patient. I am changing your life from a piece of wood to an instrument that will play heavenly music to cheer and comfort those about you. It takes time for Me to do this. Wait." Our Heavenly Father knows what He is doing. A surgeon once said to a patient, "I may hurt you, but I will not injure you."

It is easy to sing in the light when things are going well. But He has a special song He gives in the night. God made this truth gloriously real in my experience. I had gone through deep waters. Trial after trial had engulfed me. Then another blow fell. I had to face an extremely serious problem. The night before a decision was to be made, I couldn't sleep. Fear had crept into my heart. As I prayed, I asked the Lord to remove the fear and give me a promise. As I drew a promise from my "Promise Box," I read, "Let not your heart be troubled, neither let it be afraid" (John 14:27). Not only did the Lord take away all my fear, but He gave me a song that night. Joy flooded my soul. The next day a favorable decision was made. But God had given me victory the night before, when I did not know the outcome. With His victory had come "His song in the night."

6   *The eternal God is thy refuge, and underneath are the everlasting arms. Deuteronomy 33:27a*

From childhood we are afraid of falling, of losing our footing. No doubt you have experienced this in descending from a high place. Fear gripped you as you cautiously lifted your foot from one support and placed it securely on the one below.

We are promised a refuge of *safety*. A refuge is a hiding place, a stronghold. "The Lord is good, a strong hold in the day of trouble; and he knoweth them that trust in him" (Nahum 1:7). Our refuge is the eternal God Himself.

We are promised a strong *support:* "Underneath are the everlasting arms." We rest on His sustaining strength. This support is not available only once a year or once a month or merely when we need special help. His support is constant. His arms are everlasting; they are always underneath us.

Do you need a safe refuge and a strong support today? The One who is God from everlasting to everlasting is encircling you in His refuge of safety and upholding you with His everlasting arms of strength. He *is* our refuge, and underneath *are* His arms. Perhaps you are looking into the future, at tomorrow and the day after, at next month and next year. Look at the present with the assurance that *He* is your refuge *today* and that His everlasting arms are underneath you *today*.

But first gave their own selves to the Lord. II Corin-
thians 8:5

It has been said, "The gift without the giver is bare." The Macedonian Christians had discovered the secret of true giving. They first gave themselves to the Lord. They had learned that God was more interested in them than in their gifts.

Today God is looking for those who are willing to give themselves to Him. He doesn't want merely our possessions, but ourselves. He has a right to our lives, for we read, "Ye are not your own. For ye are bought with a price" (I Corinthians 6:19, 20).

The story is told of how Fritz Kreisler, the famous violinist, obtained his treasured violin, the "Heart Guarnerius." One day he heard someone playing it in a shop. He was so charmed by its tone that he asked to buy it, but he was told that the instrument had been sold to an Englishman, a collector of old violins. Kreisler said, "I must have it. What will the collector do with it?" The dealer replied, "Probably put it in a glass case for people to look at." "This is not a violin merely to look at," said Kreisler, "but an instrument to bless the world with." He went to see the Englishman, but to no avail. Week after week he pleaded with him. One day the collector allowed Kreisler to play the instrument. The famous violinist said, "I played that violin as one condemned to death would have played to obtain ransom." When he had finished playing, the Englishman, completely moved, said, "I have no right to keep it; it belongs to you. Go out into the world and let it be heard!" And Kreisler used the violin to produce the wonderful music which has blessed the world.

More than your ability, talents, money or possessions, the Lord wants *you.* A yielded life is a God-centered life; a God-centered life will be an instrument in the hands of the Master Musician. From your life He will bring forth sweet heavenly music to bless a needy world.

8   *For we have not an high priest which cannot be touched with the feeling of our infirmities; but was in all points tempted like as we are, yet without sin. Hebrews 4:15*

A woman saw a little boy holding a sparrow with a broken wing. She said, "Son, would you like me to take this sparrow home and nurse it back to health? I promise to bring it back to you." The little boy thought for a moment and then said, "If you don't mind, I'll take care of it myself, because, you see, I understand this bird." The woman didn't understand what he meant until he stood. Then she saw that his left leg was in a cast. Because he was crippled, he understood the problem of the suffering bird.

God, in the person of His Son, came to earth and lived as a man. He was subjected to all the trials and testings of life, yet without sin. Thus, as our High Priest, He can sympathize and comfort as no one else can. Someone who has been tested and tried as we have is best able to understand our feelings.

Our Saviour understands when we are heartbroken, and He shares the experience with us. He knows when we are lonely, discouraged and disappointed. He understands when we are misunderstood. He never misjudges us. He knows our weariness and loneliness. There is no one so tender and sympathetic as He. Today, whatever your temptation, whatever your infirmity, He is very near, understanding and sympathizing, bringing comfort to your heart as no one else can.

There is a lad here, which hath five barley loaves,
and two small fishes: but what are they among so
many? John 6:9

Often we hear it said, "Little is much if God is in it." This truth is vividly illustrated in John 6, where God's Word tells us about a little boy of whom we read only once, and whose name we do not even know.

One day a great multitude had been following Jesus. It was growing late and the crowd was hungry. Jesus said to His disciples, "Whence shall *we* buy bread?" Andrew found a little boy with a small lunch of five loaves and two fishes. "What are they among so many?" he asked. Andrew, like many of us, was not familiar with the arithmetic of heaven. But the little boy was willing to give Jesus what he had — only a small lunch. Jesus took it, blessed it, and shared it. Thus a great multitude was fed. Little did the boy realize how important his lunch would be in God's program that day. We may feel that we have little that God can use. But insignificant as it may seem, placed in God's hands it can become a blessing to multitudes.

A new church was being constructed. The members of the congregation apparently felt no need for a new building and were not enthusiastic about the project. They were reluctant to provide the necessary money, and the pastor became discouraged. One morning there was a knock at his door. The caller was a little boy with a wheelbarrow containing six bricks. "Here are a few bricks I thought you could use for the new church," said the lad. This encouraged the pastor. He told every person in the congregation about the six bricks. Soon the members subscribed enough money to begin construction of the building. Only six bricks — but when a little boy gave them to God, a beautiful church was built and dedicated to His glory.

10   *And the Lord shall guide thee continually. Isaiah 58:11*

On one occasion when we were visiting relatives in a distant city, friends invited us to have dinner with them at their home. When we left, we failed to get directions for returning to the home of our relatives. Soon we realized that we had made a wrong turn and were lost. As we approached a stop sign, we explained our plight to the young men in the car beside ours, and to our relief, one of them said reassuringly, "We're going in that direction; just follow us."

We have a Guide who has promised to lead us in the way we should go each day. "The Lord *shall* guide thee." Many, many times a day I need His guidance, for I do not know what to do or which way to go. I have learned to follow Him, for His way is always best. He will keep me from stumbling or losing my way. He will guide me *continually*.

If the Lord is to be our Guide, we must follow Him. Jesus said, "My sheep hear my voice, and I know them, and they *follow me*" (John 10:27). Perhaps He is saying to you today, "Take your eyes off your problems, your circumstances, your needs, and *look* up. Then your feet will follow your eyes, and you will follow Me."

*And he said, My presence shall go with thee, and I
will give thee rest. Exodus 33:14*

God took Moses up into the mountain where He had given
him the tables of the Law. While their leader was gone, the
children of Israel decided to make a golden calf to worship.
When Moses returned and discovered this, he was heartbroken,
discouraged, disappointed. Knowing that he needed encouragement, God gave him the reassuring promise that He would go
with him and give him rest.

What a comforting promise this is for us today — the assurance
of His divine presence. God says, *"My presence* shall go with
thee."* The Septuagent Version reads, "I Myself will go with you."
We have His companionship as a Friend. His presence is sure,
for He says *"shall* go." It is personal — "with *thee."* His presence
brings rest — rest from frustration, fear, tension, worry, doubt.
His presence is real.

During World War I a soldier at the front received a copy of
one of the Gospels. Although he read it, he could not accept
the reality of Christ. One night he was on sentry duty. Alone
in the presence of danger, he thought about God. How he wished
that he could believe in the reality of Christ and know that His
presence was with him there! Suddenly he was aware of someone standing behind him. To his surprise, he saw King Albert,
his king, standing sentry duty with him. This experience was
used of God to make him realize that the Lord would be as
near and as real to him as King Albert was. As a result, he became
a Christian.

No matter what calamity befalls, no matter what emergency
arises, His presence is with us, helping, encouraging, strengthening, comforting and giving wisdom. Assured of His presence, we
are assured also of His rest.

12   *Return . . . and submit thyself. Genesis 16:9*

Hagar, a slave maid in the home of Abram and Sarai, had been treated unjustly, and in her hatred and resentment had fled to the desert. The angel of the Lord found her — weary, lonely, disappointed, disillusioned — sitting by a fountain of water in that desert place.

As the angel questioned her, she told him the reason for her flight. The angel said to her, "Return . . . and submit." What a shock that must have been to the unhappy slave maid! Perhaps she was expecting sympathy; certainly she was not prepared for such advice. She couldn't be expected to return to that impossible situation and to her cruel mistress, she reasoned. Yet she was told to return and submit.

Is there a situation in your life to which you need to return and submit? Has the Lord found you running away from something? Do you feel that you have been unfairly treated? Perhaps you have asked rebelliously, "Why do I have to do that?" or "Why can't I do what I want to?" Perhaps your pride has been wounded and you have said selfishly, "Well, I won't do that" or "Well, they'd better get along without me." The "self way" never brings real peace and joy. Victory and power will come as we sweetly submit our wills and ways to God. This is not easy. Our wills are strong. But great blessing comes in returning and submitting.

But he knoweth the way that I take: when he hath tried me, I shall come forth as gold. Job 23:10

13

One of the words most frequently used by children is the little word "why." This word is often found on the lips of God's children also. "Why doesn't God hear my prayer?" "Why does this have to happen to me?" "Why do I have to suffer?" Why? Why? Why?

Things were dark for Job; hope seemed to be gone. He couldn't see *the way* ahead. He said, "Behold, I go forward, but he is not there; and backward, but I cannot perceive him: on the left hand, where he doth work, but I cannot behold him: he hideth himself on the right hand, that I cannot see him" (vss. 8, 9). It seemed as if God had forsaken him. *But God* knew his way. "He knows the way that I take — He has concern for it, appreciates and pays attention to it. When He has tried me, I shall come forth as refined gold [pure and luminous]" (Amplified). Job looked beyond the trouble and rejoiced in the assurance that God knew his way and would bring him forth as pure gold.

These are days of trial and testing for us. We know not the way ahead. Sickness, heartache, suffering — these burden us. At times it seems as if all we hold dear is being taken away. We seek a way out. Like Job, we turn to the right and to the left. We go forward and backward. Although we cannot see *the way,* we can say confidently, "but *he knoweth the way* that I take: when he hath tried *me,* I shall come forth as gold." He knows the pain, suffering, heartache and disappointment. Not only does He know; He *cares.* The way that is dark to us is light to Him. The way that is hidden to us is clearly seen by Him. As He moves upon our lives through trials, the result is gold. I once heard these wise words: "We are receiving exactly what we would request if we could see as God sees."

14   *Although the fig tree shall not blossom, neither shall fruit be in the vines . . . yet I will rejoice in the Lord, I will joy in the God of my salvation. Habakkuk 3:17a, 18*

Habakkuk was a prophet of faith. The Lord had shown him that an invasion of Judah by Babylonia was inevitable. He told him of the adverse conditions that would prevail when that occurred. Habakkuk's response to this was one of victory — "Although . . . yet." "*Although* the fig tree shall not blossom, neither shall fruit be in the vines . . . the fields shall yield no meat; the flock shall be cut off from the fold, and there shall be no herd in the stalls: *yet* I will rejoice in the Lord, I will joy in the God of my salvation," he declared confidently. He had learned to look at God, not at circumstances.

Although there might be adversity and affliction ahead, *yet* Habakkuk could say that he could rejoice. The prophet refused to be defeated by the "*although*" of circumstances but triumphed in the "*yet*" of his trust in God. He adds victoriously, "The Lord God is my strength, and he will make my feet like hinds' feet, and he will make me to walk upon mine high places" (vs. 19).

One morning a pastor met one of his parishioners and asked her how she was. "Not too bad, under the circumstances," she answered. "Why don't you get above the circumstances where the Lord is?" was the pastor's penetrating reply. What are the circumstances in your life today? *Although* you may be experiencing many trials, *yet* you, too, can declare victoriously, "I will rejoice in the Lord, I will joy in the God of my salvation."

As my Father hath sent me, even so send I you. **15**
John 20:21b

These verses are easily applied to those who are in full-time service, such as missionaries and pastors, but do these words of Scripture not apply to us also? It has been said, "Every heart with Christ in it is a missionary; every heart without Christ is a mission field." Does this limit missionary service to a special group of people? A missionary has been defined as "God's person in God's place doing God's work in God's way for God's glory." This surely includes all of us.

Jesus said, "As my Father hath sent me, even so send I *you.*" This is still our commission today. He commissions some of us to serve Him in our neighborhoods; others in our offices; others in our families. Not all of us are called to "full-time" service, but all of us are called for "lifetime" service. Wherever you are today, God can use you, for He says, "Even so send I *you.*" Have you paused to discover His purpose for you where you are?

With our Lord's commission to the disciples came His assurance of blessing for their hearts — "Peace be unto you" (vs. 21). This peace of heart would prepare them to be His messengers *in* the world with His message *for* the world.

The story is told that when the Saviour returned to heaven, an angel asked Him, "Now that You have returned to heaven, do You have a plan for taking the Gospel to all the world?" "Yes," Jesus replied. "I chose and trained a group of men to be sent out with the Gospel. Others in turn will join them in spreading the Word." "But," said the angel, "what if they fail? What other plan do you have?" "I have no other plan," Jesus answered.

16   *To be molded into the image of His Son [and share inwardly His likeness]. Romans 8:29, Amplified*

A man returned to his home town to search for his uncle whom he had never seen. Walking down the street with a friend, he said suddenly, "There goes my uncle!" "How do you know?" asked his friend. "He walks like my father," was the reply.

God desires to mold us into the image of His Son. This is His purpose for us. Someone has said, "God the Father was so pleased with His Son that He wanted a whole heaven full of people like Him. Therefore He is willing to patiently conform us into the likeness of His Son." God accomplishes this by taking a piece of human clay and carefully fashioning it into the likeness of His Son. A conforming process is necessary to accomplish this. This fact gives us insight into the reason for the trials and adversities in our lives.

When one makes a gelatin salad, the powder must be dissolved in hot water. As the liquid begins to cool, it is poured into a mold to set. There it becomes firm, conformed to the shape of the mold. If the gelatin becomes firm before it is put into the mold, it must be softened before it can be molded. Similarly, the heat of adversity may be necessary to soften the hard places in our lives so that we may be conformed to the image of Christ.

Clay conforms to outside influences. What are the outside influences to which our lives conform? Who is our mold? The world or Christ? "Don't let the world around you squeeze you into its own mould, but let God remould your minds from within so that you may prove in practice that the Plan of God for you is good, meets all His demands and moves toward the goal of true maturity" (Romans 12:2, Phillips).

Yea, he loved the people; all his saints are in thy hand: and they sat down at thy feet; every one shall receive of thy words. Deuteronomy 33:3

17

Do you have a particular spot where you like to go to escape the strain of daily living — a place that is peaceful and quiet? There the cares of life slip away and you forget everything but the joy of solitude. At least you may wish for such a place. The above verse suggests three resting places for God's children — in His heart; in His hand; at His feet.

First, we have a resting place in His great heart of love: "For the Father himself loveth you" (John 16:27a); "Yea, I have loved thee with an everlasting love" (Jeremiah 31:3). Second, there is a resting place in His hand. This is a place of security. "Fear thou not; for I am with thee . . . yea, I will uphold thee with the right hand of my righteousness" (Isaiah 41:10). Third, we have a resting place at His feet. Mary found this resting place. This is a place of fellowship with Him, a place to hear His voice, a place of instruction. Sitting at His feet, listening to Him, loving Him, we find peace and refreshment. What blessed resting places God has provided for us — in His heart; in His hand; at His feet!

One night a preacher was using as his text, "Come unto me, all ye that labour and are heavy laden, and I will give you rest" (Matthew 11:28). He asked, "What does this verse mean?" A little girl answered, "It means He wants me." Both the preacher and the people felt that no more need be said. Hearts became tender, eyes wet with tears. "He wants *me.*" Today He wants *you* — He wants *me* — in His heart; in His hand; at His feet.

18

If it be so, our God whom we serve is able to deliver us from the burning fiery furnace, and he will deliver us out of thine hand, O king. But if not, be it known unto thee, O king, that we will not serve thy gods, nor worship the golden image which thou hast set up.
Daniel 3:17, 18

In this chapter we read about three men who were facing a choice. They had to choose between bowing to an image or refusing to do so and remaining true to God. If they refused, they were to be cast into a fiery furnace. Their trust was in God. They knew He could deliver them if He so willed. They said, "*Our God* whom we serve is able to deliver us . . . . *But if not.*" Even though they should be cast into the fire, they would still believe and trust God, knowing He had a purpose to be accomplished by this trial.

These men were not delivered *from* the fiery furnace; they were cast *into* it. But something wonderful happened. The Son of God Himself came and walked with them in the furnace. They experienced the reality of His companionship. Then they were delivered *out* of the fiery furnace. However, they had the victory of trusting God before they were delivered — "Our God whom we serve is able . . . . But if not."

Have we learned the blessing of "*but if not*" in our lives? When prayers are delayed, do we fume and fret, and begin to doubt that God really cares? Or can we say as these three men did, "Our God is able to deliver us. But if not, we will go right on trusting Him"? He may not deliver us *from* problems, but He will go through them with us, and in His time and way He will deliver us *out* of them.

Pray for us unto the Lord thy God . . . that the Lord thy God may shew us the way wherein we may walk, and the thing that we may do. Jeremiah 42:2b, 3.

19

In Jeremiah 42 we read about a small remnant of God's people in Palestine who were fearful, not knowing which way to go. They were few in number. Faced by enemies on every hand, they knew their weakness. They desperately needed God's guidance. Therefore they went to Jeremiah the prophet and said, "Pray for us unto the Lord thy God . . . that the Lord thy God may shew us the way wherein we may walk, and the things that we may do."

However, merely asking for guidance was not enough. They had to *obey* God's commands. They said, "Whether it be good, or whether it be evil, we will obey the voice of the Lord our God" (vs. 6a). Are we willing to say that? Do we trust God even when we don't understand His purposes? God knows the end from the beginning, and what may seem evil to us at the beginning may later turn out for our good. "To obey is better than sacrifice" (I Samuel 15:22b).

Then the Israelites had to wait for God to bring it to pass. "And it came to pass after *ten days*, that the word of the Lord came unto Jeremiah" (vs. 7). Have we ever become impatient because the answers to our prayers didn't come immediately? Have we wondered if God really did hear our prayers? The answer may come soon; or it may come only after months or years of waiting. "And therefore will the Lord *wait*, that he may be gracious unto you . . . blessed are *all* they that *wait* for him" (Isaiah 30:18). Someone has said, "God will never arrive too late nor with too little for our needs." When we seek guidance from God and are obedient to His commands, we can wait with assurance that in His time and way He will give us the answer.

20

I have strength for all things in Christ Who empowers me — I am ready for anything and equal to anything through Him Who infuses inner strength into me, [that is, I am self-sufficient in Christ's sufficiency]. Philippians 4:13, Amplified

This inspiring declaration was written by one who had suffered much for the cause of Christ; in fact, he was in prison at the time he wrote these words. Paul's life was totally committed to Jesus Christ. He could say, "For to me to live is Christ." He had the assurance that with Christ dwelling within he had all the strength he needed to face each day's needs. Christ was the source of strength for all things in his life. He could declare boldly, "I have strength for *all* things." He was infused with this inner strength to face life. He could face prison, persecution and prosperity; he could be content wherever he was. Christ was sufficient for any situation and for any need he might have.

This strength to do "all" things is available for you today in Christ. Are there difficult places before you? Do they look like mountains? Do you feel that you can't climb over them? Through Him you are equal to anything.

On one occasion when my sister and her young son were visiting us, we took them into the mountains. Just as we started up the first steep incline, Don looked up and said, "Uncle Clarke, I don't think you can make it," but the power generated in the engine of the car moved it up the steep grade and soon we were at the top of the mountain.

Claiming the inner strength He gives you, you can begin climbing the mountain before you, knowing that His sufficiency will take you over it.

These things have I spoken unto you, that my joy might remain in you, and that your joy might be full. John 15:11

The dictionary defines the word "joy" as "a lively emotion of happiness; cheerfulness; that which causes delight." We find that our joy is greatly affected by circumstances. When everything goes smoothly, we radiate a joyful spirit. But what happens when everything goes wrong, when our world seems to fall apart around us? Our joy seems to "fly out the window."

The source of true joy is the Lord Himself. "The joy of the Lord is your strength." There is a difference between the joy that comes from peaceful circumstances and the joy of the Lord which is constant and enduring day after day regardless of the circumstances about us.

In God's Word we read of the nine Christian virtues which are the fruit of the Spirit. "But the fruit of the (Holy) Spirit, [the work which His presence within accomplishes] — is love, joy (gladness), peace, patience (an even temper, forbearance), kindness, goodness (benevolence), faithfulness; (meekness, humility) gentleness, self-control (self-restraint, continence). Against such things there is no law [that can bring a change]" (Galatians 5:22, 23, Amplified). We might illustrate this in the following way. A flower has a number of petals, and each petal is an essential part of the complete flower. Joy is one of the "petals" in the fruit of the Spirit, and without it we are not complete Christians.

The joy of the Lord transforms us and gives a cheerfulness and joyousness that is not dependent upon our outward circumstances but comes from the presence of Christ in our hearts. He gives "beauty for ashes, the oil of *joy* for mourning, the garment of praise for the spirit of heaviness . . . that he might be glorified" (Isaiah 61:3). It has been aptly said, "Joy is the flag which is flown from the castle of the heart when the King is in residence there."

22 *I am the light of the world. John 8:12a*

I remember vividly our first visit to Washington, D.C. As we walked around the city that first evening we were there, my eyes were constantly drawn back to a sight that stirred the very depths of my being. All about us was darkness; yet one thing was clearly visible. Numerous hidden spotlights were focused on one object — not the White House, not the Congressional Library, not the Senate Building, not the House of Representatives, but the dome of the Capitol Building itself. The spotlights themselves were not visible, but their powerful light enabled us to see, glowing majestically in the darkness, the beautiful dome of the building that represents the very heart of our great country.

In Genesis 1:16 and 17 we read of the greater and the lesser light, set in the heavens to give light upon the earth. Since Christ, the greater Light, has returned to heaven, we, the lesser lights, must shine for Him upon the earth. We are His "spotlights" shining in a dark world.

One day a very poor little girl slipped into a church service. The preacher spoke on "The Light of the World." After the service she went up to the pastor and said, "Sir, are you the Light of the World you were talking about?" "No," he answered, "I am just one of His lights." "Then," she pleaded, "would you please come and shine in the alley where I live? It's so dark down there."

And he must needs go through Samaria. John 4:4

Appointments are important and are made to be kept. One day God made an appointment for Jesus to keep. The *path* to this appointment took Him through Samaria. On this path was a *place* of appointment where two *persons* were to meet. God had arranged the meeting of these two — a very needy woman met the Saviour, and her life was transformed.

God's Appointment Book for me has led me on various paths to people with spiritual needs. There have been occasions when I was put in a certain place at a certain time to meet a certain person — times when I must "needs go through" my "Samaria."

I once had to change my flying schedule because of a strike. I told the girl at the airlines office that I couldn't return home on the one plane which she said was available. This was unusual for me. Ordinarily I would have been happy to get home by any route. However, I suggested a different route, and I obtained reservations on another plane. Later I knew why I "must needs go home on that particular plane." There was a needy person on it — the young hostess who needed the Saviour.

God has scheduled many appointments for us which we have missed because we did not check to find out where and when they were to be kept. Have you wondered why you accepted a position in your particular office? Or why you moved into your present neighborhood? Was it perhaps because God has an appointment for you to keep there? Be sure to check God's Appointment Book for you every day so that you will not miss an appointment He has made for you.

24   *And they took knowledge of them, that they had been with Jesus. Acts 4:13*

"It pays to advertise." Advertising is the key to American success, we are told. Why is so much money poured into this method of attracting customers? Newspapers are filled with advertisements; television screens present attractive advertising; billboards display signs; free samples are distributed; demonstrations show the advantages of one product over another. How many products do you have in your home today because you saw them demonstrated? It is said that a pleased and satisfied customer is the best advertisement for a product.

Peter and John had spoken boldly about Jesus. Those around them could see the change in their lives. Christ had become real to them. This was an intensely personal experience. "For we cannot but speak the things we have seen and heard," they declared. Those who observed them had discovered the secret of this change. "And they took knowledge of them, that they had been with Jesus."

Do you remember playing the game "New Orleans" when you were a child? One group of children would go to the second group and say, "New Orleans," to which the latter would reply, "Show us some." Today people are looking for something that is real, that really works in life. We have the privilege of "showing" them that Christianity is real, for it is a Person, Jesus Christ. We have been effective advertisements for Him if others "take knowledge of us that we have been with Jesus."

After the death of Robert McCheyne, a letter addressed to him was found among his belongings. It was from one whom he had led to Christ. Speaking of the experience, the writer made this revealing statement: "It was nothing you said that first made me want to be a Christian — it was the beauty of holiness which I saw in your face."

Lord, what wilt thou have me to do? Acts 9:6

Paul had a transforming experience in his life. He had been seeking believers in Christ so that he could have them put in prison or killed. One day on the Damascus road he had an encounter with Jesus and became a Christian. He committed his life completely to Him, saying, "Lord, what wilt thou have me to do?" This was the desire of one who was in love with Jesus Christ. He had made Christ the Lord of his life, and had yielded his whole being to Him.

The story is told of a beggar in India who sat by the roadside begging alms. As he held out his bowl, people passing by dropped a few grains of rice into it. This was his means of providing food for himself. Occasionally someone dropped a coin into his hand. One day he saw a procession coming down the road. *This is good,* he thought. *It looks as if a prince is approaching. Surely he will give me a gold coin today.* It was indeed a prince, and he stopped beside the beggar, who held out his bowl and waited eagerly to see what his royal benefactor would drop into it. To his surprise, the prince asked, "Will you please give me your rice?" "I can't do that," the beggar answered. "It is all I have." Again the prince said, "I want your rice." "No, I can't give you my rice. It is all I have to eat," was the firm reply. The prince made a third request for the rice. Slowly the beggar took *three* grains of rice out of his bowl and put them into the hand of the prince, who then reached into a bag hanging at his belt and took out *three* nuggets of gold which he dropped into the bowl. As the beggar looked at them he thought regretfully, *Oh, why didn't I turn my bowl upside down in his hand?*

26   *When I consider thy heavens, the work of thy fingers, the moon and the stars, which thou hast ordained; what is man, that thou art mindful of him? and the son of man, that thou visitest him? Psalms 8:3, 4*

One evening my husband and I were sitting in our back yard. As the stars came out we tried to count them as we had done in our childhood. Of course we soon lost count, but I remembered that God's Word says, "He telleth the number of the stars; he calleth them all by their names" (Psalm 147:4).

Can you not visualize David as he sat on the hillside and looked at the starry heavens, meditating on the glory of it all? Contemplating man and his place in this great universe, he questions, "What is man, that thou art mindful of him? and the son of man, that thou visitest him?"

God is *"mindful"* of us. This two-syllable word consists of the words *"mind"* and *"full."* Have you not looked down on the earth from an airplane or a high building and realized that man is only a speck in God's great universe? Yet the Psalmist says that God's mind is *full* of man. The God of the universe is also the God of the individual. His thoughts are centered in man and his needs. He is more interested in us than in the rest of His creation.

God proved how interested He is in us — He visited us in the *person of His Son.* "And the Word was made flesh, and dwelt among us" (John 1:14a). "For God so loved the world, that he gave his only begotten Son, that whosoever believeth in him should not perish, but have everlasting life" (John 3:16).

A vessel unto honour, sanctified, and meet for the master's use, and prepared unto every good work.
II Timothy 2:21

How many vessels do you have in your home? I am sure you have a variety of types and styles with a wide range of uses. Some are displayed prominently where people can see them. Others are seldom seen by others but are used constantly in the kitchen, and you are certain you couldn't keep house without them.

God has a variety of vessels, too. They are of various types and styles, and He has different uses for them. Some are used occasionally; others are used often. Some are in prominent places; others are in places hidden from view but are of equal importance in His work. God's requirement is that the vessels be clean and empty so that He can fill them with Himself. A vessel in the home is useless in itself; it is useful only in the hand of the master of the house. Similarly, God's vessels are to yield themselves as instruments in His hand for Him to use.

Some years ago a famous violinist was to give a concert on his Stradivarius violin for which he had paid a thousand guineas. The huge hall was filled to capacity, and the violinist played gloriously. When he had finished, there was a moment's hush and then a burst of applause, during which he smashed the instrument to pieces on the edge of the platform. There was an uproar. When quiet was restored, the great artist said, "Ladies and gentlemen, on the way to the concert hall, I bought this violin for five shillings. Now, if you will bear with me, I will play for you on my Stradivarius."

The instrument or vessel itself is not so important as its willingness to be used in the hand of the Master. "May each of us be a vessel set apart and useful for honorable and noble purposes, consecrated and profitable to the Master, fit and ready for any good work" (Amplified).

28 *Epaphras, who is one of you, a servant of Christ, saluteth you, always labouring fervently for you in prayers, that ye may stand perfect and complete in all the will of God. Colossians 4:12*

Little is known of Epaphras, but this verse of Scripture reveals his greatness before God. He was a servant of Jesus Christ. A servant is one who has yielded his will completely to his master. He serves without regard to his own interests, time or strength. He owns nothing and is nothing apart from his master. Jesus was first in the life of Epaphras.

Epaphras knew and believed in the power of prayer. We read that he labored fervently in prayer for the Colossian Christians. God had laid them on his heart and he had a real concern for them. He considered his prayer life as part of his service to God — he labored "fervently." Some people think that because they have no special talents or abilities they can do no service for God. But they forget that they can serve by praying.

Epaphras' petitions were for others. He had a prayer interest in their lives. He prayed that they might be mature and "stand perfect and complete" in the will of God. How much we need to pray for our fellow Christians! Too often we are criticizing them when we should be praying for them. May each of us say, in the words of a well-known Negro spiritual, "I'll talk about others down on my knees." May we — like Epaphras — be servants of Jesus Christ, praying fervently that others might mature into God's will for their lives. Only eternity will reveal what will be accomplished for the Lord through such lives yielded completely to Him.

In the true spirit of humility (lowliness of mind) let each regard the others as better than and superior to himself — thinking more highly of one another than you do of yourselves. Philippians 2:3, Amplified

The following story is told of General Howard, of the United States Army. Because he had led his brigade to victory, he was entitled to lead his men in the Grand Review at the conclusion of the war. One morning, however, he was told by his commanding officer that through political favoritism his predecessor in the brigade had been chosen to lead the men in the parade. The General, of course, was upset by this news and believed this privilege should be his; his men would expect him to lead them in the review as he had led them in the campaign. The commanding officer agreed, but reminded him there was nothing that could be done. He said, "General Howard, I understand that you are a Christian; perhaps you can accept this situation as a Christian." The General replied, "That makes all the difference in the world. I will not object to his leading my brigade." "Thank you," said the commanding officer. "I appreciate your attitude. We will let him take your place at the head of the brigade. But will you please meet me at the headquarters at nine o'clock in the morning? You shall march with me at the head of the army."

Someone may be given a place of service which you think you should occupy. In fact, you may even deserve it. Let us not be upset and concerned about such seeming injustices. Let us not become bitter when another receives the credit for what we have done. God's Word says, "None of you should think of his own affairs, but should learn to see things from other people's point of view" (Philippians 2:4, Phillips). We must keep ourselves humble and esteem others better than ourselves. "A good violinist is one with the ability to play first fiddle and a willingness to play second."

30   *And let the peace (soul harmony which comes) from
the Christ rule (act as umpire continually) in your
hearts — deciding and settling with finality all questions that arise in your minds — [in that peaceful
state] to which [as members of Christ's] one body
you were also called [to live]. And be thankful —
appreciative, giving praise to God always. Colossians
3:15, Amplified*

A ruler is one who directs, makes decisions, guides and controls. We see rulers of this world set up their systems and make
their plans to bring about peace. Yet world peace has not come.
In our own lives we see, too, that making our own plans, directing our own lives, does not give us inner peace.

This verse of Scripture reveals the secret of perfect peace; it
is God's formula for peace. We are instructed to "let the peace
of God *rule*" in our hearts. In Ephesians 2:14 we read that Christ
"is our peace." When He rules in our hearts, everything is in its
proper place, and peace is the blessed result. His peace is a
peace which the world cannot give or take away.

The world believes that security can give peace. But in reality
it is only peace with God that brings security. It has been well
said, "*peace* is our *privilege* when we *belong* to Christ. *Peace*
can only be our *possession* as we *believe* in Christ."

Rejoice in the Lord always — delight, gladden your-
selves in Him; again I say, Rejoice! Philippians 4:4,
Amplified

This verse is easy to memorize, but it is not easily put into practice. Yet Paul tells us to rejoice "always." We are not to rejoice merely on the calm days when everything is going smoothly; not merely on the sunlit days. But we are to rejoice also on the weary days, the gloomy days, the dark days when our hearts are heavy with grief. We are to rejoice also on the days when we have physical or financial needs.

This rejoicing is not dependent upon our circumstances; its source is in *the Lord.* To "rejoice in the Lord always" is to have a constant and abiding spiritual joy in our hearts, and our faces will glow with this radiant inner joy of His presence.

A woman was crossing a London railway station when an old man said to her, "I want to thank you." "Thank me?" she said, in surprise. "What for?" He answered, "I used to be a ticket collector here. Whenever you went through the gate you smiled at me and said 'Good morning.' No matter what the weather was, you were always the same. I wondered where you got your smile, and finally I decided it must come from within. One day I saw a Bible in your hand, and thinking that perhaps that was the source of your cheerfulness, I bought a Bible and began to read it. Soon I found Christ as my Saviour, and now I can smile, too."

1
Therefore, my beloved brethren, be firm (steadfast), immovable, always abounding in the work of the Lord — that is, always being superior (excelling, doing more than enough) in the service of the Lord, knowing and being continually aware that your labor in the Lord is not futile — never wasted or to no purpose. I Corinthians 15:58, Amplified

In the earlier part of this chapter Paul speaks of the resurrection. In this closing verse he says what the reality of the risen Lord means in the life of the believer. "And so, brothers of mine, stand firm. Let nothing move you as you busy yourselves in the Lord's work. Be sure that nothing you do for Him is ever lost or ever wasted" (Phillips).

Christ's resurrection from the dead makes it possible for Him to live within our lives. The reality of His presence prevents instability and insecurity. It makes us steadfast, unmovable, not only in our faith, but also in our service for Him. We can be steadfast regardless of our circumstances or feelings. We can be unmovable in spite of discouragement or disappointment.

The resurrection gives us a great incentive for service. We are to be always abounding in the work of the Lord." "Abounding" means "overflowing." When our hearts and lives are filled with the joy which comes from our knowing the risen Saviour, they will overflow in service. It is the overflow of our lives that touches others.

Whatever you do for the Lord is never lost or wasted. You may be serving the Lord in a small place. Your service will not be forgotten. Perhaps because of responsibilities at work and at home you can do very little. But remember that your life can have a powerful influence on those around you. Wherever you are, you can abound to overflowing.

For to me to live is Christ. Philippians 1:21a

2

What does life mean to you? For what are you living? One person might reply, "For my family and home." Another might answer, "For my work." Still another might say, "For pleasure." Perhaps someone would respond, "To save and prepare for the future." Edmund Cooke said, "This life is a hollow bubble." Browning wrote, "Life is an empty dream." Will Durant, the famous philosopher, once sent George Bernard Shaw, the great dramatist, a questionnaire in which he asked, "What is the purpose of life?" Mr. Shaw answered, "How should I know?"

Paul the Apostle knew the true purpose of life. He said, "For me, to live is Christ — His life in me" (Amplified). To him life was a Person — the Lord Jesus Christ. Some say, "Life begins at forty." Paul said, "Life begins with Christ." He was the object of Paul's love and devotion; the apostle's ambition and goal in life was to serve and glorify his Saviour.

Paul met the Lord on the Damascus road and life was never again the same for him. He was completely transformed. With Christ dwelling within him, Paul could say, "For to me to live is Christ." Someone has said, "With Christ living in us we have His feet for walking; His ears for hearing; His face for reflecting; His eyes for seeing; His lips for speaking; His life for living."

What is your ambition, your goal, your purpose in life? Is it to let Christ live His life in you? "When someone becomes a Christian, he becomes a brand-new person inside. He is not the same any more. A new life has begun" (II Corinthians 5:17, Living Letters).

3
For he satisfieth the longing soul, and filleth the hungry soul with goodness. Psalm 107:9

When Jesus appeared for the first time after the resurrection, on the first day of the week, He met Mary Magdalene. Mary had come to the tomb to see the body of the Lord, but the sepulchre was empty. Weeping, she peered into the tomb and saw two angels. "Woman, why weepest thou?" they asked. She answered, "Because they have taken away my Lord, and I know not where they have laid him."

She turned away from the angels and saw Jesus standing. He asked her, "Why weepest thou? whom seekest thou?" Mary supposed Him to be the gardener. Her eyes blinded by tears, she said, "Sir, if thou hast borne *him* hence, tell me where thou hast laid *him,* and I will take *him* away." Her thoughts were filled with *Him.* Christ was "all" to her; she was wrapped up in Him; she was completely satisfied with Him.

Are we as wrapped up in Jesus Christ Himself as Mary was? Are we completely satisfied with Him? Many times you wanted something — a new dress; a piece of furniture; a position; a home — and believed that if only you could possess it you would be completely satisfied and desire nothing more. Yet when you obtained it, you soon wanted something more. It did not completely satisfy.

When Christ becomes real and precious to us, we find that He is all we want. Someone has said, "Christ responds to special love, revealing Himself to the loving, waiting heart." *He completely satisfies.*

And there we saw the giants . . . and we were in our own sight as grasshoppers, and so we were in their sight. Numbers 13:33

4

The Israelites had been told to "go in and possess" the land of Canaan. Before they entered, however, God directed Moses to send twelve spies to search out the land. After forty days they returned with their report. They even brought back "Exhibit A" — figs, grapes, and pomegranates.

What an encouraging report they could have given regarding the fertility of the land; and two of them did present a glowing report. But ten returned fearful, defeated, hopeless. They could remember only the giants. They said dejectedly, ". . . it floweth with milk and honey . . . *nevertheless* the people be strong . . . " (vss. 27, 28).

Only two looked beyond the giants — they remembered God's promise regarding the land. Both groups were reporting on the same territory but from different viewpoints. Ten looked at the giants and were filled with fear; two looked at God and were filled with faith. The giants were great, but God was greater. To possess the land required faith in God and His promises. Ten were men of fear — two were men of faith.

The Lord has entrusted to us the "possessing of the land" for Him today. "But as we were allowed of God to be put in trust with the gospel, even so we speak" (I Thessalonians 2:4). Whether the result is victory or defeat depends on your viewpoint. Are you looking at the giants or at God? Unbelief sees the giants; faith sees God. We may ask fearfully, "Can God?" Faith answers triumphantly, "God can!" If we look at the giants, we, too, will be defeated. But if we look to God, we will be victorious. Be sure that your eyes are focused on God — not on the giants.

5   *Search the scriptures; for in them ye think ye have eternal life: and they are they which testify of me. John 5:39*

It has been said, "We must know the Word of God to know the God of the Word." Jesus emphasized the importance of knowing Him through the Word. He said, "They [the Scriptures] . . . testify of me." The Jewish leaders knew the Scriptures; they knew the letter of the Law and thought that was sufficient. But Jesus warned that merely knowing the Scriptures was not enough. Their search must lead them to Him.

We may say, "How blind they were!" But why do *you* read the Word? Do you read it because to do so is your duty as a Christian? Do you read it merely to know what it says? Jesus said that the Scriptures testify of *Him*. The Word of God becomes alive and real to us only when we read it to see Him on its precious pages and to have it reveal Him to us.

The story is told that in Washington, D.C., there is a unique copy of the Constitution of the United States. If examined closely, it appears to be simply a chaos of irregular lines and peculiar lettering. But when the visitor steps back and views it in proper perspective, he is suddenly surprised to see the face of George Washington looking out at him. The lines are spaced and the letters are shaded in such a way that one sees in them a striking likeness of the Father of our Country. As the face of Washington can be seen in this copy of the Constitution, so the face of Jesus Christ shines forth from the pages of the Bible. We can have a fresh revelation of Jesus Christ Himself each day as we read His Word.

I will bless the Lord at all times; his praise shall continually be in my mouth. Psalm 34:1

This is the "All" Psalm. David wrote it when he was a homeless exile. During this time of great trouble in his life, there was seemingly nothing for which to praise God. Yet the Psalmist praised God continually.

Can we, like David, praise the Lord at all times? Can we praise Him when sorrow comes? When heartache overwhelms us? Can we praise Him when friends fail us? When we have financial reverses? David said, "I will bless the Lord at *all* times." He could do this because he looked beyond his circumstances to the Lord. He believed the truth of Romans 8:28, "We are assured and know that [God being a partner in their labor], all things work together and are [fitting into a plan] for good to those who love God and are called according to [His] design and purpose" (Amplified).

David said, "I sought the Lord, and he heard me, and delivered me from *all* my fears" (vs. 4). David was not delivered from some of his fears, or nearly all of them, but from *all* of them, every one. He went to the source of deliverance. He "sought the *Lord*," the One who could deliver completely. What fears do you have today? The Lord can give you complete deliverance from *all* of them.

David was also delivered from *all* his troubles. "This poor man cried, and the Lord heard him, and saved him out of *all* his troubles" — not merely the great ones, or the small ones, or the majority of them, but from *all* of them. The Lord can do the same for you.

In verse 6 we note the past tense of the verbs — "cried," "heard," and "delivered." In verse 17 they are in the present tense — "cry," "heareth," and "delivereth." He who heard and answered yesterday will do the same today. We must not think that Christians will escape trouble, for we read, "Many are the afflictions of the righteous: *but* the Lord delivereth him out of them *all*" (vs. 19). How wonderful to know God, the *all*-sufficient One, and to experience the reality of His complete deliverance as we bring *all* our needs to Him.

7 *If thou canst believe, all things are possible to him that believeth. Mark 9:23*

Do you really believe that God can do *anything?* "Of course we do," we say with our lips, but do we truly believe with our hearts?

In Mark 9 we read of a boy with a physical need. His father, desperately seeking help for his son, brought him to Jesus. *"If* thou canst *do* any thing, have compassion on us, and help us," he pleaded. Jesus answered, *"If* thou canst believe, all things are possible to him that believeth."

Here are two "if's" — man's "if" versus God's "if." *"If thou* canst *do* any thing," the father said. Could not God who created the world do anything? Jesus said, *"If* thou canst *believe."* He was saying, "The problem is not My inability to do, but your inability to trust. It is not a question of what I can do, but what you can believe." The father recognized his own doubts and said, "Lord, I believe; help thou mine unbelief."

How like this man we often are! Problems, heartaches and needs arise and we say, "If You can do anything . . . why don't You do something?" Doubts crowd out faith and trust. It is not a question of God's ability — "If God can" — for *He can.* It is a question of our faith — "If we can believe."

Which "if" controls your life and mine — our "If thou canst do" or His "If thou canst believe"? If we trust we do not doubt; if we doubt we do not trust.

Being confident of this very thing, that he which hath begun a good work in you will perform it until the day of Jesus Christ. Philippians 1:6

8

"Value" is defined as "the desirability or worth of a thing; attributed or assumed valuation." Several factors determine value — the cost and effort required to obtain something; the purpose for which it is used; or the associations connected with it.

My mother-in-law had a beautiful Dresden plate which she greatly treasured. She had saved for a long time to purchase it. Today it is mine and priceless to me, not only because of its beauty, but also because it was hers. I also have an inexpensive bowl which is valuable to me because it belonged to my mother. Not only is it valuable for this reason; it is also useful in the kitchen.

What value has God placed on life? In James 4:14 we read, "Whereas ye know not what shall be on the morrow. For what is your life? It is even a vapour, that appeareth for a little time, and then vanisheth away." Jesus said, "Fear ye not therefore, ye are of more value than many sparrows" (Matthew 10:31). God has placed an infinitely great value on us. "For God *so loved* the world, that he gave his only begotten Son, that whosoever believeth in him should not perish, but have everlasting life" (John 3:16).

Our Heavenly Father wants to increase the value of our lives. He who has begun a good work wants to perfect it. The Greek word translated "will perform it" means "will evermore put His finishing touches to it." How important are the finishing touches on a dress, the final touches of color on a picture, the last artistic touches of decoration on a cake! These finishing touches transform a commonplace object into a work of art. Little touches, yes, but of great importance! So God continues to put His finishing touches on our lives to increase His investment in them and make us more valuable to Him.

9   *As thy days, so shall thy strength be. Deuteronomy 33:25b*

It has been well said, "Today is the tomorrow you worried about yesterday." Our lives are so filled with tensions, turmoil, fear and frustration that we sometimes feel we cannot face "today." We *need* a strength beyond our own. God has this strength — *His strength* — for us today. He doesn't give it to us ahead of time, but each day we receive "today's" supply. Our need for strength varies from day to day. "As thy days, so shall thy *strength* be."

Not as our weeks, not as our months, not as our years, but as our *days* shall our strength be — not as our desires, not as our fears, not as our failures, but as our days. Sometimes we forget to claim this strength that God has available for us, and we struggle along in our own weakness. Sometimes we even add tomorrow's load to today's burden. Someone has said, "The today I worried about yesterday has made a wreck of me today."

We have days filled with problems, heartaches, sorrows; days filled with too many things to do; days filled with little needs; days filled with great needs. Whatever the day, God says, "*As* thy days." He is sufficient for all our needs. He is always prepared to meet them. He is never taken by surprise.

This promise is personal; it is for *you*. "As *thy* days, so shall *thy* strength be." Are you weary today? Is your schedule so full that you wonder how you will get everything done? Claim God's promise that your strength shall "be *equal* to *your* day" (Berkeley). Isaiah says, "In quietness and in confidence shall be your strength" (Isaiah 30:15). God's strength comes to us as we rest in Him in quietness and confidence.

Furthermore, brethren, we beg and admonish you in [virtue of our union with] the Lord Jesus, that [you follow the instructions which] you learned from us about how you ought to walk so as to please and gratify God, as indeed you are doing; that you do so even more and more abundantly — attaining yet greater perfection in living this life. I Thessalonians 4:1, Amplified

How much time do we spend trying to please others? We spare no effort in seeking to please those who are near and dear to us. We are interested in the things which interest them. We enjoy what they enjoy. We do what they do, go where they go. We listen to what they have to say. Our very aim in life is to please them.

Paul wrote of his aim to please God. This was his one absorbing desire. The entire purpose of his life was to please His Heavenly Father. He writes, "We make it our aim, whether in our home or away, to *please Him*" (II Corinthians 5:9, Weymouth).

We need to re-evaluate our aims in life. What is your goal? To make a name for yourself? To please your family? To accumulate a bank account? To occupy a position of honor? This is the important question for each of us: "Is my life *pleasing to God?*"

When we love Him with all our hearts we will seek to please Him and to be obedient to His every wish. A mother is pleased when her children are obedient to her commands. But if one day one of them does something special for her, not because he has been asked to do so, but simply because he loves her, how pleased the mother is.

"Without having seen Him you love Him; though you do not [even] now see Him you believe in Him, and exult and thrill with inexpressible and glorious (triumphant, heavenly) joy" (I Peter 1:8, Amplified).

11   *But I am poor and needy; yet the Lord thinketh upon me. Psalm 40:17*

The Psalmist here describes his condition — he was poor and needy. But in the midst of his need he was encouraged because he could say with certainty, "Yet the Lord thinketh upon me." David was looking to the right source of help. He says, "*The Lord* thinketh upon me." This, we are told, could be translated, "I occupy His attention."

Often we feel completely alone and we wonder if anyone really cares. There are times when we are spiritually "poor and needy." Let us remember that *we* are in the very thoughts of God Himself. We are in His thoughts today. He knows our loneliness and is occupying Himself with *us*. He "thinketh upon *me*." "Many, O Lord my God, are thy wonderful works which thou hast done, and thy thoughts which are to usward: they cannot be reckoned up in order unto thee: if I would declare and speak of them, they are more than can be numbered" (Psalm 40:5). The One who loves us occupies Himself with us.

The words "thinketh upon me" indicate that the Lord is "busying Himself with us weaving the pattern of our lives." Moment by moment He weaves in the threads which form His pattern. Skillfully He adds a thread of joy here, a thread of sorrow there, a thread of disappointment where it is needed. Each has its place and is important. As the Master Weaver, "thinks upon us" He continues to weave until His divine pattern is complete. Not only does He think about us. He does something about it!

My heart is fixed, O God; my heart is steadfast and confident! I will sing and make melody. Psalm 57:7, Amplified

David was being pursued by King Saul. Life was uncertain and insecure for the Psalmist. Yet he had *perfect security.* He said, "My soul takes refuge and finds shelter and confidence in You; yes, in the shadow of Your wings will I take refuge and be confident until calamities and destructive storms are passed" (vs. 1, Amplified). God was his refuge and he was protected by His sheltering wings.

David had perfect security because he knew that God was able to perform all things for him. He declared confidently, "I will cry to God Most High, Who performs on my behalf and rewards me — Who brings to pass [His purposes] for me and surely completes them!" (vs. 2, Amplified). We have perfect security today in the midst of calamities when we take refuge in God and rest under His sheltering wings. Knowing that our Heavenly Father is able to perform *all things* for us, we are perfectly secure. The expression "all things" (verse 2) means exactly that.

David also had *permanent stability.* One whose security is in God can be steadfast and unmovable at all times and in any situation. When life seems to crash in upon the Christian, he can say, "My soul is bowed down, but my heart is fixed."

Perfect security and permanent stability gave the Psalmist a *precious song of victory.* David had a song in the midst of the storm. "I will sing and make melody," he said. It is easy to sing when the days are bright, but a steadfast heart can sing also in times of trouble. A fixed heart has a God-given song in the dark days.

A famous old violin-maker always made his instruments out of wood from the north side of the tree. Why? Because the wood which had endured the brunt of the fierce wind, the icy snow, and the raging storm, gave finer tone to the violin. So trouble and sorrow give to the soul its sweetest melodies.

13   *Be of good cheer; it is I; be not afraid.* Matthew 14:27

The disciples were in a storm on the Sea of Galilee. Not recognizing Jesus as He walked toward them on the water, they were frightened until He spoke. Then Peter said, "Lord, if it be thou, bid me come unto thee on the water." Jesus answered, "Come."

Fixing his eyes upon the Lord, Peter stepped out in faith and walked on the water. When he turned his eyes from Jesus and looked at the waves, he became afraid and began to sink. "Lord, save me," he cried. It was a short prayer, right to the point, and stated his need specifically. Immediately Jesus caught Peter and said, "O thou of little faith, wherefore didst thou doubt?" Peter had been filled with doubt and fear instead of faith and trust.

As storms sweep across our Sea of Circumstances and Adversity, we can either be overcome by fear and doubt and begin to sink or be filled with faith and trust and walk triumphantly on the angry waves. We can put our trust completely in Him. May each of us say with David, "O Lord my God, in thee do I put my trust" (Psalm 7:1). Fear and trust do not dwell together.

At Sunday school one Sunday the children were learning the hymn, "Trust and Obey." The next week a little fellow sang confidently "Trust and O.K." If we trust and obey, everything will be "O.K." When the waves of life threaten to engulf us, if we keep our eyes on Him we can face the storms with complete trust. "I will *trust,* and not be *afraid*" (Isaiah 12:2).

I came that they may have and enjoy life, and have it in abundance — to the full, till it overflows. John 10:10, Amplified

Surrounded by Norway's lofty mountains, with their sparkling streams and waterfalls, stood a little hotel where many found rest and relaxation. Below, at the edge of the fjord, was a small settlement of red-roofed houses. One year a clergyman, who had become very weary from his heavy burden of duties, came to the hotel for his vacation. Grateful for the seclusion, he relaxed in the friendly, homelike atmosphere. Erica, the hotel-owner's daughter, was a lovable child who quickly won the hearts of the guests.

Each evening the residents of the hotel gathered to discuss the experiences of the day. One night as the clergyman was talking with several of the guests, Erica came into the room. Seating herself at the piano, she began to play. The little pianist did very well until she reached a certain line in the piece. Repeatedly she made the same mistake. Presently a man entered the room. He listened intently. Then he quietly seated himself beside the girl and began to play the piece with her, adding chords, trills and runs which transformed the simple melody into a beautiful composition. When she reached the line where she usually made the mistake, he concealed it with beautiful harmony. This was the work of a master. Later the clergyman asked his hostess, "Who is the gentleman?" She named a well-known pianist and explained, "He comes here often to rest."

As the clergyman pondered the incident, he thought, *This is an illustration of God's grace — it illustrates the way in which He adds what is necessary to make our lives full of harmony that glorifies Him.* God knows when to add the chords, runs and trills which will make your life a symphony of praise to Him. This is the life we have from Him in abundance — "to the full, till it overflows."

April

15   *And he led them on safely, so that they feared not.*
      Psalm 78:53

I once heard about a group of children who had gone for a walk in the woods. Soon they realized that they were lost. The younger ones began to cry, but the older girl said calmly, "We are going to kneel and pray and ask God to lead us out of the woods." This they did. As they finished praying a bird lighted in front of them. The children attempted to pick up the little creature. Each time they reached for it, however, it hopped ahead of them. Soon the children were surprised to find themselves out of the woods and near their home.

So our Guide will lead us safely in the way we are to go. Perhaps we cannot see ahead. We may be uncertain of the way. But the Holy Spirit will lead us step by step. He will not only lead us, but lead us *safely*.

With such a One to lead us safely, we need not fear. As He has safely led His children down through the ages, so will He lead you this very day. Life may continue to be filled with dangers and perils, but with our Heavenly Guide we need not fear. It has been said, "Safety is not the absence of danger but the presence of the Lord." Rejoice in the assurance that God leads His dear children safely.

But when it pleased God . . . to reveal his Son in me, that I might preach him among the heathen. Galatians 1:15, 16

16

God did not reveal His Son *to* Paul but *in* Paul. So God wants to reveal His Son *in* us. "Christ in you, the hope of glory" (Colossians 1:27). We cannot understand how He does this, but we can know that in His great love and mercy He chose to be pleased to reveal Him in us who were once sinners.

God has a purpose in making His Son a living reality in us: that we "might preach him among the heathen." We are to reveal His Son not only by what we say but by what we *are*. Paul stated this truth: "It pleased God . . . to put His Son within me so that I could go to the Gentiles and *show* them the Good News about Jesus" (Living Letters).

A story is told about a water lily. It was a black bulb in the mud at the bottom of the pond. "What are you?" asked the fish and frogs. "I am a water lily," was the reply. They laughed at the bulb. "Just wait and see," answered the lily. One day the sun shone warmly on the pond, and the lily began to push to the surface of the water. It had turned from black to green. The fish and frogs asked, "What is that and who are you?" "I am a water lily," was the reply. "Is a water lily merely a green ball lying on the surface of the pond?" asked the fish and frogs. "Wait and see," answered the lily. As the bulb opened its heart to the warm rays of the sun, petal after petal unfolded until beauty bloomed on the pond and fragrance filled the air. "Now at last we know what a water lily is!" exclaimed the fish and the frogs. "It is a beautiful flower whose fragrance fills the air."

So God is pleased to reveal His Son in our lives that the beauty and fragrance of His presence might be revealed to others.

17 *For without me ye can do nothing. John 15:5*

The stone was large, the boy was small, and the day was hot. His face flushed and streaked with sweat, the lad tugged at the stone, which wouldn't budge. His father asked, "Are you doing the best you can?" "Of course I am," replied the boy. "It's a big stone." "But are you sure you're doing your best?" persisted the father. Again the boy struggled but he couldn't move the huge stone. Again the father insisted, "You still aren't doing your best; you haven't asked me to help you, and I am big enough to lift it."

How true this is in our experience! We struggle and struggle, trying to do our best. But our best is not good enough. Jesus said, "Without me ye can do *nothing*." "The flesh profiteth *nothing*" (John 6:63).

Some of us say that we "can't do anything." We can't — that's true. But perhaps we are keeping our eyes on ourselves instead of looking at the One who can do all things. Some admit that they "can't do very much"; others point out that in their "own weak way" they do what they can. But are we willing to say that we "can do *nothing*"? We may have ability, talent and training. However, unless we let God use these, it "profiteth nothing."

We must take our hands off our lives and let God have full control. We must not rely on our self-sufficiency, but on God's all-sufficiency. "Not that we are sufficient of ourselves to think any thing as of ourselves; but our sufficiency is of God" (II Corinthians 3:5).

*John did no miracle: but all things that John spake
of this man were true. And many believed on him
there. John 10:41, 42*

Jesus had gone into the region beyond Jordan where John the
Baptist had carried on his ministry. As the crowds gathered
about Jesus, He very likely reminded them of John, and they said,
"John did no miracle: but all things that John spake of this
man were true." As a result, "many believed on him there."

F. B. Meyer speaks of the ministry of John as "The Work of the
Ungifted Worker." John was a God-chosen man, one "sent from
God" (John 1:6). He was one of whom Jesus said, "There hath
not risen a greater than John the Baptist." Yet what else do we
read concerning him? He "did no miracle." He was not known
for his spectacular achievements; yet in God's sight he was great.

Meyer said, "True greatness consists in doing the appointed
work of life from the platform of a great motive." John had a
great motive. Speaking of Christ, he said, "He must increase,
but I must decrease" (John 3:30). He did not seek to perform
miracles; his eyes were on Jesus, and his aim was to glorify Him.

What, then, did John do? He "spoke of this man." He talked
about Jesus. His conversation was full of Him. "And I saw, and
bare record that this is the Son of God" (John 1:34). What he
said concerning Jesus was "true."

Today God is looking for those who will speak about Jesus;
those who will share with others what Jesus has done for them.
To speak about Him we must know Him. To know Him we must
read of Him in His Word, we must commune with Him, we must
spend time with Him. We can introduce others to Christ only
if we know Him ourselves. You may think of yourself as ungifted,
but you have a very important work to do — the task of talking
about Jesus and introducing Him to others.

19   *For Israel hath forgotten his Maker. Hosea 8:14a*

Frequently we read in the Old Testament that the children of Israel had forgotten God. They chose their own kings, and even made idols to worship. They had forgotten their Maker, turning from Him and putting other things in His place. They grieved the heart of God but He patiently waited for them. When they turned back to Him He lovingly forgave them.

Not only is it true that nations forget God, but individuals forget Him as well. The word "forgotten" in this verse can be translated "mislay." Have you ever mislaid something? It wasn't really lost, but other things were piled on top of it. Temporarily you weren't sure just where it was. You may have forgotten about it because it was out of sight. Perhaps we have allowed into our lives things which have pushed God out of His place, causing us to forget or "mislay" Him for a time.

Perhaps you have "mislaid" your Maker. He may have been crowded out by activity, self-will, indifference, or sin. Over and over God reminded the Israelites that if they would seek Him they would find Him: "And ye shall seek me, and find me, when ye shall search for me with all your heart" (Jeremiah 29:13). Seek Him with all your heart. Then you will have the joy of finding Him and experiencing again the peace of His presence.

It is good for me that I have been afflicted; that I might learn thy statutes. Psalm 119:71

20

In this verse David states that affliction was good for him. As he reflects on God's dealing in his life, he realizes the reason for the affliction: "Before I was afflicted I went astray." He recognizes that God in His goodness has disciplined him, and he declares, "Thou art good, and doest good." Then he confesses, "It is *good* for me that I have been afflicted." David was grateful for God's discipline.

Some lessons are learned only in the valley of tears. God has to wash our eyes with tears so that we can see clearly. Without the trials we might have missed the sweetness of having God's hand of love wipe away our tears. I can remember that in my childhood days when I was hurt I would run to my mother and she would kiss away the tears. I felt her strength and love and was comforted. So it is with God.

Affliction has a place in God's training program. Norman B. Harrison said, "When God tests you He is honoring you with the opportunity of putting Him and His promises to the proof." The great George Mueller said, "The only way to learn strong faith is to endure great trial. I have learned faith by standing firm amid severe testing."

The story is told of a German baron who made an Aeolian harp by stretching wires between the towers of his castle. When the harp was completed, he listened for its music, but in the calm of the summer the wires were silent. When the autumn breezes blew, however, he heard faint sounds of music, and when winter came with its strong winds, the harp gave forth beautiful harmonies.

21 *And the angel of the Lord spake unto Philip, saying, Arise, and go toward the south unto the way that goeth down from Jerusalem unto Gaza, which is desert. Acts 8:26*

Philip had been preaching in Samaria. Great things had been happening there. How surprised Philip must have been when he was told to leave this place where many people were giving heed to his preaching and to go into a desert place. Should he not stay here where much was being accomplished? Why go to a desert place? Who could be reached for God there? But Philip was sensitive to the leading of the Holy Spirit. God's command was to arise and go; Philip's response was to obey.

God had a purpose in taking him there. God knew that an Ethiopian official with a seeking heart would be going down that road. He was reading the fifty-third chapter of Isaiah. God directed Philip to go near the chariot. He arose and went. Then he had the opportunity to point this man to Christ. The individual is important to God. He may call a person from ministering to a crowd and send him to guide one needy seeker in a desert place.

Today there are many people on the road of life who have deep spiritual needs. God may have a divine plan for you to meet one of them — perhaps in some unexpected place. Have you wondered why you may be in some "desert" place? If God tells you to "Arise, and go," you must be quick to obey. Today there may be some seeking soul to whom God wants you to minister. Listen for His voice.

Master, carest thou not that we perish? Mark 4:38c

While Jesus and His disciples were out on the Sea of Galilee, a violent storm suddenly arose. The disciples were frightened and feared that they would perish in the huge waves. To their dismay, they found Jesus asleep, undisturbed by the storm. They cried, "Master, carest thou not that we perish?" Jesus arose, rebuked the storm, and said, "Peace, be still." In the Greek this means "Be silent; be muzzled." Immediately the wind ceased and the sea became calm. The Master turned to His disciples and said, "How is it that ye have no faith?"

Most of us have probably had experiences similar to this. Things seem to be going along smoothly when suddenly a storm breaks over our lives, and we almost sink under the fury of it. Sometimes we feel forgotten of God. We feel He no longer cares. Perhaps we are saying by our attitude, if not by our words, "Master, carest thou not that we perish?" We become more occupied with the storm than with the One who is in the boat with us.

We are safer in the storm with Him than in the calm without Him. As we sail on the sea of life, storms will come. But we need have no fear with Him on board. Someone has said, "With Christ in the vessel, I smile at the storm." Fear sees the storm; faith sees God in the storm. "Christ is no security against storms, but He is perfect security in storms. He does not promise an easy passage, but He guarantees a safe landing."

When the *Titanic* was built, it was called the "unsinkable ship." Yet the world soon learned that this was not true, for the vessel sank after hitting an iceberg. With Jesus in the ship of your life, no matter how severe the storm, you are "unsinkable" with Him as your Pilot.

23   *And therefore will the Lord wait, that he may be gracious unto you . . . blessed are all they that wait for him. Isaiah 30:18*

Today are you waiting for God to do something for you? Are you puzzled by the delay? Do you think that perhaps He has forgotten you? God does not always answer us when we think He should. Sometimes He waits because He knows it is not the right time for the answer. He may be waiting that He may enlarge your capacity to receive and thus give you an even greater answer to your prayer. He may be waiting because you must learn needful lessons before He can answer your prayer. But He waits that He may do His very best for you.

"And therefore the Lord (earnestly) waits — expectant, looking and longing — to be gracious to you . . . . Blessed — happy, fortunate and to be envied — are all those who (earnestly) wait for Him, who expect and look and long for Him [for His victory, His favor, His love, His peace, His joy and His matchless, unbroken companionship]" (Amplified).

The Hebrew word translated "wait" twice in this verse is *chakah,* meaning "adhere to." This indicates the sticktoitiveness of waiting. The Bible speaks of many who had this ability to wait on the Lord. Joseph, for example, endured a long period of waiting, for he did not become a ruler in Egypt until many years after he had been sold by his brothers. Yet he continued to wait for God, and he could say to his brothers, "But God meant it unto good."

It has been well said, "His delays are not denials." The Lord is waiting that He may be gracious unto you.

For the Lord shall be your confidence, firm and strong, and shall keep your foot from being caught [in a trap or hidden danger]. Proverbs 3:26, Amplified

Hezekiah was the godly king of Judah, doing what was right in the sight of the Lord. The Assyrians had conquered much territory around Judah and now turned their attention to acquiring it. They used propaganda as their method of attack. Sennacherib, king of Assyria, sent a message to Hezekiah. His messengers were insolent to Hezekiah's men, trying to undermine their trust in God. They made light of Hezekiah's trust in God and asked scornfully, "What confidence is this wherein thou trustest?" (II Kings 18:19). They even said that God had sent them. Hezekiah went to God with his need. God answered and gave him victory.

When there is no human solution to our problems, where do we place our confidence? In our own strength? In our friends? In our money? We are told in Proverbs 3:25a, "Be not afraid of sudden terror and panic" (Amplified). Such courage is possible when the Lord is our confidence.

Confident that He will watch over us, we can come to Him in the assurance that He will hear and answer our prayers. "And this is the confidence — the assurance, the [privilege of] boldness — which we have in Him: [we are sure] that if we ask anything (make any request) according to His will (in agreement with His own plan) He listens to and hears us. And if (since) we [positively] know that He listens to us in whatever we ask, we also know [with settled and absolute knowledge] that we have [granted us as our present possessions] the requests made of Him" (I John 5:14, 15, Amplified).

We can be confident of His keeping power and His ability to answer prayer when we are certain of our own personal relationship to Him. We can *know Him.* "These things have I written unto you that believe on the name of the Son of God; that ye may know that ye have eternal life, and that ye may believe on the name of the Son of God" (I John 5:13).

25   *My times are in thy hand. Psalm 31:15a*

David's life was full of trouble. He said, "Have mercy upon me, O Lord, for I am in trouble" (vs. 9). But he confidently turned from trouble to trust. *"But* I trusted in thee, O Lord: I said, Thou art *my* God" (vs. 14). His trust was in the One who could help him in time of trouble — "in thee, O Lord."

The Psalmist stated specifically what he entrusted to God. He trustingly turned his life over to God. He placed his "times" — his needs, heartaches, problems — in God's hand.

Today troubles may come to you as they did to David. What assurance comes as you say, "But I *trusted* in thee." What comfort you experience as you place yourself in His hand! What peace comes as you trustingly say to Him, "I do not know what lies ahead, but I place my life, my times, moment by moment, in Your strong hand." He knows every step ahead. Confidently you can follow Him.

As you yield your life to Him, you are like a pen whose owner fills it, cleans it when necessary, and uses it as he desires. You are like a pen in the hand of God. He cleanses you of yourself and fills you with Himself. Then He uses you where and when He wishes.

As you relax in His constant care, you can say, "*My* times are in *thy* hand."

But God hath chosen the foolish things of the world to confound the wise; and God hath chosen the weak things of the world to confound the things which are mighty. I Corinthians 1:27

In the secular world, when an employer seeks a worker to fill a certain position, he makes every effort to find someone qualified, and trained in that particular field. God does the opposite; He chooses the weak and foolish ones. We look at the outer qualifications, but God looks at those within. He will use natural ability but it must be yielded to Him. God will use people who will not glory in what they do but in what He does.

Some of you may be using your weakness and inability as an excuse for not doing the work God wants you to do. You are trying to "ease out" because you consider yourself inadequate. Perhaps you take pride in saying, "I have no talents. I can't do anything." Regardless of your ability or lack of it, what God wants is your yielded life. Someone has said, "There is no limit to what God will do through one who is willing and who doesn't care who gets the credit."

A great pianist was to give a recital. While the guests were assembling, they heard someone playing *Chopsticks*. One of the mothers immediately recognized that the pianist was her little son. She hurried to stop him, but a man had heard the playing, too, and had gotten to the little fellow first. Putting his arms around the boy, he whispered, "Keep right on playing, Sonny," so the lad continued to play on the black keys while the man used the entire keyboard to demonstrate the thrilling possibilities of the instrument. "Who is it?" the audience asked, captivated by the artistry of the performer. The reply was, "Paderewski, the master of the piano, who is giving the recital tonight."

This illustrates what God will do with your life if you will let Him. Keep playing on the black keys and let God supply the beautiful melodies that will bring glory to Himself.

27 *But Simon's wife's mother lay sick of a fever, and anon they tell him of her. Mark 1:30*

The disciples had learned of the illness of Peter's wife's mother. She was someone with a need, and immediately they did the one thing they could to help her. They went to Jesus and "told him of her." How simple it was! They had direct and instant access to Him, the Source of true help. The Bible doesn't say that they used flowery language. They simply told Him that she was sick.

When they told Jesus of this woman's need, He quickly went to her aid. "And he came and took her by the hand, and lifted her up; and immediately the fever left her, and she ministered unto them" (vs. 31). The disciples had not been too busy ministering to the crowds to see one person with a need. Jesus, too, left those He was with and went to the sick woman.

There are many about us today who are spiritually sick — members of our families, neighbors, those with whom we work. Many are carrying burdens and heartaches — and do not know where to turn for help. They need someone to care about them, someone to love them. Most of all, they need someone who has access to Jesus — the Source of their help — someone who will faithfully remember them in prayer, someone to "tell Him of them." May we not become so busy in our activities each day that we forget this important ministry. Let *us* tell *Him* of *them*.

Bring forth therefore fruits meet for repentance. Matthew 3:8

John the Baptist was preaching in the wilderness when the Pharisees and Sadducees came to hear him. Perhaps they came to investigate. He knew they had not repented; they did not really believe what he was preaching; they had no desire to do the will of God. John said to them, "Bring forth fruit that is consistent with repentance — let your lives prove your change of heart" (Amplified).

Repentance brings a change of heart which results in a changed life. When we have a personal relationship with Jesus Christ as Saviour and Lord, a change takes place in our lives; we make a complete turnabout and go God's way. This is what the world wants to see — a life transformed through a change of heart, a life so lived as to prove that a change has taken place. The world wants to know if Christianity really works.

Missouri is known as the "Show Me State." It is said that the people of this state must be "shown" before they will believe something to be true. The world is looking at the Christian and saying, "If what you say is true, show us. If you have what you say you have, if it really works in your life and meets your problems and needs, we want to see it in action."

We must show in our lives fruit consistent with the change that has taken place in our hearts. We talk much about peace, but the world wants to see if we actually have this peace in all the distressing situations that arise in our lives. We must bring forth peace consistent with and proving our change of heart. This is also true of joy, love, gentleness — all the Christian virtues which are the fruit of the Spirit. The Pharisees and Sadducees had an outward form — but not the inner reality. Jesus said, "Ye shall know them by their fruits." As we let the Holy Spirit control our lives, He will enable us to show to the world the reality of the change that took place when Jesus became our Saviour, and the fruit of our lives will prove the change in our hearts.

29   *I, the Lord, will instruct you and teach you in the way you should go; I will counsel you with My eye upon you. Psalm 32:8, Amplified*

God, our Divine Instructor, has enrolled us in His Great University as His pupils. He has promised to instruct and teach us in the way we should go. He imparts to us the knowledge we need if we are to walk in the light of His will. Teaching includes a training course. Our Heavenly Teacher says, "I will instruct you and train you" (Berkeley). He trains us to apply His instruction to our daily lives.

God also promises to guide us with His eye upon us. He sees us at all times and knows what we need. It may be a look of love that we need; or possibly of encouragement; or perhaps of reproof. We read of the look of reproof that broke Peter's heart after he had denied the Lord. Our Lord is always ready to counsel us.

One day a man watched a black ant crawling along. He dropped a piece of cracker nearby to see what the tiny insect would do. It started in the other direction. He blocked its way with his finger, and the ant turned in another direction. Again the man guided it with his finger. Doubtless the ant considered this a trying interference. However, in reality one with higher intelligence was attempting to guide the insect to a source of good.

Oftentimes God sets a seeming obstacle in our path that He may instruct and teach us concerning His way for us and give us counsel regarding it.

Now when Daniel knew that the writing was signed,
he went into his house; and his windows being open
in his chamber toward Jerusalem, he kneeled upon
his knees three times a day, and prayed, and gave
thanks before his God, as he did aforetime. Daniel
6:10

How many of you have appointment books? In these busy
days most of us find this necessary. We make every effort to
keep these appointments. Today is your most important appointment recorded on your calendar? It is your prayer appointment
with God.

When a lad, Daniel was brought to Babylon as a captive. He
had a strong faith in God and had learned the importance of
keeping regular prayer appointments with his Heavenly Father.
Throughout his life he proved the sufficiency of God. When
King Darius appointed him to the highest position in the land,
those under him were jealous and they devised a plot against
him. It was decreed under Darius' signature that during the next
thirty days whoever prayed to anyone but the king would be
cast into a den of lions. What would Daniel do? This decree
threatened his prayer life.

Daniel knew that he had regular daily prayer appointments
with God and that He would be waiting to meet him. Therefore,
"he went into his house . . . kneeled upon his knees three times a
day, and prayed . . . as he did *aforetime.*" He could have missed
his appointments for the month, or prayed silently, and no one
would have known. But, no, he continued to pray openly — just
as he had been in the habit of doing — three times a day.

Do you have a regular daily appointment to meet God in
prayer? Is it scheduled on your calendar? Are the windows of
your life open toward heaven? Or have busyness, indifference,
and doubts closed your windows? It is important that these
appointments with God be scheduled on your calendar. But it
is more important that you don't miss them. God doesn't; He is
waiting for you.

1   But it is good for me to draw near to God: I have
       put my trust in the Lord God, that I may declare
       all thy works. Psalm 73:28

In this Psalm we read about a man who was confused, troubled, and perplexed. As he looked about him, there were many things he couldn't understand. Why did some people have so much more than others? Why did some get ahead whereas he didn't? Why were some free from trouble?

Do any of these questions come to your mind? Do you wonder why someone at the office was promoted instead of you? Why some of your neighbors seem to have more than you do? Why some of your friends seem to be free from trouble whereas one trial after another seems to afflict you?

The more Asaph thought about the problem, the more upset he became. At last he found the solution to his confusion and perplexity. He said, "When I thought to know this, it was too painful for me; *until* I went into the sanctuary of God; then understood I their end" (vss. 16, 17). He discovered that he had been looking at the present. God was considering the end from the beginning. When God gave him the answer, it brought peace to his heart. Then Asaph could say, "It is good for me to draw near to God."

We, too, will find the answers to our questions and our problems as we draw near to God. As we draw near to Him, we can place our trust in Him as Asaph did. Then each of us will say, "I have put my trust in the Lord God, that I may declare all thy works."

O thou that hearest prayer, unto thee shall all flesh come. Psalm 65:2

2

The doorway into the secret place of the Most High is always open to the soul in need. Prayer puts us in contact with God.

Someone has said, "Prayer is a conversation between the soul and heaven." It has been likened to a two-way telephone conversation. I have noticed that when a person makes a call from a telephone booth he usually closes the door so that he can hear clearly. He deposits a dime, the price required, before he is connected to the line. Then he hears the dial tone and dials the number. The connection is completed and the business transacted.

In our prayer time with God we need to close the door to the things of this world so that we can hear Him speak. "But, thou, when thou prayest, enter into thy closet, and when thou hast shut thy door, pray to thy Father which is in secret." However, before we can dial the number, the price must be paid. God, through His Son, paid the price that we might have access to His presence. Jesus said, "No man cometh unto the Father, but by me" (John 14:6). We must accept Jesus as our personal Saviour before we have the right to "dial" heaven.

We must "dial" correctly. There are certain prayer conditions to fulfill. "And whatsoever we ask, we receive of him, because we keep his commandments, and do those things that are pleasing in his sight" (I John 3:22). Also read Mark 11:24; John 14:14; I John 5:14, 15.

There is an open line to heaven for us. When we have accepted God's price and fulfilled His conditions for prayer, then we can dial with confidence, knowing that God is on the line ready to hear and answer us.

3   *The entrance of thy words giveth light; it giveth understanding unto the simple. Psalm 119:130*

Have you ever entered an unfamiliar room in the dark? As you groped for the light switch, you may have stumbled over something. The furniture may have cast shadows in the room. You groped along the wall where you thought the switch might be. Suddenly your hand touched it and you snapped it on. How different the room looked as the light flooded it!

God's Word does this for our lives. Often we read and reread some portion of Scripture and suddenly one day it sheds a new light on some problem which is troubling us. Or perhaps some new experience in our lives imparts a deeper meaning to a Scripture verse or passage. All may seem dark ahead. We may be unable to see the way. We may desperately need a solution to a problem. Suddenly light shines from the Word and new understanding floods our souls.

Not only does the Word give light and understanding, but it is continually unfolding in our lives. The Holy Spirit is our Teacher and continues to reveal the Word to us and apply it to our needs. A Chinese scholar was once asked to read Psalm 119 in the original and then translate the 130th verse into the English language without consulting the King James Version. After studying the passage for a few minutes, he said, "The Bible says; God speaks; a light comes! This makes a dumb man a wise one."

As newborn babes, desire the sincere milk of the   **4**
word, that ye may grow thereby. I Peter 2:2

Someone said to a little boy, "Johnny, how you do grow!" "Of course I does," he replied. "I wouldn't be real if I didn't." As soon as a baby is born, if it is normal, growth begins. It is natural to grow. When we become Christians we should also begin to grow. Growth is evidence of new life within.

In our physical lives one essential for growth is food. This is true also in our spiritual lives. "Man shall not live by bread alone, but by every word that proceedeth out of the mouth of God" (Matthew 4:4). The requirements vary, depending on the progress we have made. Milk, bread, meat — all are necessary at different stages in our development. But the desire for food must develop into action. We must partake of it in order to benefit from it. As a baby has a regular feeding schedule, so we must have a regular feeding schedule in the Word.

There should be a direction or goal in our growth. An eight-year-old girl was attempting to teach her little brother to ride a bicycle. After trying a number of times, he steadied himself as he wobbled from side to side, and called, "I'm moving!" His sister looked at him and said, "Yes, you're *moving*, but you aren't *going*."

Second Peter 3:18 indicates the direction of our growth. "But *grow* in spiritual strength and become better acquainted with our Lord and Saviour, Jesus Christ" (Living Letters). We are to grow in knowledge of Him and become like Him.

Do you remember when your parents stood you against a door and marked your height? Later they stood you there again to check your growth. Measure yourself today by God's "yardstick." Are you showing growth?

5

And they come unto him, bringing one sick of the palsy, which was borne of four. Mark 2:3

Jesus had returned to Capernaum. When the people heard this, a large crowd gathered to see and hear Him. Before long there was no more room in the house.

Four men, hearing of Jesus' return, brought their sick friend, believing that Jesus could heal him. What a feeling of expectancy they must have had as they approached the home where Jesus was! But their hope soon turned to disappointment when they found that because of the crowd they couldn't get him into the house. What were they to do? Must they give up? No, they were determined to get their sick friend to Jesus in spite of this obstacle.

The four persistent men decided to let him down through the roof. "They removed the tiles from the roof over Jesus' head and let down the paralytic's bed through the opening. And when Jesus saw *their faith,* He said to the man on the bed, My son, your sins are forgiven. Get up, pick up your bed and go home" (Phillips). First Jesus met his spiritual need; then he supplied his physical one.

Today there are people all about us who are spiritually sick. Are we as determined to get them to Jesus as these four friends were? Will we persist as they did until all obstacles are removed? Prayer is our great source of power to remove obstacles.

When Jesus saw their faith, He healed the man. Are we praying in faith? "Only it must be in the faith that he asks, with no wavering — no hesitating, no doubting. For the one who wavers (hesitates, doubts) is like the billowing surge out at sea, that is blown hither and thither and tossed by the wind" (James 1:6, Amplified).

And it shall come to pass, as soon as the soles of the feet of the priests that bear the ark of the Lord . . . shall rest in the waters of Jordan, that the waters of Jordan shall be cut off from the waters that come down from above; and they shall stand upon an heap.
Joshua 3:13

The Israelites were about to enter the Promised Land. This meant that they must cross the Jordan River when it was at flood stage. God told Joshua, the leader, that *"As soon* as the feet of the priests would *rest* in the waters of the Jordan, they would part in a heap." The way would open before them when their feet rested in the water — not a minute before or a minute after. This implied a step of faith in obedience to God's orders.

Can you not see them coming closer and closer, right down to the edge of the river? Still the river rushed by. Dare the priests actually rest their feet on the water? As they obeyed, God performed a miracle, making a way through. Contrary to nature, the water stood in a "heap." The waters didn't divide while they were still in camp — nor as they marched down — but when they rested their feet on the water.

Are you facing a hopeless situation? Are the waters of trouble rushing by? Is there no way through? Commit your need, whatever it may be, to Him, and trust. As He brings you right up to your problem, you can step out in faith, knowing that as you rest your feet on the water of trouble, He will make a way through. Instead of being defeated by despair, you can rejoice in a victory of faith.

Perhaps you are saying, "But you don't know the problems in my life — you don't know the rivers of trouble before me. My situation is impossible." It may be impossible for you, but there is One who has promised to make a way through for you. Your part is to *rest* your feet; His part is to *open* the way.

7   *The effectual fervent prayer of a righteous man availeth much. James 5:16*

It was Sunday morning and the church service was about to
start. The organist attempted to play but no sound came from
the instrument, and the church service had to start without the
help of the organ. The trouble was soon located, and the repair-
man estimated that the organ would be functioning by the time
the pastor had completed the morning prayer. The following note
was sent to him: "The power will be back on after prayer."

How true this is! Power will be on in our lives — and in our
Christian activity — after prayer. "The earnest (heartfelt, continued) prayer of a righteous man makes *tremendous power available* — dynamic in its working" (Amplified).

Dr. P. F. Forsyth, the great Scotch preacher, once said, "Prayer
is the highest use to which speech can be put." We need genuine
earnestness in our petitions; we must not merely "say prayers."
There must be deep concern for the fields, white unto harvest
which challenge us on every side.

It has been said, "It is not the arithmetic of our prayers, how
many they are; nor the rhetoric of our prayers, how eloquent
they are; nor the geometry of our prayers, how long they are;
nor the music of our prayers, how sweet our voice may be;
nor the logic of our prayers, how argumentative they may be;
nor the method of our prayers, how orderly they may be, which
God cares for. Fervency of spirit is that which availeth much."

Is your prayer life availing much?

So then faith cometh by hearing, and hearing by the   *8*
word of God. Romans 10:17

Frequently we hear someone say, "If only I had more faith." But we can't produce faith by *our* own efforts or by repeating over and over again, "My faith is increasing."

The Word of God is the source of *faith*. The more we read the Word, the better we know God; the better we know God, the greater is our faith. If we feel weak in faith or lacking in it, we must saturate ourselves with the Word. We must search God's promises. Then as needs arise day by day we can claim these promises. God makes good His promises.

As we study the lives of great men in the past who have exhibited great faith, we find them to be Christians who spent much time reading the Word of God. Thus they came to know God better. This strengthened their faith.

Dwight L. Moody said, "I prayed for faith and thought that some day faith would come down and strike me like lightning. But faith did not seem to come. Then one day I read in Romans 10 that 'faith cometh by hearing, and hearing by the word of God.' I had closed my Bible and prayed for faith. I now opened my Bible, began to study it, and faith has been growing ever since."

George Mueller, in speaking of faith, said, "My faith is the same kind of faith that all of God's children have had down through the ages." When someone asked him how to increase faith, his answer was, "Study the Word of God and believe its blessed promises." His faith grew as he became increasingly familiar with the Bible. He fed his faith on the promises of God and it kept growing from day to day.

Someone has well said, "When you get wrinkled with care and worry, it is time to get your faith lifted."

9

For we are the sweet fragrance of Christ [which exhales] unto God, [discernible alike] among those who are being saved and among those who are perishing. II Corinthians 2:15, Amplified

Perfumes are very interesting and revealing. I once read of a million-dollar display of perfume exhibited at the John Wanamaker Store in Philadelphia. In the collection were perfumes from many countries. The most expensive bottle sold for a thousand dollars. On a certain television program a panel member was blindfolded and asked to guess the identity of a certain guest. She was the wife of one of the panel members. Almost immediately he guessed who it was. When asked how he identified his wife so quickly, he replied, "I recognized her perfume."

Paul tells us something about the importance of perfume. We are the sweet fragrance of Christ, spreading and making evident the fragrance of the knowledge of God everywhere. We are "perfume-bearers," carrying the sweet fragrance of our precious Lord. If we are to do this, His fragrance must first permeate our lives. We must spend time with Him. When I returned from Hawaii, I had some flowers in my suitcase. When I opened it on arriving home, I discovered that the pungent odor of the flowers had permeated my clothing, and for months I was aware of their fragrance. It is impossible to linger in our Lord's presence without carrying His fragrance.

Wherever we go we are to be a sweet fragrance for Him. When Mary broke the alabaster box of spikenard, the perfume filled the room. When we are broken of self and His presence fills our lives, His fragrance will permeate the world wherever we go.

But the fruit of the Spirit is . . . gentleness. Galatians 5:22

10

What constitutes greatness? Family name, position, wealth, talent — the world believes that these make a man great. But God has a different standard. In Galatians 5:22 and 23 He tells us what qualities make a man truly great.

"Gentleness" is defined as "kindness, graciousness, consideration." Christians should be the kindest, most considerate and courteous people in the world. God's Word tells us to be gentle — "And the servant of the Lord must not strive; but be gentle unto all men, apt to teach, patient" (II Timothy 2:24). A gentle person forgets about self and considers others. David realized what gentleness had accomplished in his life. He said, "Thy gentleness hath made me great" (II Samuel 22:36).

Gentleness, courteousness and consideration exert a greater influence and power over others than does a harsh, dictatorial manner. Do you remember the story of the argument between the wind and the sun? Each believed it had greater power than the other. To settle the controversy the wind said, "See that man walking down the street with his coat on? Let each of us try to get him to remove his coat. First I will blow; if I fail, you may try." So the wind blew its strongest. But instead of taking off his coat, the man only hugged it more tightly to him. The sun then shone quietly upon the man. The intense heat of its rays soon forced him to remove his coat. So in our lives gentleness is more effective than force.

We are to be gentle not only with some, but with all; not only with the docile, but also with the difficult. The Holy Spirit within gives us the gentleness of our lovely Lord. Then we can say as David did, "Thy gentleness hath made me great."

11   *Blessed are the meek: for they shall inherit the earth. Matthew 5:5*

The word translated "blessed" means "happy." We usually think that happiness is the possession of those who have wealth, position or talent. Yet many who have these are not happy. Their happiness is the happiness of the world. True happiness is the deep joy that comes from fellowship with God.

Who are the meek? We often think of a meek person as one who is wishy-washy and timid. But this is not so. A meek person is not weak. Moses was a meek man. Scripture says of him, "Now the man Moses was very meek, above all the men which were upon the face of the earth" (Numbers 12:3). Yet he was one of the strongest leaders.

A meek person is humble, submissive, gentle and patient. He doesn't assert his rights, doesn't give offense, refrains from condemning others, or does not judge the actions or motives of another. One person may be born with a gentler and more patient disposition than another. But Jesus is speaking here of the one who is yielded to God and whose life is controlled by Him. When we realize that of ourselves we are nothing and have nothing of which to boast, we humble ourselves and are willing to turn our lives over to Him.

A very proud lawyer once asked a farmer, "Why don't you hold up your head in the world as I do?" The farmer replied, "See that field of grain? Only the heads that are empty stand up. Those that are well filled are the ones that bow low." "For whosoever exalteth himself shall be abased; and he that humbleth himself shall be exalted" (Luke 14:11).

Casting the whole of your care — all your anxieties, all your worries, all your concerns, once and for all — on Him; for He cares for you affectionately, and cares about you watchfully. I Peter 5:7, Amplified

Life today is filled with cares, worries, anxieties. But we have a great Caretaker — God Himself. *"He"* cares for you. He is interested in and concerned about you and everything pertaining to your life. He *"careth"* for you. His care is personal; He careth for *"you."* Someone has said, "With Him there is care for you."

Many today are burdened with the load of their cares. God's Word tells us to *cast* the whole of our care upon *Him.* This includes *all* of our cares — the big ones, little ones, easy ones, hard ones. "Casting" means "rolling." We are to cast, or roll, all of our cares on Him — not on our families, or friends, or neighbors, but on *Him.* Roll them on Him once and for all. Often we take our burdens to Him in prayer and then carry them back with us.

An old Negro woman was asked the secret of her excellent health and long life. She replied, "When I works, I works hard; when I sits, I sits loose; and when I worries, I goes to sleep."

Someone has said, "His eye is upon you; His ear is open to you; His hand is sufficient for you; His heart is sympathetic with you; His angels are round about you; His treasures are laid up for you."

Some years ago an officer in the Royal Navy told this interesting story. His ship's flag had these words on it: "In the care of God." Whenever the ship was in heavy engagement the men aboard would look up, see the flag flying, and take courage. They knew the ship was still "in the care of God." In the Song of Solomon we read, "His banner over me was love" (2:4b). This banner flies from the ship of your life. On it are these words: "In the care of God." When problems mount, heartaches bring tears, and cares seem heavier than you can bear, you will be comforted as you look up and read, "In the care of God."

13   *But we will give ourselves continually to prayer, and to the ministry of the word.* Acts 6:4

Someone was asked the question, "Do you have camel's knees?" This was a strange inquiry. However, I wonder if you have ever seen the callouses on the knees of a camel. According to an early Christian tradition, it was said that the Apostle James had "knees like a camel." He had spent so much time kneeling in prayer that his knees bore a marked resemblance to the calloused knees of that beast of burden.

The early Christians served the Lord boldly and accomplished great things. The secret of this power is found in their prayer life. They said, "We will continue to devote ourselves steadfastly to prayer and the ministry of the Word" (Amplified). They were steadfast in their prayer life as they ministered the Word. "Prayer is not the coating of our plans, but the very foundation of the work."

S. D. Gordon says, "Prayer is power. The time of prayer is the time of power. The place of prayer is the place of power. Prayer is tightening the connection with the divine dynamo, so that the power may flow freely without loss or interruption."

How about the steadfastness of your prayer life? Do you have "camel's knees"? You may not have actual callouses on your knees, but do they show the marks of your steadfastness in your prayer life? On your knees you can be a power in the world today. It has been said, "Where prayer falls, power focuses."

The Lord is with thee, thou mighty man of valour.
Judges 6:12

The Midianites were invading Israel and caused them to flee to caves in the mountains. One day an angel of the Lord appeared to Gideon and said, "The Lord is with thee, thou mighty man of valour" (vs. 12). Gideon replied, "If the Lord be with us, *why* then is all this befallen us?" (vs. 13). Does this have a familiar ring? How many times have you asked this?

God was calling Gideon to deliver the Israelites. Yet he seemed an unlikely candidate, unsure of himself, timid, fearful, with no apparent ability. "And the Lord *looked* upon him and said, Go in this thy might, and thou shalt save Israel from the hand of the Midianites" (vs. 14). This might was in the One who had called him. Someone has said this was "the strength-giving look of the Lord."

Is God calling you to some task that seems too great for you? Do you feel incapable of performing it? Are you saying, "Lord, You know I am timid and afraid; I am not as capable as Mrs. . . . or Mary . . . I can't do it." With His call, however, comes His enabling. He is looking on you with *His* strength-giving look and saying, "Go in this thy might."

Not only did the Lord say "Go" to Gideon, but He also asked, "Have not I sent thee?" (vs. 14). In effect He was saying, "You can go in My might and strength because I am sending you." Then He encouraged Gideon by promising, "Surely I will be with you" (vs. 16). Not only does He send us but He goes with us.

Today He may be calling you to a particular task. You may be fearful because of your insufficiency. Look to the Lord and see in Him your all-sufficiency. God's "strength is made perfect in weakness" (II Corinthians 12:9). It has been said, "Pray not for tasks equal to your strength but for strength equal to the tasks God gives you to do."

God said to Gideon, "Go in this thy might. I am sending you. I will be with you." Today He promises to give you His strength for a divinely appointed task and assures you of His unfailing presence.

15

Have not I commanded thee? Be strong and of a good courage; be not afraid, neither be thou dismayed: for the Lord thy God is with thee whithersoever thou goest. Joshua 1:9

Joshua was the newly chosen leader who was to take the children of Israel into the Promised Land. He recognized his weakness and inability to do the job before him. The Israelites were entering into an unknown land and facing strong enemies. He must have been frightened as he realized the responsibility that was to be his.

With God's call to Joshua came encouragement. He wanted Joshua to be assured that he would have power for the task — "Be strong and of a good courage." Joshua would have peace of heart as the Israelites went forth to face the enemy — "Be not afraid, neither be thou dismayed." Joshua would have the divine presence with him constantly, for God promised, "The Lord *thy* God *is* with thee whithersoever thou goest."

Often we, too, feel weak and unable to face life and its responsibilities. We may be carrying burdens too heavy for us. God's encouraging words come to us today: "Be strong and of a good courage; be not afraid, neither be thou dismayed." Ephesians 6:10 says, "Be strong in the Lord, and in the power of *His* might." God promises us His abiding presence in the midst of our needs: "For the Lord *thy* God *is* with *thee* [today] whithersoever thou goest."

"Have I not commanded you? Be resolute and strong! Be not afraid, and be not dismayed; for the Lord your God is with you everywhere you go" (Berkeley).

And the soul of the people was much discouraged because of the way. Numbers 21:4

The Israelites had been traveling through the desert wilderness to the Land of Promise. The way was hot, sandy and rough; there was little water. But God had promised that He would guide them and provide for them. However, like many of us, they became discouraged. If only they had trusted God's promise that He who had led would continue to lead, if only they had believed that He who had supplied would continue to supply, instead of being discouraged they would have been encouraged. Discouragement turns to encouragement when we look away from our circumstances and focus our eyes upon the Lord.

In I Samuel 30 we read about David in the midst of trouble. The Amalekites had burned Ziklag, his private property and residence. But his distress drove him to the Lord. "David encouraged himself in the Lord" (vs. 6). Someone has said, "To look around is to be distressed; to look within is to be depressed; to look up is to be blessed."

Today our way may be through the wilderness. It may be easy to become discouraged. Discouragement is a tool of Satan. The story is told that Satan was "going out of business." All of his tools were offered for sale. They were attractively displayed on a table. What an array — hatred, envy, jealousy, deceit! One harmless-looking one, much worn, was priced higher than any of the others. "What is that tool?" someone asked. "Discouragement," was the reply. "Why is it so expensive?" Satan answered, "Because it is more useful to me than any of the others."

Will our distress drive us to despair and discouragement or to God? May we, like David, "encourage ourselves in the Lord."

17 *Sir, I have no man, when the water is troubled, to put me into the pool. John 5:7*

There was once a man who had been a helpless cripple for thirty-eight years. How hopeless life must have seemed to him! On this particular day Jesus found him lying beside the pool at Bethesda. It was said that at a certain time an angel came down to the pool and stirred up the water. "Whosoever then first after the troubling of the water stepped in was made whole of whatever disease he had," Scripture tells us. This poor man had no one to put him into the pool. Day after day he lay there, hoping that someone might care enough to let him down into the pool so that his body could be healed. When Jesus spoke to him, he said, "I have *no man* . . . to put me into the pool."

Many people passed by but were too busy to help him. Some said, "That poor man — too bad he's so crippled!"; others asked, "Why doesn't someone in his family do something for him?" Then they went on their way. They were too involved with their own plans and problems to give assistance. No one really cared enough to help him. We might say, "Surely there was someone who could have taken time to help." But do *we* take time to help those in need?

Today we are often too busy to see those about us who are in spiritual distress. It has been said, "Busyness — the great American excuse; the great American boast." We rush about so frantically that we fail to see those whom God has put in our path; those who need to be brought to the Saviour for the healing of their souls. How tragic if we, too, pass them by without helping! May God challenge us with this question today: "Is it nothing to you, all ye that pass by?" (Lamentations 1:12).

Ye are the light of the world. Matthew 5:14

Jesus said that we are the light of the world — light-containers through whom *He* can shine. Your place may be dark, but remember that the darker the night, the brighter the stars shine. If God has placed you in a dark place, He has done so that you might shine there for Him.

Lights are not all the same. There are various kinds for various purposes. Some lights are very bright and illumine entire rooms. Others are lamps placed in certain places to give concentrated light for reading. Some are beautiful chandeliers; others are small lights intended for closets; some are tiny night lights. But each is important in its place. So it is with us. We have a responsibility to shine wherever God places us, and each of us is important in his particular place.

In a little village in southern Europe there is a gray-stone church on the summit of a hill. It is called "The Church of Many Lamps." Legend says that this church was built in the sixteenth century by a duke who had several daughters whom he loved dearly. As he grew older, he wanted to perpetuate his memory in some way. He decided to build a church so beautiful that men would desire to worship God as soon as they entered it. He drew up the plans and eagerly watched the construction of the magnificent building.

At last the church was finished. The duke took one of his daughters to see it. She admired the beautiful carvings and the stained-glass windows. "But, Father," she said, "you have forgotten one thing. Where are the lamps to hang?" "There will be no hanging lamps," he replied. "There is a small bronze lamp for every person in the village. Each will carry his own lamp. If he doesn't come to church, his place will be dark."

Today are there places in the world which are dark because we have not brought them the Light of the World?

19   *God shall give Pharaoh an answer of peace.* Genesis 41:16b

Joseph was God's man of the hour — God's messenger with God's message. God had allowed Joseph to be put in prison. But through this experience Joseph had learned a most important lesson, that of his insufficiency and God's all-sufficiency.

Pharaoh wanted someone to interpret his dream. His butler remembered Joseph, who had interpreted a dream for him. When he told Pharaoh about Joseph, the ruler sent for him, asking him to interpret his dream. Joseph said, "*God* shall give Pharaoh an answer of peace."

God is the One who can give an answer of peace today. People are trying in every way to secure it. They consult psychiatrists, they take tranquilizers, they change positions, they move to different surroundings in their constant search for peace of mind.

God's answer to the peace question is His Son, the Lord Jesus Christ, "for *he* is our peace" (Ephesians 2:14a). He is our peace for every situation in our lives, "for he will speak peace unto his people" (Psalm 85:8). "The peace of God, which passeth all understanding, shall keep [our] hearts and minds through Christ Jesus" (Philippians 4:7).

We, too, can be God's men today in a peace-seeking world. Our message to such seekers is, "God shall give an answer of peace."

What is that in thine hand? Exodus 4:2

God had chosen Moses to deliver the children of Israel from Egypt. But Moses immediately began to enumerate all the reasons why he was not qualified to assume such leadership. Then the Lord asked him, "What is that in thine hand?"

When Moses looked at his hand, what did he see? A rod — a dead stick. What could be done with it? It was only a rod in Moses' hand, but when it was given to God it became a rod of power to deliver the Israelites.

Through the years God has challenged His children with the question, "What is that in thine hand?" Many have answered and accepted this challenge. An inspiring example is David Livingston, who came from the coal mines of Scotland. When God said to him, "What is that in thine hand?" he offered Him his heart of love for Africa and accepted His challenge to missionary service. Through him that continent was opened to the Gospel.

God is saying to you today, "What is that in thine hand?" He sees your talent and ability. Placed in God's hand these can be a "rod of power" for Him to use. Your answer to Him may be, "Nothing — nothing that You can use." But God does not look at your hand as you do. Lift your seemingly empty hands to Him and He will use you. He is more interested in your *availability* than in your ability. He uses the weakest instruments to accomplish His mightiest works. When God calls, He enables.

The great violinist Paganini was to give a concert. As he was about to begin his program, to the great horror of those present, he deliberately broke all except one of the strings on his violin. Then as he held up his instrument, he said, "One string and Paganini." What indescribably beautiful music the great musician played on the violin with one string!

What glorious harmonies the Great Musician can bring forth from a life — with its abilities and inabilities — which is yielded completely to Him!

21 *Launch out into the deep, and let down your nets for a draught. Luke 5:4*

One day as people were pressing about Jesus, eager to hear Him, He climbed into Peter's boat to talk to them. Then He turned to Peter and said, "Launch out into the deep, and let down your nets." Although they were expert fishermen, and had been fishing all night, they had failed completely. Peter said, "We have toiled all the night, and have taken nothing" (vs. 5).

Jesus told Peter to go back to the place where they had been fishing, launch out and let down their nets. Peter might have said, "Why should we do that? We have fished there all night. If there were fish at that place, wouldn't we have caught them?" But he didn't say that. He didn't continue to dwell on their failure. He looked to the Lord and said, "Nevertheless at *thy word* I will let down the nets." This time they were successful. They had a multitude of fish in their nets. What made the difference? At first they had toiled all night with no results. But when Jesus directed them, they were successful.

There are many people today in the deep waters of fear, discouragement, despondency, sin. Jesus is saying to us, "Launch out into the deep, and let down your nets." When our plans for reaching the troubled multitudes start with "we," failure is inevitable. However, when our plans start with "nevertheless at thy word," we will succeed for His glory.

Thou wilt keep him in perfect peace, whose mind is   **22**
stayed on thee: because he trusteth in thee. Isaiah
26:3

This is a familiar and encouraging verse. It promises a *state* of perfect peace. "Thou wilt keep him *in perfect peace.*" This is complete peace, with no room at all for worry. It is a continuing peace.

This peace is possible because its *source* is in God. "*Thou* wilt keep him in perfect peace." This peace is not the result of human effort but is a gift from God. "Peace I leave with you, my peace I give unto you" (John 14.27). Not only does He give us this peace, but He *keeps* us in it. "Thou *wilt keep.*"

The *secret* of peace is the possession of him "whose *mind* is *stayed* on" God. The mind which is stayed on the Lord has perfect peace. A free translation of this verse is "Thou wilt keep him in perfect peace whose mind stops at God." It is not the staying of our minds on God that gives the peace, but the One on whom we stay our minds. When you "stop" at God you will leave all in His care.

The *steadfastness* of this peace comes from trusting. The one who steadily trusts has undisturbed peace.

Perhaps distressing news has come; sorrow or trouble may have brought heartache. Your very life may be completely shaken. God "will guard him and keep him in perfect and *constant* peace whose mind [both its inclination and its character] is stayed on You, because he commits himself to You, leans on You and hopes confidently in You" (Amplified).

Each of two artists was to paint a picture illustrating peace. The first painted a scene showing a still lake with mountains in the distance. The second drew a thundering waterfall with a slender branch of a tree bending over it. At the fork of the branch, which was wet with the spray of the waterfall, sat a robin on its nest. This was an excellent way to illustrate peace. To rest in the storm is to have perfect peace.

Someone has said, "Mental rest brings heart peace."

23 *Who are kept by the power of God through faith unto salvation ready to be revealed in the last time.*
I Peter 1:5

How much effort is expended to keep our possessions, our valuables, and ourselves safe! Yet despite every safety device and method known, human efforts fail.

What a comfort to know that we are kept by the power of God! What security this provides for us! Peter experienced this keeping power of God. Although he was very likely a physically strong and robust man, yet he was spiritually weak. His intentions were good, but often he failed the Lord. However, when he truly committed his life to God and His keeping power, he became one of the most courageous followers of Christ.

In Psalm 62:11 we read, "Power belongeth unto God." This power never fails. This is the power that created the universe, that keeps the stars in place, that raised the Lord from the dead. How foolish to worry and fret when we are in His keeping power!

Not only am I being kept by the power of God, but all I need is being kept for me in His great storehouse. I have His protection — He is keeping me; and I have His provision for my life — He is keeping what I need.

God's Word speaks frequently of His power to keep us: "And, behold, I am with thee, and will *keep* thee in all places whither thou goest" (Genesis 28:15a); "He will *keep* the feet of his saints" (I Samuel 2:9a); "For he shall give his angels charge over thee, to *keep* thee in all thy ways" (Psalm 91:11).

Pause and thank Him for His keeping power today.

Now unto him that is able to do exceeding abundantly above all that we ask or think, according to the power that worketh in us. Ephesians 3:20

This story is told of an old Army captain, Tom. One day he said to his trusted servant, "Stay with me and I will take care of you. When I die I will provide for you." The servant was pleased with the arrangement and remained with the captain. One day Captain Tom died, leaving John provided for as he had promised.

As John grew older, he became sick and weak and was unable to work. He was almost starving one day when a friend of the captain visited him. "John," he said, "why don't you go down to the bank and get some of the money Captain Tom left you?" "But I don't know how to get it," said John. "All you have to do is go down to the bank and tell them that you need some of the money," the visitor explained.

John went to the bank. He approached the cashier and asked, "Did Captain Tom leave some money for me?" "Yes, he did. He left five thousand dollars in an account for you," was the reply. "How much can I get? I am almost starving. Can I have fifty cents for a sack of meal?" "Yes," said the cashier. "How do I get it?" "Write a check." The cashier helped him write a check for fifty cents and cashed it. John bought a fifty-cent sack of meal, and returned to his small house to make his hotcakes — with $4,999.50 still in the bank.

Can we not apply this illustration to ourselves? We have all the wealth of heaven at our disposal; yet we live meagerly. God has limitless riches for us; yet we limit Him. "Ye have not, because ye ask not" (James 4:2). He is ready to do exceeding abundantly above all that we *ask* or *think*.

25   *That he might sanctify and cleanse it with the wash-*
ing of water by the word. Ephesians 5:26

One day as I was shopping the girl who waited on me looked at her hands and said, "I just can't keep clean around here." Later I thought, *It is difficult to keep our lives clean in this world of today. Yet our bodies are the temples of the Holy Spirit. How important it is that they be clean!*

As I work about my home, I have to wash my hands often. The same is true of our lives. They must be cleansed frequently from the daily contamination of this world. As a mirror tells us when our faces are dirty, so God's Word reveals to us our need for cleansing.

It may be that resentment has crept into our hearts. A critical attitude, envy, pride — these have perhaps come into our lives. As we read the Word, the Holy Spirit convicts us of our sins. As we confess them, we are cleansed. Someone has said that "we should keep short accounts with God, confessing and being cleansed as soon as something is revealed to us."

A man was asked what the pastor had preached about that Sunday. "I can't remember exactly," he replied, "but I know that I went home and took the false bottom out of my measuring basket."

It has been well said, "We need to look into the Word until the Word looks into us."

A land which the Lord thy God careth for: the eyes
of the Lord thy God are always upon it, from the
beginning of the year even unto the end of the year.
Deuteronomy 11:12

The children of Israel were soon to possess the Promised Land. It was a land that God promised to care for. He said that He would *always* keep his eyes upon it, from the *beginning* of the year even to the *end*.

When we start a new year we do not know what lies ahead. However, we know that it will be filled with new experiences, new blessings, new problems. But we go forward in the assurance that He has promised to keep His eyes upon us from the beginning of the year to the very end.

As the year moves on and the needs arise and the problems and heartaches come, it is sometimes difficult to believe His promise that His eyes are upon us not merely at the beginning of the year, not merely for part of the year, but from the beginning *even* unto the end of it. His eyes are not upon us merely when we feel well, or when we have no problems, or when everyone loves us. His eyes are upon us *always*. This includes the days when we are in turmoil, the days when we are ill and in great pain, the days when our hearts are breaking, the days when we are discouraged. "Always" includes "*even today.*" With His eyes of love upon us He goes with us everywhere.

Once a young boy had to go a considerable distance on an errand. When he was ready to start, he said in a trembling voice, "Mother, it's so far, and I don't know the way very well. I'm not really afraid, but would you go just a little way with me?" The mother caught the anxiety in his voice and said, "I will go with you all the way." With his hand in hers he walked all the way without fear.

27   *Evening, and morning, and at noon, will I pray, and cry aloud: and he shall hear my voice. Psalm 55:17*

David knew God, for he spent much time with Him. F. B. Meyer said, "Blessed is the one who retires from the hubbub of the street as did David and Daniel, three times a day."

We are careful to eat three times a day. Shouldn't we pray as often as we eat? God's availability is constant. David didn't pray only when a need arose. He didn't pray merely on the days when he felt like praying. He had regular prayer times.

Constant prayer should be the occupation of the believer. We are not limited to one time and one place. There is no limit to the time we can spend on our knees. What a comfort in these trying days to know that evening, morning, and noon we have entrance into the presence of One whose ear is open to us and who is sensitive to our needs.

Christians everywhere have experienced the strength derived from a constant and instant access into God's holy presence through prayer. I read that someone once asked John Charles Thomas, the famous singer, to what or to whom he owed his success. He quickly replied, "God." He was the son of a minister, and his Christian training profoundly influenced his musical career. Before a concert he would sometimes spend as much as thirty minutes in prayer that God might use his voice to bless others.

And Jesus looking upon them saith, With men it is impossible, but not with God: for with God all things are possible. Mark 10:27

28

My husband was responsible for electrical and mechanical jobs in the shop at his place of business. Many who worked there discovered that he could do many jobs that at first seemed impossible. I found this true at home also. No matter what job challenged him, he usually was able to do it, although, of course, there were limits to his ability.

God has a "specialty shop" which specializes in the impossible. God, the One who can do the impossible, is the Specialist. There is no problem too great or too small to bring to Him.

The above verse declares man's inability — "with men it is impossible." It also declares God's ability — "with God all things are possible." It has been said, "You have only proved the sufficiency of God when you have asked of Him the impossible."

God's specialty shop offers service twenty-four hours a day seven days a week. His shop never closes, but we may have to wait occasionally. When one takes his car to the garage for repairs, there is often a delay. So in God's workshop. There may be something He has to accomplish in our lives before He can take care of our needs. It has been said, "Sometimes He delays answering our requests in order to enlarge our capacity to receive."

Be sure to take your needs to the Great Specialist who can do all things, with whom not one thing is impossible.

29 *And the Lord was with Joseph, and he was a prosperous man . . . . And his master saw that the Lord was with him, and that the Lord made all that he did to prosper in his hand. Genesis 39:2, 3*

Prosperity is the yardstick by which we often measure a person's success. Usually we think of prosperity in terms of material possessions. In God's Word we read of a man who was prosperous but in a different sense.

Joseph was the pampered son of a wealthy family. He had been sold as a slave into Egypt and served in Potiphar's house. But we read that he was prosperous — prosperous because God was with him. "And the Lord was with Joseph, and he was a prosperous man . . . . The Lord made all that he did to prosper in his hand." He experienced the "prosperity of God's presence."

God was interested in Joseph, watching over him and caring for him. He may have been homesick and lonely, yet he had with him One who was closer to him than any member of his family could be. Instead of pitying himself and pining away, Joseph was cheerful and lived in such a way that those about him were aware of God's presence in his life. He might have become discouraged, defeated, depressed and embittered. Instead his life reflected the strength of his faith. Later Joseph could look back on this experience and say to his brothers, "But as for you, ye thought evil against me; but God meant it unto good" (Genesis 50:20). He saw God in all his circumstances.

God has also promised to be with *you* and *me*. We, too, can experience the "prosperity of God's presence" with us, "for he hath said, I will never leave thee, nor forsake thee" (Hebrews 13:5).

O our God, wilt thou not judge them? for we have no might against this great company that cometh against us; neither know we what to do: but our eyes are upon thee. II Chronicles 20:12

Jehoshaphat, king of Judah, was threatened with war. The enemy was besieging the land. It was a time of grave crisis. Jehoshaphat could have done a number of things. He could have attempted to recruit more men; he could have tried to secure additional equipment; he could have improved his military strategy. But he knew there was only one real source of assured help. "And Jehoshaphat feared, and set himself to seek the Lord . . . . And Judah gathered themselves together, to ask help of the Lord" (vss. 3, 4).

Jehoshaphat knew it was important that his people turn their *eyes* in the right direction. As he heard the news of the enemy's advance and as he turned his eyes to the resources he had, he was afraid. But he knew where to look. He looked to God in prayer. "For we have no might against this great company that cometh against us; neither know we what to do: *but our eyes are upon thee*" (vs. 12).

The Spirit of the Lord came upon Jahaziel and God spoke through him. "The battle is not yours, *but God's* . . . . The Lord will be with you" (vss. 15, 17). What an encouragement this was! First the people praised God for the victory that was to come. Then they obeyed God by going forth, believing that He would give the victory, and He did.

The direction of *our* eyes is important. When we are besieged by the enemy, when needs arise, when troubles and heartaches come, we turn our eyes upon them. Then we begin to fear. We realize that we have no might against them. But we, too, can say as Jehoshaphat did, "*Our eyes* are upon thee." The battle is not ours, but God's.

It has been said, "When we go to man we get only what man can do; but when we go to God we get what God can do."

31   *And Jesus stood still, and called them, and said, "What will ye that I shall do unto you?" They say unto him, Lord, that our eyes may be opened. Matthew 20:32, 33*

One day two blind men were sitting beside the road as Jesus passed by. They cried out, "Have mercy on us, O Lord." Jesus asked, "What will ye that I shall do unto you?" They replied, "That our eyes may be opened." Jesus had compassion on them and touched their eyes. They received their sight and followed Him.

Our eyes were darkened by sin until we invited Jesus, the Light of the World, into our lives. Then each of us could say as did the blind man of whom we read in John 9:25b, "One thing I know, whereas I was blind, now I see."

As Christians, our spiritual eyes need to be opened to all that God has for us. If Jesus would ask us, "What will ye that I shall do unto *you?*" what would be our reply? Our answer should be, "Open our eyes to more of the truth of God's Word." Each of us should make this request of God: "Open thou mine eyes, that I may behold wondrous things out of thy law" (Psalm 119:18). We should ask that our eyes be opened to our need for a deeper prayer life and a greater concern for those who need the Gospel. Let each of us pray earnestly, "Lord, open *my* eyes to my own spiritual needs and to the needs of those about me."

Fear thou not; for I am with thee: be not dismayed; **1**
for I am thy God: I will strengthen thee; yea, I will
help thee; yea, I will uphold thee with the right
hand of my righteousness. Isaiah 41:10

One day while traveling on a plane, I was sitting with a young man, a university student. As we discussed world conditions he said, "We young people of today might as well confess that we are afraid."

God tells us over and over again, "Fear not." In the above verse He assures us that we need have no fear. This assurance is personal to us, His children: "Fear *thou* not."

We need not fear for we are promised *His presence:* "Fear thou not; for I *am* with thee." We have the power of *His Person* in our lives: "Be not dismayed; for I am *thy God.*" We have *His promise* to keep us from fear: "I will strengthen thee; yea, I will help thee; yea, I will uphold thee with the right hand of my righteousness." He is waiting to strengthen, help and uphold us.

Have you not seen a youngster holding onto his father's hand as they walked together? Suddenly the little one stumbled but the father held the child's hand tightly in his strong one and kept him from falling.

So the Lord holds your hand in His — your weak one in His all-powerful one. When we come to the rough spots in the way, He keeps us from falling. He holds us up as we stumble over our problems, our needs, our sorrows, our heartaches. Thus we can face each day unafraid as we rest in Him. "I will trust, and not be afraid" (Isaiah 12:2).

2

I will hear what God the Lord will speak: for he will speak peace unto his people, and to his saints. Psalm 85:8

Hearing is a very common daily experience. If when evening came we could play a tape-recording of everything we had heard that day, would God's voice be recorded on the tape? God has something to tell us each day, but we must be "tuned in" if we are to hear His words.

God's message to His people is a message of peace. Eight days after Jesus had risen from the dead He appeared to His disciples as they were in a room with all the doors shut. He stood in the midst and said, "Peace be unto you." He speaks these same words to us today. But we must be quiet enough to hear Him.

In this world of tension and strain, we can relax as we hear Him speak to us. Tradition says that a hunter once found the aged Apostle John seated on the ground playing with a tame quail. He expressed surprise that such a saintly man should be spending his time so profitlessly. John looked up and said, "Why is the bow on thy shoulder unstrung?" The hunter replied, "If I kept it always taut, it would lose its spring." "For the same reason," said John, "I play with this bird." We do not know if this actually occurred, but the truth illustrated by the story can be applied to us. We need to take time to "unstring our bows."

God's word of peace gives a heart of peace.

As ye have therefore received Christ Jesus the Lord,   *3*
so walk ye in him: rooted and built up in him, and
established in the faith, as ye have been taught,
abounding therein with thanksgiving. Colossians
2:6, 7

The verbs in this verse — "walk," "rooted," and "built up" — characterize our relationship with God. Paul was concerned that these Colossian Christians not only be strong in faith but that they reflect this faith in their daily lives. They were to practice as well as possess this faith.

He said, "Walk ye *in Him.*" Walking denotes motion and direction; it indicates progress and attainment. Walking with Him suggests progress (one moves when he walks); walking with Him suggests companionship (He walks with us each step of the way); walking with Him suggests a destination (our walk leads us into His presence). All of this is summed up in the words, "Walk ye in him." Our walk should match our talk.

We are also to be "rooted . . . *in him.*" In this verse our Christian experience is likened to a tree. If we are to grow upward, our roots must reach downward. A tree grows and becomes strong as its roots reach down to the very source of supply and are nourished.

Furthermore, we are told that we are to be "built up *in him.*" We are to be built up in His likeness. Remember these three illustrations of our Christian development — walking, growing, building. Walking goes *on* — indicating progress day by day. Have you made progress today? Roots go *down* — indicating inward growth as we reach downward and nourish ourselves through His Word. Are you growing inwardly? Building goes *up* — indicating outward growth into His likeness. Can He be seen in your life?

Going onward, growing inwardly and showing Him outwardly — what a privilege!

4   *Moreover, it is [essentially] required of stewards that
a man should be found faithful — proving himself
worthy of trust. I Corinthians 4:2, Amplified*

In these days it is difficult to find those who will assume responsibility and be dependable. God's Word tells us that His stewards are to be faithful. A steward is defined as "a person entrusted with the management of affairs not his own." As stewards of God, we are entrusted with the Gospel. "But as we were allowed of God to be put in trust with the gospel, even so we speak; not as pleasing men, but God, which trieth our hearts" (I Thessalonians 2:4).

It is not required that a steward be popular, or successful, or wealthy, or have a high position, but he must be faithful. A steward's capability is not of primary importance, nor is the scope of his service, but his dependability is the most important requirement.

Stewards of God have a great trust — the Gospel of Jesus Christ — and they must be trustworthy, dedicated to God's service. Talents and abilities have been given them by God. The eyes of the faithful steward are on the Master, and his one desire is to please Him.

The story is told of a great violinist who presented a concert in a huge auditorium filled to capacity. As the last note of his beautiful music died away, there was a moment of complete silence. Suddenly the audience broke into enthusiastic applause. However, the artist scarcely seemed to hear it. He was looking intently into the balcony. There in a corner sat his teacher. As the instructor nodded his head in approval, the famous musician turned and acknowledged the applause of the audience. His first concern had been to please and win the approval of his teacher.

And I will give thee the treasures of darkness, and hidden riches of secret places, that thou mayest know that I, the Lord, which call thee by thy name, am the God of Israel. Isaiah 45:3

5

God gave Cyrus this promise which can be a blessing to us today. Many people are going through a time of darkness. This is not a pleasant experience and our natural reaction is to rebel against it. We ask to be removed from it or to have it removed from us. Yet this verse speaks of the "treasures" of darkness. The dictionary defines "treasure" as "something valuable, something on which a high value is set, something very precious." So God allows darkness to come into our lives to bring something valuable to us.

It is said that night is nature's growing time. In the fall I sometimes plant bulbs in pots inside the house. If these bulbs are to produce flowers, however, I must keep them in the dark for two or three weeks so that they will develop strong roots. When I bring them out into the light they begin to grow with amazing rapidity.

Spiritual growth also occurs in the darkness. Instead of saying, "*When* am I going to get out of this dark place?" you should ask, "*What* am I going to learn from this dark place?" In the night God draws near in a special way. "Thou hast proved mine heart; thou hast visited me in the night." Instruction comes in the night. "My heart instructs me in the night seasons" (Psalm 16:7, Amplified). God gives us a special song for the night. He "giveth songs in the night" (Job 35:10). In the darkness we often experience a greater desire for God Himself. "With my soul have I desired thee in the night" (Isaiah 26:9). God has a great purpose in allowing darkness to enter your life: "That thou mayest know that I, *the Lord*, which call thee by thy name, am the God of Israel" (Isaiah 45:3b).

6

But the fruit of the (Holy) Spirit, [the work which His presence within accomplishes] — is . . . patience (an even temper, forbearance). Galatians 5:22, Amplified

Long-suffering is included in the fruit of the Spirit. It is produced by the Holy Spirit; it is His work, not ours. The Old Testament contains many references to God's long-suffering. His long-suffering enabled Him to wait patiently and lovingly for us to turn from our own ways. "The Lord does not delay and be tardy or slow about what He promises, according to some people's conception of slowness, but He is long-suffering (extraordinarily patient) toward you, not desiring that any should perish, but that all should turn to repentance" (II Peter 3:9, Amplified). In spite of our weaknesses and failures, God is infinitely patient, gracious and long-suffering toward us. F. B. Meyer said, "It is impossible to exhaust the patience of God."

Long-suffering, patience and endurance result when the love of God fills our lives. "Love endures long and is patient and kind" (I Corinthians 13:4, Amplified). "This love of which I speak is slow to lose patience" (Phillips). Even though wronged, love forbears and is silent. It does not strike back. The Holy Spirit produces such love in our lives.

Our Lord's love — unlike ours — is perfect. It never yields to anger, is never impatient. Someone has said, "He is the Original Photograph; we are the reprints." The Apostle Paul declared, "But I obtained mercy for the reason that in me, as the foremost [of sinners], Jesus Christ might show forth and display all His perfect long-suffering and patience for an example to [encourage] those who would thereafter believe on Him for [the gaining of] eternal life" (I Timothy 1:16, Amplified).

He shall come down like rain upon the mown grass: 7
as showers that water the earth. Psalm 72:6

In this verse we read of rain which comes down on the mown grass. However we are told that the expression "mown grass" does not refer to the grass which has been cut but to the stubble which remains. As the rain comes down upon this stubble, it heals and revives it. The stubble begins to grow again, becomes green, and is eventually harvested. I have heard, in fact, that the second cutting of hay is usually better than the first.

God sometimes prunes our lives. This pruning leaves our hearts bruised and bleeding. Then the tender and gentle rains of His love and comfort come down upon these wounds. The Holy Spirit pours upon them the Balm of Gilead with its healing power. Rain on mown grass is not more gentle than His loving touch on human souls. The wounds begin to heal, growth begins again, and there is an abundant second crop to His glory.

A Christian had two cut-glass dishes. They were alike in size and weight, but one was coarsely cut and the other was finely cut. When the latter was placed in the sunlight, it sparkled with all the colors of the rainbow. The finely cut dish was the more beautiful. The same is true of us. Many of us are not willing to endure the painful cutting process in our lives, but it can make us choice and beautiful vessels to reflect the beauty of our lovely Lord. "Now no chastening for the present seemeth to be joyous, but grievous; nevertheless afterward it yieldeth the peaceable fruit of righteousness unto them which are exercised thereby" (Hebrews 12:11).

8   *For the Lord God is a sun and shield: the Lord will give grace and glory: no good thing will he withhold from them that walk uprightly. Psalm 84:11*

The sun brings light, dispelling darkness. Perhaps today there is darkness ahead of you. The Lord is a sun for your darkness today. The light may not shine very far ahead of you, but as you go forward step by step, it will shine on your way, scattering your darkness.

The Psalmist also says that God is a shield. A shield is a piece of armor that protects from danger. He is our protection from danger — from the strong onslaughts of our enemy. He said, "Fear not, Abram: *I* am *thy* shield" (Genesis 15:1). God Himself is our shield. No other shield could give us better protection.

David also tells us that the Lord will give grace — unmerited favor from Him — and glory — the light of His presence. Furthermore, the Psalmist assures us, "*No* good thing will he withhold from them that walk uprightly." If He withholds something, He does so for our good. When a little child asks us for a pair of sharp scissors, do we give them to him? Of course not. We know that such a thing would not be for his good, and we withhold what he requests, despite his tears and protests.

God holds back only what is not good for us; He is willing to give us everything that is for our good.

Jesus Christ the same yesterday, and to day, and for ever. Hebrews 13:8

9

It has been said that "God is the God of every tense — past, present and future. He is the help of our past; the hope of our future; and the great *I am* of today."

In I Samuel 7 we read that the Israelites were in battle with the Philistines. After they had defeated their enemies, they "took a stone, and set it between Mizpeh and Shen, and called the name of it Ebenezer, saying, *Hitherto* hath the Lord helped us" (vs. 12). As we look at God's leading in the past, we can praise Him for our past blessings. This gives us assurance of future blessings. God has been our *help* in the *past*.

In Genesis 22:14 we read of Jehovah-jireh — "The Lord *will* provide." The verse does not say He *may* provide, or that He *could* provide, but that He *will* provide. As God has provided in the past, so will He provide in the future. God is the *hope* of the future.

Sometimes, however, it is the "today" that gives us the most difficulty. The problems and needs of today give us a defeated spirit and bring discouragement. We must remember that God *is* going to work for us today as He did in the past and as He will do in the future. He is God, El-Shaddai, the All-Sufficient One, for this very moment. "The Lord *is* my helper, and I will not fear what man shall do unto me" (Hebrews 13:6). God is the great *I am* of *today*.

George Mueller had the following motto on his wall: "And Today." Each of us can also claim "And Today" as our day-by-day motto. Our God is the God of the past, the future, *and* the present. Our trust is in "Jesus Christ, the same yesterday, *and* to day, and for ever."

10   *But God led the people around by way of the wilder-*
ness toward the Red Sea. And the Israelites went up
marshaled (in ranks) out of the land of Egypt. Exodus
13:18, Amplified

I learned a valuable spiritual lesson from an incident which occurred when we were making a trip to the Northwest. Early one morning we were driving into Seattle on a busy dual highway. Suddenly the four lanes of traffic halted from both directions. We wondered, of course, what had caused this. To our surprise, we saw a mother duck and six little ducklings calmly crossing the highway. The little ducklings were following the mother duck in a straight line, one behind the other. Following closely behind their mother, trusting her as their guide, they were oblivious to danger.

What an illustration of God's guidance! The Israelites experienced divine guidance when they were leaving Egypt. Before them lay the Red Sea. Pharaoh and his men were pressing in from the rear. There seemed to be no way out. But God "stopped traffic" for them.

"And Moses stretched out his hand over the sea; and the Lord caused the sea to go back by a strong east wind all that night, and made the sea dry land, and the waters were divided. And the children of Israel went into the midst of the sea upon the dry ground: and the waters were a wall unto them on their right hand, and on their left" (Exodus 14:21, 22).

As God led the Israelites through the Red Sea, so will He lead us. Are you completely hemmed in? Is there no way out, around or through your problems? Do not fear or lose heart. Your way out is *up*. He will make a way where there is no way. He will "stop traffic" to lead you through.

To day, if ye will hear his voice, harden not your **11**
hearts. Hebrews 3:7, 8

How exciting it is to answer the telephone and hear the voice of a loved one! It is even more wonderful to answer our "royal telephone" and hear God's voice speaking to us.

"If ye will *hear his* voice . . . " we read in this verse. Christ is our connection from God's "telephone line." "God . . . hath in these last days spoken unto us by his Son" (Hebrews 1:1, 2). We have twenty-four-hour-a-day service on this line — it is open night and day.

When riding in a cab, you have probably observed that the driver has an open line to his office. Thus he can hear any message intended for him. If he turns off the connection, however, he can't hear. We, too, can hear God's voice as long as we keep our line to heaven open. But if we turn off our connection, we are unable to hear His message for us.

"Harden not your hearts," this verse tells us. What are some things that harden our hearts and close the connection to Him? Perhaps our busy schedules or the pressure of business or the problems of our home or family keep us from hearing His voice. Disobedience to God, indifference, delay, or even unbelief may close the connection. *"Today* if ye will hear his voice," says our Scripture verse. God will speak the word we need today. It may be a word of comfort, instruction, correction or strength. Hear His voice *today*.

A man worked quietly at the foot of a telephone pole located on a noisy street corner. He seemed to know exactly what tools were needed by his fellow worker at the top of the pole, and the two worked in complete harmony. This was possible because the workman on the ground was wearing headphones. As the sounds around him were shut out, he could hear the voice above and follow the instructions given to him by the workman at the top of the pole.

As we shut out the sounds of the world, we can hear God's voice giving us our directions so that we can work in complete harmony with Him.

12   *Let us go on unto perfection. Hebrews 6:1b*

God's Word tells us that we are to go on to "perfection," which means "full growth." We are to mature spiritually.

The student does not want to stay in the same grade year after year. However, before he can be promoted he must take final examinations, pass some kind of test, or in some way give evidence that he has satisfactorily completed the work required.

The goal of our spiritual maturity is stated in Ephesians 4:13-15: "Till we all come in the unity of the faith, and of the knowledge of the Son of God, unto a perfect man, unto the measure of the stature of the fulness of Christ: that we . . . may grow up into him in all things, which is the head, even Christ." Our goal in life is maturity in Christ. Let us go on to full growth. We will never reach the limit of the growth which is possible in Christ, but God wants us to continue to grow spiritually. We must not be satisfied to stay where we are. The Amplified New Testament reads, "Let us go on . . . advancing steadily toward the completeness and perfection that belongs to spiritual maturity" (Hebrews 6:1). Bishop Wescott said that this could mean, "Let us be borne or carried on." Jesus Christ is ready to carry us on to full growth.

We are to go on, showing progress in our spiritual growth; we are to advance steadily, and to be borne on toward the goal of maturity in Christ.

In what grade are we spiritually?

Behold, thy servants are ready to do whatsoever my Lord the king shall appoint. II Samuel 15:15

13

Absalom, the son of David, through clever scheming was stealing the hearts of the men of Israel. He was conducting a campaign to set himself up as king. He even persuaded David's trusted counselor, Ahithophel, to join his ranks. One day a messenger came to David, saying, "The hearts of the men of Israel are after Absalom." David knew it was time for him and his servants to flee for their lives. When he presented the choice to the servants, they chose to obey and follow him, their king. They were ready to obey him, to follow him, and to do whatever he suggested.

Today we are constantly having to make choices. There are many decisions to make. Are we ready to say to our King of kings, "I am ready to do whatever You want me to do"? Or have we permitted scheming "Absaloms" to steal our hearts away from our love and loyalty to our King? Busyness, indifference, lack of compassion, self — these are Absaloms that may creep into our hearts.

On whose side are you? Absalom's or the King of kings? Are there Absaloms in your life that have stolen your heart away from the Lord? Can you say as did the servants of David, "Thy servant is *ready to do* whatsoever my Lord shall appoint"? Let Him be King in every avenue of your life.

14   *Deliver me, I pray thee, from the hand of my brother.*
Genesis 32:11a

Jacob was a trickster. He had cheated his brother Esau out of his birthright and blessing and had fled to the home of his Uncle Laban. As he was making the journey, God spoke to him, telling him He would bring him back again to his homeland. Jacob lived with his uncle. Later he married Laban's daughters and had a family. Laban was as much of a schemer as Jacob was, and the two constantly tried to outwit each other.

One day God said, "Return unto thy country, and to thy kindred, and I will deal well with thee." In obedience, Jacob began to plan his return trip. But instead of consulting God he began to make his own plans. He remembered Esau's hatred for him. Would his brother now carry out his threat to kill him? Not yet having learned to trust God completely, Jacob became fearful.

After he had made plans, he paused to pray. How like many of us today! We make our own plans and then ask God to bless them. One day my sister-in-law was making candy. It didn't harden. She said to her little son, "Let's pray and ask God to make it hard." He said wisely, "We should have prayed first."

Jacob was eventually driven to prayer by circumstances without and fears within. God had said "Return," and he was returning. Obedience to God puts us on praying ground. He humbled himself before God. He knew he had no merits of his own by which he could approach God. He admitted, "I am not worthy of the least of all the mercies" (vs. 10).

Jacob then brought his need to God. "Deliver me, I pray thee, from the hand of my brother," he pleaded (vs. 11). His prayer was simple and direct; right to the point; a cry from the heart. He reminded God of His promise: "And *thou saidst*, I will surely do thee good." God heard and answered Jacob. He still had many things to learn, but God undertook for him.

Let us pray and accept God's plan rather than make our own plans and then pray. It has been said, "We lie to God in prayer if we do not rely on Him after prayer."

And he said, Thy name shall be called no more Jacob,
but Israel: for as a prince hast thou power with God
and with men, and hast prevailed. Genesis 32:28

15

This is an age of power. We are aware of the great power man has at his command today. But we must remember that God's Word says, "Power belongeth unto God" (Psalm 62:11). God's power is available for His children. It strengthens us for service and enables us to be witnesses for Him. It makes our lives fruitful.

From the life of Jacob we learn lessons which will help us to become channels of power for God. Jacob was a schemer and a planner; it was difficult for Him to pray and leave the results with God. But he finally had to decide who was going to direct his life — God or himself.

After sending his family across the brook Jabbok, he was alone. The angel of the Lord appeared to him and wrestled with him all night. God brought him to the end of himself, to the place where he recognized his helplessness. He had to learn that in his weakness was God's strength.

After Jacob had wrestled all night with the angel, God suddenly touched his thigh and he was utterly powerless, broken of self. He clung to God and said, "I will not let *thee* go, except thou bless me" (Genesis 32:26). From "Jacob the Supplanter" his name was changed to "Israel," "The one God commands." Then God said to him, "For as a prince hast thou *power* with God and with men, and hast prevailed."

We, too, need "power with God and with men." But perhaps we are like Jacob. We plan our lives in our own way. We must be broken of self. Our strength must be touched and broken that His power may be perfected in our weakness.

Are you a "power with God" in prayer? Then you will be a "power with men" in His service.

16 *Then went king David in, and sat before the Lord, and he said, Who am I, O Lord God? and what is my house, that thou hast brought me hitherto?* II Samuel 7:18

David was a great man. Not only did he want God's best, but he wanted to give his best to God. He had a longing to build a temple for God. His desire was good, yet it was not God's plan for him. He must have had a feeling of disappointment. Yet he did not murmur or complain. Instead, he did what was evidently his habit. He went to God in prayer. He "sat before the Lord."

Like a pupil before his teacher, he sat at the feet of the Lord. He took time to sit quietly in God's presence, meditating on His greatness. He prayed, "Who am I, O Lord God? and what is my house, that thou hast brought me hitherto?" His own plans faded away when he was in God's presence. In quiet submission he was ready to exchange his will for God's. God had a better plan for him. Instead of building a temple for God, he established a family line through which the Saviour came.

We plan what we want to do for the Lord. But He may have other plans for us. Do we begin to murmur and complain, or are we like David? Do we go in and sit before the Lord, ready to do His will?

Someone has said, "There is no disappointment to one whose will is lost in God's will."

And he said unto them, Come ye yourselves apart **17**
into a desert place, and rest a while: for there were
many coming and going, and they had no leisure so
much as to eat. Mark 6:31

An interested observer was watching a workman make an amber necklace. He put a piece of rough amber on the lathe, shaved off a few fragments, and then laid it aside. This he did with every piece he planned to use in the necklace. Then he returned to the pieces, rounding them a little, but working only a short time on each bead. He repeated this process until all the beads were shaped and polished as he wanted them. Since the workman had learned that amber will "fly to pieces" if one works on it for more than a brief time, he let each piece rest after he had worked on it.

This is also true of our lives. We need a time of resting to keep us from "flying to pieces." This rest is in the Lord. "Come unto *me*, all ye that labour and are heavy laden, and I will give you rest" (Matthew 11:28). We let ourselves become tense and troubled instead of resting in Him.

When the disciples returned from their mission, they "gathered themselves together unto Jesus" (vs. 30). They had many things to share with Him. Then crowds began to gather, and the disciples had no time to eat. Jesus knew that they must have rest if they were to minister effectively to the crowds about them.

Our Lord said, "Come ye yourselves apart . . . and rest a while." Note that He had said, "*Come* and rest" not "*Go* and rest." True rest is found in companionship with the Lord. Resting is not merely ceasing from toil but coming apart and fellowshiping with Him.

A time "apart" is necessary for physical and spiritual rest and also for preparation for the work ahead. We must forget the successes and failures of the past and rest in Him so that we will be prepared for the future.

We must "*come* apart" or we will "come *apart*."

18 *If ye abide in me, and my words abide in you, ye shall ask what ye will, and it shall be done unto you.* John 15:7

Are you satisfied with your prayer life? Are you spending as much time in prayer as you think you should?

This verse gives us the secret of an effective prayer life. First, we must abide in Him: "If ye abide in me." To abide in Him is to live in constant fellowship with Him, to "make our home" in Him. Second, His words must abide in us: "And my words abide in you." We are to feed on His Word, appropriating it in our lives. We are to be guided and controlled by it.

This puts us in the place where God answers prayer. "Ye shall ask what ye will, and it shall be done unto you." If we live in Him and let His Word control our thoughts and actions, our desires and requests will be in harmony with His will and our prayers will be answered.

F. B. Meyer said, "The temple of prayer is guarded from the intrusion of the unprepared footstep by many tests. At the foot of the marble steps, we are challenged for the watchword. If we do not speak in harmony with God's glory, our further passage is peremptorily stayed. The key, engraven with the name of Jesus, will only obey the hand in which His nature is throbbing. We must be in Him if He is to plead in us. His words must prune, direct and control our aspirations. His service must engage our energies. Out of the abundance of the heart the mouth speaks; and when the mouth is opened in prayer and supplication, the heart speaks."

For God alone my soul waits in silence; from Him comes my salvation. My soul, wait only upon God and silently submit to Him; for my hope and expectation are from Him. Psalm 62:1, 5, Amplified

19

David's life was filled with trouble, discouragement and heartache. Friends and family had turned against him. Even his life was in danger. He knew what it was to have enemies. But he also knew God and had learned to wait only upon Him.

What do we do when burdens press in upon us? To whom do we go? Sometimes we try to work out the answer ourselves or we go to another person. We go to God only when all else has failed. We need to do what David learned to do — we must wait *only* upon God.

We are to wait "in silence" (vs. 1, Amplified) and to "silently submit to Him" (vs. 5, Amplified). A literal translation is, "Only on God wait thou all hushed, my soul." We are to wait in silence before Him that we might be aware of His holiness and majesty. We need to be still in His presence that we might worship Him for who He is and what He has done. In the hustle and bustle of living we often rush into His holy presence and out again without pausing to wait on Him. We do not take time to tune our souls to Him.

Several missionaries had to make a trek into the bush country. They secured the services of several native guides. The first few days they traveled long hours. One morning the missionaries discovered that the guides had made no preparation for the day's journey and refused to move. When asked why they would not travel that day, the guides answered, "Our souls must catch up with our bodies."

20   *And the word of the Lord was precious in those days. I Samuel 3:1b*

How precious God's Word is to us today! However, if it is to be a power in our lives, we must read it and meditate on it. As we read through the Psalms we find that David habitually meditated on God's Word. According to the dictionary, "to meditate" means "to think in view of doing." Have you asked yourself how much meditating you really do? Do you read the Word with the intention of putting it to work in your life? "Be ye doers of the word, and not hearers only" (James 1:22a).

Meditation is the secret of prosperity. "This book of the law shall not depart out of thy mouth; but thou shalt *meditate* therein day and night, that thou mayest observe to do according to all that is written therein: for then thou shalt make thy way *prosperous*, and then thou shalt have good success" (Joshua 1:8). It is also the secret of fruitfulness. "But his delight is in the law of the Lord; and in his law doth he *meditate* day and night. And he shall be like a tree planted by the rivers of water, that bringeth forth his *fruit* in his season" (Psalm 1:2, 3).

Someone has said, "Study is gathering information; meditation is viewing it from all angles and relating it to our life. Study leads to conclusions; meditation to convictions. We study for serving; we meditate for living. Study alone brings growth of mind, but meditation brings growth in the inner man." "Meditate upon these things; give thyself wholly to them; that thy profiting may appear to all" (I Timothy 4:15).

Meditating in the Word makes the Lord Jesus Christ more real to us, and makes us more like Him. "My meditation of *him* shall be sweet: I will be glad in the Lord" (Psalm 104:34).

Hear me when I call, O God of my righteousness: **21**
thou hast enlarged me when I was in distress; have
mercy upon me, and hear my prayer. But know that
the Lord hath set apart him that is godly for himself;
the Lord will hear when I call unto him. Psalm
4:1, 3

"To call" means "to send out the voice in order to attract another's attention, either by word or by inarticulate utterance," the dictionary tells us. Calling implies a need, a cry for help.

David was being pursued by his enemies. Even his son had turned against him. He called out to God — to attract His attention. "Hear me when I *call*, O God of my righteousness," he said. He called to Him with the expectation that he would be heard: "Hear *me*." Many others were calling out to God at the same time, yet He heard David's cry.

David remembered how God had enlarged him in his distress. "Enlarged" means "set at large" or "set free." "You have freed me when I was hemmed in and enlarged me when I was in distress" (Amplified). Because God had undertaken for his past needs, David was encouraged that He would do so again. "Have mercy [now in my present need] upon me, and hear my prayer," he pleaded.

Today, in the midst of the complexities of life, we have an open line of communication to God. He is listening. David said, "The Lord listens and heeds when I call to Him" (Amplified). His ear is open to your *call* also. Even though thousands of God's children may be calling to Him at the same time, yet He hears each one and will answer every prayer. You're just a call away from God.

22 *Every Scripture is God-breathed — given by His inspiration — and profitable for instruction, for reproof and conviction of sin, for correction of error and discipline in obedience, and for training in righteousness [that is, in holy living, in conformity to God's will in thought, purpose and action], so that the man of God may be complete and proficient, wellfitted and thoroughly equipped for every good work. II Timothy 3:16, 17, Amplified*

One day my husband mentioned an interesting comment which had been made at work. One of the men had said, "When everything else fails, read the instructions." I said, "Isn't that true in our Christian lives also? When everything else fails, then we turn to the Lord and to His Word. As a last resort we seek His direction. How much better it is to read the Bible, God's Instruction Book, first! How many mistakes and heartaches would be avoided if we did so!"

All Scripture is God-given and is profitable for our lives. It is "profitable for instruction." It teaches us. It is profitable "for reproof and conviction of sin." It shows us what is displeasing to God. It is profitable "for correction of error and discipline in obedience." It shows us how to correct what is wrong in our lives. It is profitable "for training in righteousness [that is, in holy living, in conformity to God's will in thought, purpose and action]." It gives us instruction and training which enable us to please God and do His will. The purpose of all this is that we may be "complete and proficient, well-fitted and thoroughly equipped for every good work."

God's Word is extremely important for our lives. It is profitable for us. Study it carefully; study it prayerfully. It will teach you how to achieve maturity.

Our Father which art in heaven, Hallowed be thy name. *Matthew 6:9*

When Jesus' disciples said, "Lord, teach us to pray," He gave them a model prayer which began with the words, "Our Father." This prayer is effective only if it is prayed by those who have the right to say, "*Our* Father." This indicates a family relationship, a Father-child relationship. A child becomes a member of a family through birth into that family.

This is also true of our spiritual lives. We have the right to call God "our Father" only through the new birth. Only when we receive Jesus Christ as our Saviour does God become our Father. Then we have the right to say, "*Our* Father."

As we kneel in His presence and lovingly pray, "Our Father which art in heaven, hallowed be Thy name," what a sense of nearness we experience! As we tenderly and reverently approach Him in love, calling Him "our Father," our one desire is to do His will. We are praying to a Person, and there are no words sweeter than "our Father" to express our faith and confidence in Him.

A man was walking in his garden. He was carrying his little blind daughter in his arms. A business acquaintance came into the garden. He reached out and took the little girl from her father, who asked her, "Aren't you afraid?" "No," she replied calmly. "But you don't know who has you," he said. "No, I don't," she agreed, "but you do, Father."

You, too, can have this same confidence in your Heavenly Father. You can look to Him in trust, saying, "My Father, my times are in Your hands; You know best, and I can commit my life to You, knowing that you never make a mistake."

24 *Save thy people, and bless thine inheritance: feed them also, and lift them up for ever. Psalm 28:9*

David was a man of prayer. His prayer life is an example to us and can enrich our prayer lives. He had the joy and peace of a life lived in communion with God. Before making his needs known to God, he took time to hear his Heavenly Father speak to him. "Unto thee will I cry, O Lord my rock; be not silent unto me," he said (vs. 1).

After communing with God, he brought his petitions to Him. "Hear the voice of my supplication, when I cry unto thee," he prayed. Sometimes we try everything else before we finally resort to prayer. David had learned from personal experience that God hears and answers prayer. So, too, God wants us to take our needs to Him. David remembered to thank God for answered prayer. Often we forget this. "Blessed be the Lord, because he hath heard the voice of my supplications," he declared gratefully.

David was moved to pray for others also. His heart was tender toward them and their needs. "Save them, bless them, feed them and lift them up," he prayed. He asked God to preserve and keep them. David prayed that God's children might be well nourished. Food is necessary for life. When we do not eat, we become weak. Malnutrition and lowered resistance to disease result from lack of food. The same is true in our spiritual lives. We must be fed if we are to be spiritually strong and well. As we are nourished our spirits are lifted and our strength is renewed. In Psalm 3:3 we read, "But You, O Lord, are a shield for me, my glory, and the lifter up of my head" (Amplified).

Communion, petition, intercession — these had a place in David's prayer life. May they have a place in yours also.

Fear not, Abram; I am thy shield, and thy exceeding great reward. Genesis 15:1

Abram had passed through a trying time. He had gone with his servants to rescue Lot. Returning home, he was met by the king of Sodom who offered to let him keep the goods he had brought back. Abram refused, for he wanted to lean not on the arm of flesh, but on God. When the Possessor of heaven and earth filled Abram's vision, the things of earth had no attraction for him. His life was not centered in his possessions but in the Possessor of all things.

It was "after these things" that the Lord appeared to him. First, He spoke words of *reassurance*. He said, "Fear not." Berkeley translates this, "Have no fear." Perhaps Abram needed this encouragement because he feared that these kings might return to trouble him. God says, "Fear thou not; for I am with thee: be not dismayed; for I am thy God: I will strengthen thee; yea, I will help thee; yea, I will uphold thee with the right hand of my righteousness" (Isaiah 41:10). What reassurance and encouragement these words give us today!

Second, the Lord promised to be his *refuge:* "I am thy shield." God promised Abram that He would surround him and protect him from the enemy. He is a safe and ready shield for His own even today. The Breton sailor used to say when going to sea, "My God, protect me; my boat is so small and Thy sea is so great."

Third, the Lord promised to be Abram's *reward:* "I am . . . thy exceeding great reward." After Abram had rejected the gifts of the king of Sodom, God said, "I, Myself will be your reward." God rewarded Abram with a fresh revelation of *Himself.* Who could receive a greater reward than this? Is He not enough? He who is the Possessor of heaven and earth, He who fills heaven and earth — cannot He fill a heart and satisfy it with Himself? To have God is to have all. No shield is stronger, no reward greater. He defends without and satisfies within.

26   *Strengthen thou me according unto thy word. Psalm 119:28*

The Bible is a dependable guide for life, for it always points in the same direction. We must not only read the Word but study it and search it. We must not study it haphazardly but purposefully.

We are to see Jesus in the Word. We cannot see Him in the flesh, but we can see Him in God's Word. "And these [very Scriptures] testify about Me!" (John 5:39, Amplified). Do you want to see the preciousness of Jesus more clearly? Then search the Word.

We are to grow through the Word. Food is essential to our physical growth; we must also eat if we are to grow spiritually. "Eat God's Word — read it, think about it — and grow strong in the Lord" (I Peter 2:2, Living Letters). How many are anemic because they lack spiritual food? How many are suffering from spiritual malnutrition?

The Word equips us for God's work. "Every Scripture is God-breathed . . . so that the man of God may be complete and proficient, well-fitted and thoroughly equipped for every good work" (II Timothy 3:16, 17, Amplified). The Word can produce works that are pleasing to God.

We are to study to be approved. "Study and be eager and do your utmost to present yourself to God approved (tested by trial), a workman who has no cause to be ashamed" (II Timothy 2:15, Amplified). God's approval — not man's — is the goal we must seek.

There hath not failed one word of all his good promises. I Kings 8:56b

One day a man went to his employer and told him he could no longer work for him without pay. His wife had lost her job, he explained, so the family would have no income. His employer knew he had been receiving excellent wages. "What have you been doing with your paychecks?" he asked. "Oh, those little white slips of paper? I have been saving them. I didn't know they were as good as money," was the reply.

Sometimes we do this with God's promises. We fail to cash them in. In this world of insecurity and uncertainty, how comforting it is to know that "there hath not failed one word of all his good promise."

I have read that the Bible contains enough promises for us to claim one for each day in the year. Adoniram Judson said, "The prospects are as bright as the promises of God." These promises are given to us to use. We can claim them for our own personal needs and hold onto them as we wait for God to make them good.

His promises are made available to us through Christ Jesus. "For all the promises of God in him are yea, and in him Amen, unto the glory of God by us" (II Corinthians 1:20). The promises are "yea" in Jesus Christ. The "amen" to the promises is our response to them. It is our acceptance of them and obedience to them.

God has not failed to make good one of His promises. Andrew Murray said, "When you get a promise from God, it is worth as much as a fulfillment." May we not fail to say "Amen" to His glorious promises as we claim our needs day by day.

28 *Wherefore God also hath highly exalted him, and given him a name which is above every name: that at the name of Jesus every knee should bow. Philippians 2:9, 10a*

A name is something which each of us possesses. Some names are more common than others. Check a telephone directory and see for example, how many Joneses and Smiths are listed. When a personal interest or love is associated with a name, even though it is very common and ordinary, it is transformed into one which is most precious and important.

While Jesus lived on earth, His name began to be spread abroad. People began to hear about Him and the great miracles He performed. They desired to see this One whose name was *Jesus.*

But there was a deeper meaning attached to His name. It was associated with salvation. "Thou shalt call his name *Jesus:* for he shall save his people from their sin" (Matthew 1:21b). God sent Him to earth to become the Saviour of the world.

Even after Jesus returned to heaven, His name was to be made known. Paul was one chosen for this task. "He is a chosen vessel unto me, to bear my name before the Gentiles, and kings, and the children of Israel" (Acts 9:15b).

We, too, have the honor of being "bearers" of that name. "Because of the savour of thy good ointments thy name is as ointment poured forth" (Song of Solomon, 1:3a). We are bearers of the ointment of His name; it is not to be kept only for ourselves but is to be poured forth as a sweet fragrance to bless others. Today He is only a name to many; but to us who know and love Him, He is as precious ointment to be poured forth from our lives as a sweet savor of His presence.

He first findeth his own brother Simon . . . and he **29**
brought him to Jesus. John 1:41a, 42a

One day a pastor met a parishioner who had missed church the day before. "What did you preach about yesterday, Pastor?" he asked. "I preached about Andrew," was the answer. "Andrew? He wasn't very important, was he? What was remarkable about him?" The minister replied, "I do not suppose many would classify him as great. But there is something significant about him. He is mentioned just three times in the Bible. But in each instance he was introducing someone to Jesus."

John 6 tells us that it was Andrew who brought the little lad with his lunch to Jesus. In John 12 we read that when the Greeks came to Philip and said, "Sir, we would see Jesus," he "cometh and telleth Andrew: and again Andrew and Philip tell Jesus" (vss. 21, 22). The third reference to Andrew is found in John 1: "He first findeth his own brother Simon . . . and he brought him to Jesus" (vss. 41a, 42a). We do not read that Andrew was a spectacular person. But when he was introduced to Jesus, He became intensely real to him. Andrew then had a burning desire to introduce others to the Saviour.

Perhaps we think there is little we can do for the Lord. However, we can bring others to Jesus. We can dedicate our lives to introducing others to Him. Andrew was willing to work right where he was. He saw those all around him who desperately needed Jesus. You, too, can be an Andrew, introducing others to Jesus Christ as you tell them what He has done for you and what He means to you. Or perhaps you will introduce them to Christ as you pray to Him for them. It may be that you will introduce them to the Saviour as they see Him revealed in your life day by day. One of the great joys in heaven will be the thrill of hearing someone say, "I am here because *you* introduced me to Jesus."

30

Now to Him Who, by (in consequence of) the [action of His] power that is at work within us, is able to [carry out His purpose and] do superabundantly, far more and above all that we [dare] ask or think — infinitely beyond our highest prayers, desires, thoughts, hopes or dreams. Ephesians 3:20, Amplified

This Scripture verse gives us an overwhelming sense of God's greatness. He is *able* to do *above* all that we ask — *abundantly* above all that we ask — even *exceeding* abundantly above all that we ask or even think.

In the Greek, this verse tells us that God "is able to do superabundantly above and beyond what we ask or think, and then some on top of that." Have we availed ourselves fully of these exceeding abundant resources of God? Our petitions can never exceed God's ability to grant them.

There is no limit to what God is *able* to do. We impose the limitations. His Word says that He is able to do all this "according to the power that worketh in us." We limit the work of God in and for us by not yielding completely to Him. The Spirit of God can do in our lives only as much as we allow Him to do.

F. B. Meyer said, "The power of God without is always commensurate with His power that works within." He is "able to do exceeding abundantly above" our prayers or thoughts "according to the power that worketh in us."

There is no limit to what God can do. He is *able:* the power is available. May we not limit Him but, rather, ask Him to increase our outreach to a needy world today and to use us in fulfilling our request.

And as he prayed, the fashion of his countenance **1**
was altered, and his raiment was white and glister-
ing. Luke 9:29

Jesus took Peter, James and John with Him into a mountain to pray. Someone has called this a top-level conference — a summit meeting. On the mount the disciples were eyewitnesses to a great transformation. As Jesus was transformed before them, they saw the glory of the Son of God shining through His humanity.

This place of prayer became a place of transformation for the disciples. "And when they had lifted up their eyes, they saw no man, save Jesus only" (Matthew 17:8). We, too, need a place of prayer where we can be alone with Him; where we can have fellowship with Him; where we can meditate on Him. As we lift up our eyes to Him, all else fades away and He fills our vision. As we fix our gaze on Him, a change takes place in us. We become like Him. Our place of prayer, too, becomes a place of transformation.

"But we all, with open face beholding as in a glass the glory of the Lord, are *changed* into the same image from glory to glory, even as by the Spirit of the Lord" (II Corinthians 3:18). At the place of prayer we become radiant. "They looked to Him, and were radiant" (Psalm 34:5, Amplified). It has been said, "There will be more reflection of Christ when there is more reflection on Him."

These disciples were being prepared to be witnesses. They needed to see Christ as the Son of God. Then their service would be effective. So we, too, need a vision of Him if we are to be effective witnesses. We must not become so busy serving the Lord that we forget the Lord of our service.

The following slogan was used to advertise a certain type of firebrick manufactured in England: "For every hour of saturation, there is a corresponding hour of illumination." The brick was soaked before being used. If it was soaked for an hour, it burned for an hour. We are a reflection of Christ in proportion to the time we spend with Him.

2

And he . . . pitched his tent, having Bethel on the west, and Hai on the east: and there he builded an altar unto the Lord, and called upon the name of the Lord. Genesis 12:8

Abraham's life was one of obedience. When God called, he responded. The above verse reveals Abraham's obedience and faith. He pitched his tent with Bethel on the west and Hai on the east. There he built an altar to the Lord and called on Him. "Bethel" means "house of God," and is a symbol of communion with God. Hai symbolizes the world.

Abraham was going forth to a new land. His life would be a testimony of his faith in God. Therefore it was important where he pitched his tent. It was located between Bethel, the place of communion with God, and Hai, the world. If his life was to be an influence for God in Hai, the world, he must have a place of communion with God, at Bethel.

Where is your tent pitched? Someone has said, "The measure of the worth of our public activity for God is the private communion we have with Him. Rush is wrong every time. There is always plenty of time to worship God." Is your tent pitched close enough to Bethel, your place of communion with God, so that your life can be a great influence for God as you go out into Hai, the world?

I exhort, therefore, that, first of all, supplications, prayers, intercessions, and giving of thanks, be made for all men; for kings, and for all that are in authority. I Timothy 2:1, 2a

3

Today the greatest need of our country is *prayer*. It is also the greatest need of national and world leaders today. As we recognize the seriousness of these times we need to turn to God in intercessory prayer.

How often in the past, events of history have been changed because of prayer. Prayer is of primary importance. The above verse says that "*first* of all" prayer, with thanksgiving, is to be made.

We are reminded to pray for all men — everywhere. I have read that if we prayed for one country each day, we would pray for the entire world three times a year. We are also told to pray for kings and those in authority. We live in a world governed by men. To us God has given the privilege of praying for them.

A schoolteacher and her class were discussing the fact that a father may occasionally permit his boy or girl to take the wheel of the car. The teacher emphasized that the parent places his big hands over the child's small ones so that there will be no danger of an accident. Some time afterward one of her pupils, a little eight-year-old, was asked if he would like to pray. "Dear Lord, please put Your hands over the hands of our President so he will know how to turn the wheel for our country," he prayed.

Our country desperately needs our intercession in these days. May we join hearts in prayer for our beloved United States of America!

4

Blessed is the nation whose God is the Lord; and the people whom he hath chosen for his own inheritance. Psalm 33:12

Our country was founded on its belief in God. In the summer of 1776, delegates from thirteen colonies met to consider the future of the new country. Suggestion after suggestion was offered and rejected. Finally the discouraged delegates turned to Benjamin Franklin for his opinion. Hesitating a moment, he slowly rose and delivered a brief but powerful message based on Psalm 127:1. "Except the Lord build the house, they labour in vain that build it: except the Lord keep the city, the watchman waketh but in vain." He suggested a time of prayer. A spirit of unity resulted and the Declaration of Independence was written. As the Liberty Bell rang for the first time in Independence Hall, it proclaimed the birth of the United States of America on July 4, 1776.

Eighty-seven years later, during a time of great crisis, President Lincoln, in his famous Gettysburg Address, challenged the people of America to resolve "that this nation, under God, shall have a new birth of freedom — and that government of the people, by the people, for the people, shall not perish from the earth." There are forces at work today which are trying to take away this freedom. These enemies are strong. Unless America acknowledges her dependence on God, we could lose this freedom so dear to us.

Prayer has changed the course of history in the past. It is still as powerful today. "If my people, which are called by my name, shall humble themselves, and pray, and seek my face, and turn from their wicked ways; then will I hear from heaven, and will forgive their sin, and will heal their land" (II Chronicles 7:14).

The late President Kennedy, in his inaugural address, said, "Do not ask what your country can do for you, but ask what you can do for your country." *Pray* that our United States of America may continue as a nation "under God."

Continue in prayer, and watch in the same with thanksgiving. Colossians 4:2

5

Someone has said, "You can do more than pray *after* you have prayed, but you cannot do more than pray *until* you have prayed."

In the above verse of Scripture we are told to "continue in prayer." You may say, "I can't always be on my knees." No you can't, but he who prays only on his knees doesn't pray enough. We breathe constantly, unceasingly. The same is true of prayer. When we pray we breathe the very atmosphere of heaven.

We are to pray *unceasingly,* not merely occasionally or when we feel inclined to do so. "Be earnest and unwearied and steadfast in your prayer [life], being [both] alert and intent in [your praying] with thanksgiving" (Amplified). We may become weary *while* praying but we must not become weary *of* praying. We are to "continue in prayer" for our loved ones and friends; for our country; for those in Christian service. We must not forget that we are to pray with thanksgiving.

Ten mission stations had several pressing needs. Their missionary director, learning of this, requested each of ten prayer groups to pray for one of the mission stations. Later eight of the stations gave glowing reports of God's moving in their midst. Two, however, were still struggling. The director contacted the prayer groups. Eight of them were continuing to pray faithfully each day. Two groups were not. Yes, as you have probably surmised, the struggling stations were the ones assigned to the two groups which had not been faithful in prayer.

Is some work or some person weak and struggling because we have not continued steadfast in prayer?

6   *Rest in the Lord, and wait patiently for him. Psalm 37:7a*

Many people seem to get up as tired as when they went to bed. Much of this weariness is caused by the pressures of life and a lack of rest in the inner man.

Rest is necessary for the body and the mind. There is a great need, too, for rest within. This Psalm mentions several steps which lead to this inner rest: "Fret not" (vs. 1); "Trust in the Lord" (vs. 3); "Delight thyself also in the Lord" (vs. 4); "Commit thy way unto the Lord" (vs. 5).

The source of this rest is in the Lord. Instead of being irritable, and fuming and fussing, we can have the inner quietness of resting "in the Lord." This is a rest we can possess even in the midst of ceaseless activity. A. B. Simpson speaks of "rested workers." He said, "There is an energy that may be tireless and ceaseless and yet still as the ocean depths."

Perhaps you are faced with a particularly busy day at home. The telephone rings — someone needs a word of comfort. Later a friend comes with a problem to discuss. About that time one of the children is hurt and demands attention. Or perhaps you have an exceptionally busy day at the office. In the midst of it a customer comes in with a complaint that you must satisfy. Then you are asked to do some extra work which must be completed immediately.

Such interruptions can upset and annoy us. Yet we can have a quietness in the midst of these irritations. We can "rest in the Lord." Accept the day with its changes as from Him. Instead of becoming irritable, thank Him for the changed schedule and say, "My times are in thy hand" (Psalm 31:15).

Casting all your care upon him; for he careth for you. I Peter 5:7

We are living in a careworn world. As we talk with people we find that most of them have problems, heartaches, needs. Many feel that no one really cares about them. Yet the great God of creation has a personal interest in each individual life. *He cares for you.* Today He knows all about your heartache and pain. His heart is filled with love and sympathy for you. He who knows when even a sparrow falls, knows and cares for the smallest details of our lives.

The children of Israel were in bondage as slaves in Egypt. When they finally cried out to God, He showed His care for them. "And the children of Israel sighed by reason of the bondage, and they cried, and their cry came up unto God by reason of the bondage. And God heard . . . and God remembered . . . and God looked upon the children of Israel, and God had respect unto them" (Exodus 2:23-25).

We are to cast *all* our care on Him — not merely the light burdens, but *every* one. Spurgeon said, "What seems to you a crushing burden would be to Him as the small dust of the balance."

In our city there is a sign which reads, "Why pray when you can worry?" No, I haven't misquoted it. You see, sometimes our actions justify such a question. One time as I sat in a train station I noticed a woman who was apparently having difficulty getting her reservations and ticket. Finally she took a seat beside me and told me everything that had gone wrong. Then she asked, "Can you think of anything I should be worrying about that I am not?" Do you ever have the feeling that you should be worrying about something?

F. B. Meyer said, "There is no surer path leading to rest than to pass on to Jesus all the anxieties of life, believing that He takes what we give at the moment of our giving it; that it instantly becomes a matter of honor with Him to do His best for us."

Trust and prayer lessen care.

8   *For Ezra had prepared his heart to seek the law of the Lord, and to do it, and to teach in Israel statutes and judgments. Ezra 7:10*

Ezra had a heart which was prepared "to *seek* the law of the Lord." A prepared mind will not take the place of a prepared heart. This is the kind of heart God is seeking. "For the eyes of the Lord run to and fro throughout the whole earth, to shew himself strong in the behalf of them whose heart is perfect toward him" (II Chronicles 16:9). It is not enough to have a knowledge of the Word. His Spirit must prepare our hearts to seek Him in His Word.

Not only was Ezra prepared to seek the law of the Lord; he was prepared "to *do* it." He was not satisfied merely to know God's Word — he was willing to *submit* to living in obedience to the Word. He had more than a merely intellectual interest in it. We read in James 1:22, "But be ye *doers* of the word, and not hearers only, deceiving your own selves."

Ezra did not merely seek God's Word and obey it — he was ready to *share* it with others. He was ready "to teach in Israel statutes and judgments."

May we prepare our hearts to seek God's Word and submit to it. Then we will be prepared to share it with a world in need. Are you seeking? Submitting? Sharing?

And he shall be like a tree planted by the rivers of water, that bringeth forth his fruit in his season; his leaf also shall not wither; and whatsoever he doeth shall prosper. Psalm 1:3

We are familiar with the poem that ends with the line, "But only God can make a tree." The Psalmist compares the Christian to a tree, a God-made tree.

We are *planted* trees — "he shall be like a tree planted." When we plant a tree we select the spot where we want it and the type of tree best suited for that location and for the purpose we had in mind. God knows where He wants to plant us and He has a purpose in planting us there. It may not be the place of our choice but it is the place of His choosing.

God *provides* for His trees — He plants them "by the rivers of water." Wherever we are planted, God's River of Life flows by. Our roots can reach down and constantly draw nourishment from it. We must drink of it regularly.

We are to be *productive* trees — ". . . that bringeth forth his fruit in his season." We must be productive in due season, bringing forth God's fruit in God's season. "When our lives take deep rootage in Christ, we will bring forth rich fruitage for Him."

God's trees will be *perpetually alive* — "his leaf also shall not wither." We will be ever-living, trees of unfading beauty radiating the loveliness of our lovely Lord. God's Word says of Him, "He is altogether lovely." One definition for "altogether" is "permanently." So in Him we are permanently lovely.

We are *prosperous* trees — "whatsoever he doeth shall prosper." We mature in Him. Rooted in Christ, nourished by the Word and refreshed by the Spirit, our lives become blessings to others.

10   *And he said, The God of our fathers hath chosen thee, that thou shouldest know his will, and see that Just One, and shouldest hear the voice of his mouth. For thou shalt be his witness unto all men of what thou hast seen and heard. Acts 22:14, 15*

People are constantly striving to be chosen for special honors conferred for outstanding achievement in various fields such as medicine or science. Young men train strenuously to earn awards in the field of athletics.

Paul was chosen for a high honor. God said to Ananias, "He is a chosen vessel unto me, to bear my name before the Gentiles, and kings, and the children of Israel" (Acts 9:15).

God's vessels have been chosen (1) to "know his will" — that they "might be filled with the knowledge of his will in all wisdom and spiritual understanding" (Colossians 1:9). They have also been chosen (2) to "see that Just One." Have you ever wished you had lived when Jesus was on earth and had looked upon His face? Through the eyes of faith we can see Him now. God's vessels have been chosen (3) to hear His voice. What a thrill it is to hear the voice of someone near and dear to us! We want to hear every word he says. What a privilege it is to hear the voice of our Saviour! Mary sat at Jesus' feet and heard His words. So, too, can we. God's vessels have been chosen (4) to be witnesses of what they have seen and heard. Our outer lives of witnessing can only be as powerful as our inner lives. We are to be witnesses of what *we* have seen and heard.

Chosen vessels are important for they are bearing that precious name of Jesus to the world today. One meaning of "bearing" is "displaying." Are you, as a "chosen vessel," displaying in your life the beauty of His?

For I know whom I have believed, and am persuaded that he is able to keep that which I have committed unto him against that day. II Timothy 1:12b

Not long ago I heard someone say, "The older I grow, the less sure I am of what I really know." He was a learned professor; yet the more knowledge he acquired, the more he realized the limitations of his own wisdom.

God tells us in His Word that we can know with certainty. In the above verse Paul says, "I *know*" — not "I *hope* I know," or "I *suppose* I know," or "I *think* I know," or "I *may* know," but "*I know.*" The apostle was not speaking of intellectual knowledge but of the certainty that he had a personal relationship with Jesus Christ. He says, "I know *whom* I have believed" — not "I know *what* I have believed." Paul had the assurance of knowing Jesus Christ personally as his Saviour and of having the gift of eternal life. He declared confidently, "For I know — I perceive, have knowledge of and am acquainted with Him — Whom I have believed (adhered to and trusted in and relied on)" (Amplified).

Paul was also confident of God's power to keep all that was committed to Him. In the Greek the word "commit" as used here has the meaning of "deposit." Suppose that I were to open a savings account in a bank to deposit my money for safe-keeping. I select a bank in which I have confidence. I make a deposit. Then I fear for its safety so the next morning I draw out the money. Then I am afraid it is not safe at home so I deposit it again at the bank. You say that such behavior would be extremely foolish. Yes, it would be. But many of us are equally foolish in our failure to trust God's power to keep what we have committed to Him. We trust our salvation to Him when we become Christians, but we must also deposit our needs, our loved ones, and our lives with Him.

Have you made a total commitment of your life to Him? Have you handed everything over to Him? Can you say with certainty, "I am [positively] persuaded that He is able to guard and keep that which has been entrusted to me and which I have committed [to Him], until that day"? (Amplified).

12

For ye are the temple of the living God; as God hath said, I will dwell in them, and walk in them; and I will be their God, and they shall be my people.
II Corinthians 6:16

We are overwhelmed when we read that the great God of the universe will live in the lives of His own children. Scripture tells us that we are "God's temple, the home of the living God." He does not merely make an occasional visit, but at our invitation He comes into our lives to reside. "I will dwell in them, and walk in them."

God, our Heavenly Father, loves us as no earthly person does; He is ready to provide for our every need. He walks in us as our Guide, Helper and Comforter, encouraging us along the way. He shares all of our problems. He is *our* God through His Son Jesus Christ, and we are *His* people.

An old woman who lived in an almshouse in England was asked, "Does the Queen ever visit here?" "Yes," was the reply. "Her Majesty comes to see me." "And does the King of kings visit you here?" "No," the old woman replied, "He doesn't visit here; He *lives* here."

Remember that today He lives in *your* life. He wants to be your constant companion and provide His best for you. Have you allowed Him to be at home in every part of your life? Or have you reserved parts of it for yourself alone?

Jesus saith unto them, My meat is to do the will of him that sent me, and to finish his work. John 4:34

13

The Bible says, "The Father sent the Son to be the Saviour of the world" (I John 4:14). Jesus told His disciples that His meat was to do the will of His Father. Talking to people about their spiritual needs was our Saviour's greatest source of satisfaction.

Jesus died on the cross to finish His work. But he entrusted to His disciples the task of helping to finish the work of spreading the Gospel. "Say not ye, There are yet four months, and then cometh harvest? behold, I say unto you, Lift up your eyes, and look on the fields; for they are white already to harvest" (vs. 35). We, too, have a responsibility in helping to finish this work of reaching the world with the Gospel.

A young man was leaving home for the first time to work in another city. Although a Christian, he was not allowing God to use his life. As a last favor to her before he left home, his mother asked him to view a certain picture hanging in an art gallery. When he stepped inside the gallery, he saw someone praying. He quickly withdrew. Several times he looked in but the man was still praying. Finally he decided to slip in quietly and view the painting. It portrayed Jesus praying in Gethsemane. The young man stood looking at the painting for some time, deeply moved by it. That night he talked to his mother about the picture. She said, "Jesus had chosen and trained a small band of men to take the Gospel to the world. Could He have been praying that they and others down through the ages would be faithful in finishing their part of this work?" The next day the young man and his mother went to see the painting. As the son looked at it, he squared his shoulders and said, "Jesus, I am ready to do my part in finishing the work of bringing the Gospel to the world."

14 *Now the Lord had said unto Abram, Get thee out of thy country, and from thy kindred, and from thy father's house, unto a land that I will shew thee: and I will make of thee a great nation, and I will bless thee, and make thy name great; and thou shalt be a blessing.* Genesis 12:1, 2

In these two verses I have noted especially three phrases: "I will shew thee"; "I will make of thee"; "I will bless thee."

God had called Abram out of Ur of the Chaldees and sent him to a new country that He might make of him a new nation. The people of that day did not have the superhighways and convenient methods of travel that we have. It was, therefore, a much more difficult undertaking for Abram to go to a new land than it would be for us today.

God promised to show Abram the land, but he had to be willing to start out on the journey. God said, "Get thee out." Only if Abram obeyed this command could He show him the new country. As Abram was willing to obey, God could promise, "I will make of thee." God used His "making process" in Abram's life that a new and great nation might come through him.

Perhaps God wants to send you forth today. He is saying, "If you will go, I will show *you*." As you are obedient, He will prepare you — make you ready — for the work you are to do. Only then will the blessing be yours. What a joy it will be to hear Him say, "I will bless *you*"!

Show me Thy ways, O Lord; teach me Thy paths.
Guide me in Thy truth and instruct me: for Thou
art the God of my salvation: for Thee I wait all day.
Psalm 25:4, 5, Berkeley

15

Before taking a trip, we study maps and plan our entire route. Then we make more detailed plans and get as much helpful information as we can. As we travel we stop from time to time for further directions and instructions.

God has a plan for each of us as we journey through life. Every one of us needs to pray, "Show me *Thy* ways, O Lord." We may not see a great distance ahead, but He will lead us step by step if we but wait on Him.

David asked God to teach him. Who could be a better teacher than the One who made us and who knows all our ways from the beginning to the very end? In Him is all wisdom and knowledge. The Holy Spirit will reveal God's will to us and make it real in our daily lives as we search the Word and pray.

As we travel through life we need to stop for guidance and direction so that we won't make a wrong turn or lose our way. The Holy Spirit will use the Word, prayer and circumstances, to guide us on our journey through life.

A member of the Salvation Army was faced with a perplexing decision. On a table in a room where he was staying was an open Bible. His attention was captured by this text: "The God of my mercy shall prevenet me." "Prevenet" is an Old English word for "go before." Someone had written in the margin another rendering, "My God in His loving-kindness shall meet me at every corner." These words assured the man that God would enable him to make the right decision.

We, too, can face the future unafraid, knowing that God will meet us at every corner to show us and guide us in His way.

16   *And in their mouth was found no guile: for they are without fault before the throne of God. Revelation 14:5*

How important our conversation is! Perhaps we do not realize how closely people are listening to what we say. On the night Jesus was betrayed, several people were talking to Peter. They said to him, "You certainly are one of His disciples, too, for your accent shows you up." By his speech they knew that he was a follower of Jesus. Peter denied their assertions, but his speech had betrayed him.

The importance of our conversation was impressed upon me by an unforgettable experience in my own life. I once knew a girl about whom I was deeply concerned. One day I made a rather frivolous remark in the office where she worked. She looked at me in surprise and said, "That doesn't sound like you." I realized that she had been listening to what I said and had been influenced by it. Later I went to my knees before the Lord, confessing to Him and asking Him to guard my conversation so that it would always honor and glorify Him.

This experience taught me a lesson I never forgot. People around us — in the office, in the home, in the neighborhood — are listening to what we say. Can it be said of us, "And in their mouth was found no guile: for they are without fault before the throne of God"? We have the great privilege of showing forth Christ by our speech each day. May it be said of each of us, "Certainly you are a Christian, for your speech shows that you are."

Moreover as for me, God forbid that I should sin against the Lord in ceasing to pray for you. I Samuel 12:23a

17

It has been said, "The secret of all failure is prayerlessness." I am sure that most of us realize that we do not pray as much as we should. In the morning the duties of the day begin to crowd in upon us and we fail to take time to pray. Each day we find it easier to neglect our quiet time with God.

It is natural for Satan to attack us by keeping us from prayer, for it is on our knees that our victories for God are won. Satan will do everything he can to keep us from praying, and he has won his victory if he can accomplish this. He would rather keep us busy in service than in prayer. He would rather have us study the Word than pray. Service for the Lord is important, and we need to read the Word, but these must be accompanied by a life of prayer.

Perhaps we need to revise our schedules so that we can have time for prayer. We may be overoccupied with "things" which are unimportant. We may have to rise earlier in the morning so that we can spend time in prayer and communion with our Lord.

I know many who regret that they are unable to spend as much time on their knees as they would like to. But we must not forget that we can also pray while we are doing other things. What do you do when you are ironing, washing dishes, walking down the street? There are many times during the day when we can spend a few minutes in prayer.

Two prominent ministers were asked, "Should Christ come now, what would be your keenest regret?" Each of them replied, "That I did not spend more time in prayer."

18 *One thing have I asked of the Lord, that will I seek after, inquire for and [insistently] require, that I may dwell in the house of the Lord — in His presence — all the days of my life, to behold and gaze upon the sweet attractiveness and the delightful loveliness of the Lord, and to meditate, consider and inquire in His temple. Psalm 27:4, Amplified*

In this day of speed, of hustle and bustle, how often we experience annoying delays. We are delayed by traffic; delayed by the telephone; delayed by weather. Yet because of our haste we often miss the blessings of life. We are too busy to stop and gaze at one of God's sunsets, too busy to listen to the song of a bird, too busy to give a smile and a cheery word to those who cross our path, too busy to give a listening ear to those who are carrying heartaches and problems.

The great need today is for those who will take time to linger in the presence of the Lord. David did so. His great desire was to dwell in the Lord's presence, to gaze upon His loveliness and to meditate on Him. Moses lingered in the presence of the Lord at the burning bush. Mary lingered at the feet of Jesus. Through the years those who have carried the fragrance of Jesus have been those who have lingered in His presence.

May we take time to linger with Him, dwelling in His presence, gazing on His loveliness and meditating on Him. Then as we leave His presence we will carry with us the fragrance of the Rose of Sharon.

I know that, whatsoever God doeth, it shall be for ever: nothing can be put to it, nor any thing taken from it: and God doeth it, that men should fear before him. Ecclesiastes 3:14

I once heard a talk on investments. The speaker told how money could be safely invested in such a way as to pay the greatest possible dividends in old age. As I listened to him I reflected upon the fact that although many people make careful provision for the future, yet when they reach the end of life their earthly investments do not pay dividends in eternity.

Consider now the greatest investment we can make — the investing of our lives for God. There are several questions we must ask regarding an investment. Is it sound? What dividends do we receive? When does it mature? Let us consider these important questions as they relate to the investment of a life for God.

First, is it sound? Yes, it is the soundest investment that can be made. God is eternal — He never fails. He has never had a bank failure. "Whatsoever God doeth, it shall be forever."

Second, what dividends does our investment pay? The more money invested, the greater the dividends. So with the investment of our lives — the greater the investment, the greater the dividends. In Mark 4, which speaks of fruit-bearing, we read that some dividends yield 30 per cent, some 60 per cent, and some 100 per cent. Will our dividends pay 30 per cent, 60 per cent, or 100 per cent — minimum, average, or maximum returns? God wants us to receive the greatest possible returns on our investment, but He can pay dividends only on what we invest.

Third, what is the maturity date of our investment? It matures in eternity. Scripture says, "Lay up for yourselves treasures in heaven, where neither moth nor rust doth corrupt, and where thieves do not break through nor steal" (Matthew 6:20). But today is our day of opportunity. We must make "the very most of the time — buying up each opportunity — because the days are evil" (Ephesians 5:16, Amplified). You have a life to spend for yourself or for God. Which will it be? The decision is yours.

20   *But I give myself unto prayer. Psalm 109:4*

David was in the midst of enemies on every hand, but he had learned the secret of a quiet heart. He gave himself to prayer. He had learned that there is no other way we can accomplish so much with so small an expenditure of time.

Often we are more willing to give our money and our talents than to give ourselves to a ministry of prayer. We give ourselves to business; we give ourselves to our families; we give ourselves to pleasure; but do we truly give ourselves to prayer? The Amplified translation reads, "But I resort to prayer."

Through the years there have been many precious saints who have resorted to such a life of prayer. Hudson Taylor said that the remarkable work of the China Inland Mission was accomplished through prayer. John Knox prayed, "God, give me Scotland or else I die." It is said that the life of Adoniram Judson was one of answered prayer. These were men who gave themselves to prayer.

There is an old church in Europe in which may be seen a picture of a plowman who has left his plow and turned aside to pray. But while he prays, an angel is plowing for him. The artist had grasped the truth that no time is ever lost when we pray. We work better and more effectively after we have prayed. Prayer gives us strength and power which can be derived from no other source. God's presence radiates from such a life of prayer. Do not lose precious time by neglecting to pray.

Workers together with him. *II Corinthians 6:1*

Two men may form a business partnership. A senior partner may select a junior partner who can share the work. There may be a number of partners in a business, each contributing something to the firm. One may have financial resources; another may have prestige which would be advantageous to the firm; another may have unusual executive ability. But each contributes to the success of the business.

So it is in God's work. We are in partnership with Him, each making a definite contribution. God has not given all of us the same talents. He doesn't use all of us in the same way or in the same place. Some have conspicuous places of leadership. Others are in hidden places but are equally faithful in their service. Some He uses often; others only occasionally. But it is of the utmost importance that we be where God wants us to be when He wants us there. This may seem insignificant to us, but it is important to God. Someone has said, "The right place for you is empty if you are in the wrong place."

There was once a piccolo player who was a member of a famous orchestra. In one of the compositions he had only one note to play. He decided it was not worth arranging his score and tuning his instrument to play only one note. No one would miss it, he concluded. The conductor raised his baton and the concert began. When it was time for the piccolo player to play his one note, the conductor pointed to him, but he did not respond. The conductor stopped the entire orchestra and demanded angrily, "Where is the piccolo player?"

Remember that every worker is important to God — even the "one-note" worker.

22   *For the love of Christ controls and urges and impels us, because we are of the opinion and conviction that [if] One died for all, then all died.* II Corinthians 5:14, Amplified

The truth of this verse was a great reality in the life of Paul. He was so gripped by this love that nothing else mattered. Christ's great love for him had so *captured* his heart that he said, "For to me to live is Christ." This love so filled his life that he had no desire, no choice, no ambition but to live for Christ. No longer did he live for self. He was willing to give his all to Christ.

The love of Christ so possessed Paul that it *controlled* his life. It *compelled* him to action, driving him forward with great urgency. This love had transformed Paul and made him a new creature with a new purpose. "But all things are from God, Who through Jesus Christ reconciled us to Himself (received us into favor, brought us into harmony with Himself) and gave to us the ministry of reconciliation — that by word and deed we might aim to bring others into harmony with Him" (vs. 18, Amplified). God had brought Paul into harmony with Himself that he might bring others into harmony with God.

This is God's purpose for our lives, too. We are to be Christ's ambassadors that "by word and deed we might aim to bring others into harmony with Him."

Upon hearing a missionary tell about the love of Jesus, an Egyptian woman said, "It is a wonderful story. Do the women of your country believe it?" Then she added quickly, "I don't think they do, for if they did, they would not be so long in coming to tell us."

*[Not in your own strength] for it is God Who is all
the while effectually at work in you — energizing and
creating in you the power and desire — both to will
and to work for His good pleasure and satisfaction
and delight. Philippians 2:13, Amplified*

God has a pattern for our lives. He knows how to fit the pattern to us and to adjust us to the pattern. This requires pinning and cutting. Needlework is necessary to make us according to His pattern. Finishing touches, such as embroidery, help to make us more beautiful "samplers" for Him. Gay colors — pinks and blues and greens — are needed, but touches of black, too, are necessary to set off the beauty of the needlework.

God's pattern for our lives is the accomplishment of His will. He desires to work out His will in us. Only by doing His will can we find peace, joy and satisfaction. Someone has said, "Good is ill if it keeps us from the best." Sometimes we refuse to do His will. We may become rebellious. Not only does He work in us to do His will, but He gives us the willingness to do it.

F. B. Meyer told of the time when God asked him for the keys to his life. One by one he gave them to Him — all except one. This key was something in his life which he was not willing to give to God. He found no peace until finally he prayed, "God, I am not willing to give this key to You, but I am willing to be made willing."

God can make us willing if we let Him. Then we can say as David did, "I delight to do thy will, O my God" (Psalm 40:8a).

24   *Whatever may be your task, work at it heartily (from the soul), as [something done] for the Lord and not for men. Colossians 3:23, Amplified*

A teacher had been telling the story of Jesus and the fishermen of Galilee and was showing the children a beautiful picture of Christ and His disciples. Each pupil took the picture, looked at it and passed it to the next child. When the teacher took it back, she said, "Has everyone seen the picture?" "I didn't," said one little fellow. "I didn't see the picture. I only saw Him."

Paul had been telling servants how to serve their masters: "in simplicity of purpose (with all your heart) because of your reverence for the Lord and as a sincere expression of your devotion to Him" (vs. 22). Whatever they did was to be done "heartily, as to the Lord, and not unto men."

We, too, are to please the Lord, and not men, in our service. We are to be enthusiastic. "Whatsoever ye do, do it heartily." We are to be sold on what we do. "Work whole-souledly" (Berkeley). We are to put every part of our being into what we are doing.

We must have the right motive. We must view our tasks "as [something done] for the Lord and not for men." This is true not only of our Christian activity but of everything we do. We must do our housework heartily as to the Lord. In our offices we must work heartily as to the Lord. We must keep our eyes on Him, watching for His direction in what we do; our one desire must be to please Him above all others.

Are you doing your service heartily, whole-souledly? Is your one desire to please Him? Do you see *Him?*

But he answered and said, It is written, Man shall **25**
not live by bread alone, but by every word that
proceedeth out of the mouth of God. Matthew 4:4

I once read about the Chinese Imperial Cookbook. It is a
unique book — probably the largest book in the world. It contains ninety-six volumes and weighs a ton. What an imposing set
of books! But think of the most important Book, the Bible. It is
the world's Best Seller. Recently I heard an announcer say,
"How wonderful it would be if the 'Best Seller' would also be the
'best read' Book of the world."

Someone has well said, "The Bible is the traveler's map, the
pilgrim's staff, the pilot's compass, the soldier's sword, and the
Christian's charter."

George Mueller made this thought-provoking statement: "The
vigor of our spiritual life will be in exact proportion to the place
held by the Word in our life and thoughts." If we try to serve
God without giving His Word its proper place, we will be anemic
Christians. Yet if we spend all our time in the Word without living lives of service, we will develop indigestion. There must be
a balance between the two.

The Bible is God's Manual of Operation for our lives. There is
no situation for which there is not some word of comfort,
strength, admonition, or instruction. D. L. Moody said this concerning God's Word: "If you are impatient, sit down quietly and
commune with Job. If you are strong-headed, read of Moses and
Peter. If you are weak-kneed, look at Elijah. If there is no song
in your heart, listen to David. If you are a politician, read Daniel.
If your faith is low, read Paul. If you are getting lazy, read
James."

It has been said, "Faith views all in Christ; hope expects all
from Christ; love gives up all for Christ. The nourishment of
faith, hope and love is the Word of God."

26

We continually give thanks to God the Father of our Lord Jesus Christ, the Messiah, as we are praying for you. Colossians 1:3, Amplified

Paul was thankful to God for the Colossians. He calls them "saints" (vs. 2). "Saintliness" has been defined as "Christlikeness" in the everyday lives of those who know Christ personally as Saviour. Then the apostle enumerates several characteristics of their lives for which he is thankful. These same characteristics should be seen in our lives.

Faith is the first characteristic Paul mentions. He says, "We have heard of your faith in Christ Jesus [the leaning of your entire human personality on Him in absolute trust and confidence in His power, wisdom and goodness]" (vs. 4a).

Love is the second characteristic mentioned by the apostle. God is love. If we are like Him, we will love others. It is easy to love those who are lovable, but God's love reaches out to the unlovely ones, the difficult ones. "We have heard of . . . the love which you [have and show] for *all* the saints (God's consecrated ones)," Paul says (vs. 4b).

Hope is the third characteristic. Hope is "taking hold of things to come." Paul speaks of "the hope [of experiencing what is] laid up — reserved and waiting — for you in heaven" (vs. 5a).

Fruitfulness is the fourth characteristic of saintliness. God desires that we be fruitful in carrying the Good News to others that their lives might be transformed as ours were. "The same Good News that came to you is going out all over the world and changing lives everywhere, just as it changed yours that very first day you heard it" (Colossians 1:6a, Living Letters).

Faithfulness is the fifth characteristic to which Paul refers. Epaphras is spoken of as a faithful minister of Christ. Can it be said that you are a faithful minister of Jesus Christ?

Do *you* possess these characteristics of saintliness?

And he said unto me, My grace is sufficient for thee. **27**
II Corinthians 12:9a

Paul had an infirmity, a thorn in the flesh. Three times he asked the Lord to remove it, but the answer was not the one he sought. God answered, "My grace — My favor and loving-kindness and mercy — are enough for you, [that is, sufficient against any danger and to enable you to bear the trouble manfully]" (Amplified).

The thorn had been given to keep the apostle from being "exalted above measure," to keep him humble. But with the thorn God gave His grace. He promised Paul that moment by moment His grace would be sufficient for every need. When Paul realized that the thorn was not to be removed, he accepted it and let it become a blessing. Someone has said, "This took the sting out of the thorn."

Most of us probably have thorns in our lives today. God will use such thorns for our spiritual perfection if we allow Him to do so. Sidlow Baxter says, "God does not just want to grant prayer — He guides lives." He may not remove the thorn but He will give something better — His grace. His grace is sufficient. "Sufficient" means "enough." His grace is enough for every situation, for every need. It *is* sufficient — enough — today for *you* personally. We learn that even though everything is taken from us, God is enough. He will fill the empty place with Himself.

George Matheson, the blind Scottish preacher, said, "My God, I have never thanked Thee for my thorn. I have thanked Thee for my roses, but not once for my thorn. I have never thought of my cross as itself a present glory. Teach me the glory of my cross. Teach me the value of my thorn. Show me that my tears made my rainbow."

28

For my strength is made perfect in weakness. II Corinthians 12:9b

We try various ways of becoming stronger physically. We exercise; we eat foods which give us strength; we take vitamin pills.

We have a sure source of spiritual strength. God tells us that His strength (from *dyunamis*, meaning "dynamite") is made perfect in our weakness. His strength — my weakness. "Made perfect" is the connecting expression. It is the same word that Jesus used when He said, "It is finished," as He hung on the cross. So God's strength is "finished" or "completely made perfect" in our weakness.

Paul's weakness enabled God to work in his life. It is not human strength or confidence that God chooses to use, but human weakness. William Wilberforce, the great Christian reformer, appeared to be very frail, but he was strong in the Lord. Someone who heard him speak made this comment: "I saw what seemed to me a shrimp stand up to speak, but as I listened, he grew and grew until the shrimp became a whale."

Fanny Crosby testified, "If I had not lost my sight, I could never have written all the hymns God gave me." It has been strikingly stated, "Into the hollows of our nothingness God fits the dynamos of His power." Our Lord says, "For My strength and power are made perfect — fulfilled and completed and show themselves most effective — in [your] weakness" (Amplified). God's strength has an opportunity to become effective in our weakness. His strength is sufficient for our needs today. When God sends a trial with one hand, He gives grace with the other. Trial is then turned to triumph in our lives.

Most gladly therefore will I rather glory in my infirmities, that the power of Christ may rest upon me. II Corinthians 12:9c

29

God became increasingly real to Paul through his infirmities. He wanted whatever was necessary, even his thorn, that he might have the sufficiency of God's power in his life. He gloried and took pleasure in his infirmities because of their results in his life. Through them he experienced the very power of Christ; they enabled him to be strong. He said triumphantly, "So for the sake of Christ, I am well pleased and take pleasure in infirmities, insults, hardships, persecutions, perplexities and distresses; for when I am weak (in human strength), then am I [truly] strong — able, powerful in divine strength" (vs. 10, Amplified).

When we are self-sufficient we do not depend on Christ's strength. But when we kneel at His feet in complete weakness, He has His opportunity. His power can rest upon us. As we rise, we can face life in His strength. We can glory in our trials, realizing that when we are weak, God bestows on us the power of Christ. The weight of trials is necessary to turn us from our self-sufficiency and to cast us on the sufficiency of God's grace and power.

There was once an old grandfather clock which had a heavy weight that had to be pulled to the top of the timepiece each night to keep it running. Its new owner thought, *The clock shouldn't have to bear that heavy weight. I'm going to take it off,* so he removed it. At once the clock stopped ticking. "Why did you do that?" the clock asked. "I wanted to lighten your load," replied the owner. "Put the weight back," said the clock. "That is what keeps me going."

30

But ye shall receive power, after that the Holy Ghost is come upon you: and ye shall be witnesses unto me both in Jerusalem, and in all Judea, and in Samaria, and unto the uttermost part of the earth. Acts 1:8

This verse outlines God's plan of service for us. We are to be His witnesses. Someone has said, "People cannot be contacted from heaven. If you want them to be with you there, they must be reached for Christ down here."

A witness must be a *person* and that person is you. "*Ye* shall be my witnesses," God says. We have the privilege of being His witnesses. He has given us the *program* for witnessing. God says, "Ye shall be witnesses *unto me*." A witness tells what he knows about something. We can tell what we know about Him. John said, "That which we have seen and heard declare we unto you" (I John 1:3). Not all of us can be mighty preachers or great missionaries, but we can all be witnesses for Him.

The *place* for us to carry on our program of witnessing is world-wide in its scope: "in Jerusalem, and in all Judea, and in Samaria, and unto the uttermost part of the earth." Some are to witness close at home. Others may be called to witness in some far-distant corner of the globe.

God has made provision for *power* to enable us to carry on the ministry of witnessing for Him. The Holy Spirit will empower us and use us. We are told that the population will increase by at least eighty million in the next twenty years. This makes us realize that we must be about our Father's business. As the song says, "There is so little time and so much to do." We need to "let go — and let God."

The steps of a [good] man are directed and established of the Lord, when He delights in his way [and He busies Himself with his every step]. Psalm 37:23, Amplified

Walking is a common everyday experience. It is so much a part of life that we give little thought to it. How many steps do you think you take each day?

There is a Chinese proverb that says, "A journey of a thousand miles begins with just one step." Our life of faith is a step-by-step journey.

The above verse tells us that "the steps of a [good] man are directed . . . of the Lord." This doesn't imply that we are good; in ourselves we cannot qualify. None of us are good enough to meet God's perfect standard. But He has made it possible for us to be "good" through our personal faith in Jesus Christ as Saviour. He is our "righteousness" or our "goodness."

God delights to direct the steps of His own children. Sometimes He turns on the "green go-light," giving us a clear direction to go ahead. At other times we see the "red stop-light." We then have to wait until the light changes again. He controls the switches and knows when to turn on the one and turn off the other. "The *stops* of a good man are ordered by the Lord as well as his steps."

God busies Himself with every one of our steps. How tenderly and lovingly parents watch over their children! They reach out a hand to keep them from stumbling and they lift them up if they fall. All through our lives God busies Himself with us, lifting us up if we fall, encouraging and strengthening us along the way.

It has been said, "I know not the way He leads me, but well do I know my Guide."

1   *God is our refuge and strength, a very present help in trouble. Psalm 46:1*

What assurance is promised us in this verse for time of great need. Life may seem to be going along smoothly. We're happy and contented, serving the Lord, busy with the many things that daily living brings.

Then suddenly life changes completely. It seems that everything we hold dear is taken from us. What do we do? God in His great love whispers, "(God) is our refuge and strength [mighty and impenetrable to temptation] a very present and well-proved help in trouble"(Amplified).

Somehow the truth of this verse gets through to us. As we fly to Him, our refuge, we find Him strengthening us to face the future. We may wonder what to do, we may not see our way out, but He reminds us, "I *am* — right now, this very moment — *your* present help." It has been said of us, "It takes trouble for God to get our attention."

Hudson Taylor said, "It does not matter how great the pressure, it matters only *where* the pressure lies, whether it comes between you and God, or whether it presses you closer to His heart."

A vessel was almost driven onto a rocky coast during a storm, threatening to sink it with all of its passengers. Contrary to orders, one man went on deck. He saw the pilot holding the wheel unwaveringly, slowing turning the ship, so near shipwreck, back out to sea. When the pilot saw the man, he smiled. The man went below, saying, "All is well. I saw the face of the pilot and he smiled."

By looking into the face of our Pilot in the midst of trouble, seeing His smile, we can be assured that with Him as our Pilot, all will be well for us.

By faith Abraham, when he was called to go out into a place which he should after receive for an inheritance, obeyed; and he went out, not knowing whither he went. Hebrews 11:8

Abraham is an outstanding example of a walk of faith. One day God spoke to him, saying, "Get thee out of thy country and from thy kindred and from thy father's house, unto a land that I will shew thee" (Genesis 12:1).

By faith Abram obeyed and departed. His was a "march of faith" — going out under sealed orders and going willingly. "[Urged on] by faith Abraham when he was called, obeyed and went forth to a place which he was destined to receive as an inheritance; and he went, although he did not know or *trouble his mind* about where he was to go" (Amplified).

He didn't know the distance, difficulties or dangers but He trusted the One who said, "Get thee out." Faith doesn't know where it is being led, but it does know and love the One who is leading. Oswald Chambers said, "Faith is in the One whose character we know because it has been revealed to us in Jesus Christ."

A little girl asked her mother for a new dress. The mother agreed she needed one and said, "I will go down town later today and get one for you." The little girl hurried out to her little friend and said, "Oh, I have a new dress." "Let me see it," replied her friend. "I don't have it yet," the little girl replied. "But mother is going to get it for me." Andrew Murray said, "Tarrying at one of God's promises and claiming it is as good as a fulfillment."

Are we a part of God's "March of Faith" today? Each day is a going forth in faith, not knowing where we are going and not troubling our minds about it.

May we go forth each day in faith, believing God and asking no questions.

3   *And let us not be weary in well doing: for in due season we shall reap — if we faint not. Galatians 6:9*

Once when I was in New York City I read this inscription on the Post Office Building, "Neither snow, nor rain, nor heat, nor gloom of night, stays these couriers from the swift completion of their appointed rounds." This is the motto of the postal service. Through the years how faithful have been those with the responsibility of getting the mail delivered, regardless of weather or circumstance of any kind.

God's children are to be just as faithful in getting God's Word out. We are to minister to the spiritual needs of others. Sometimes we will see little or no results and will wonder if it is worth continuing. Perhaps we will become impatient, thinking the effort is too great. Sometimes we will become so weary we may just want to give up, feeling we cannot go on.

But we are reminded here that we are not to become weary in our well doing, for in His own time, in due season, we will reap if we have fulfilled the condition — "if we faint not."

Are you weary today, discouraged and ready to give up? Ask God to renew your vision, concern and strength. As you faithfully sow the seed and water it, fainting not, you will reap a harvest for God.

"And let us not lose heart *and* grow weary *and* faint in acting nobly and doing right, for in due time and at the appointed season we shall reap, if we do not loosen *and* relax our courage *and* faint" (Amplified).

For we know that all things work together for good   **4**
to them that love God, to them that are called
according to his purpose. Romans 8:28

This is one of God's promises on which we can rest when the world about us has fallen apart, a promise we can believe and trust even when we do not understand. Days of adversity as well as days of prosperity can bring us blessings if we let them.

God says He will work all things together for our good. When we let God enter the picture, He will take all of our experiences and work them out for our good. The Bible says *all things* — not some things, or most things, but all, every one.

We wonder how the great tragedy or heartache or pain we're experiencing can bring good to us. And the isolated experiences themselves may not be good, or bring good to us. *But God* will *work* them *together* for our good.

God will do all of this for "those who love God" and "those who are called according to His purpose." We may not know how good comes from our adversities, but to know that good does come, should be sufficient. Not all things are good but He will transform them for our good. God is behind His promise to make it good.

A piece of white onyx was brought to a lapidary to be polished and set. On examining it, he discovered an ugly stain of iron rust across it. What could he do in order to use it? As he studied it an idea came of transforming it into something of beauty. Out of the white part he formed a goddess. He did it in such a way that the iron rust became a tigerskin robe for the goddess. Thus what seemed a flaw in the stone was worked into something that increased its beauty.

5   *And it came to pass, when I heard these words, that I sat down and wept, and mourned certain days, and fasted, and prayed before the God of heaven. Nehemiah 1:4*

A lady once wrote to Gypsy Smith, asking him to speak at a meeting. She wrote, "It is a small meeting and will take nothing out of you." He answered, "I cannot come and it would be of no use if I did. If it takes nothing out of me, it will do nobody any good. Real service costs."

It is a privilege to serve God. Yet real service costs something. Salvation cost God the sending of His Son to redeem mankind. It cost Jesus Christ His death on the cross to become the Saviour. Can our service for God be effective if it takes nothing out of us? If it costs us nothing?

Nehemiah was one who experienced the cost of real service for God. He learned that building for God costs. For him it meant a willingness to go back to Jerusalem, leaving the ease of the King's Palace. It meant having the burden of the needs of his people in Jerusalem laid on his heart. When he learned their tragic condition, he was filled with great compassion for them.

Nehemiah wept and fasted. His heart went out to them in sympathy. It cost him not only compassion, but prayer. Tears alone were not enough. Intercession in behalf of a people in need was necessary.

We, too, are builders for God. Do we have the compassion for the spiritual needs of people as Nehemiah did? Such a life of intercession will cost — time, compassion, prayer, perhaps even the ease of our present life. But it will count for eternity. It means giving ourselves unreservedly to God.

"But first gave their own selves to the Lord" (II Corinthians 8:5b).

So we built the wall; . . . for the people had a mind   **6**
to work. Nevertheless we made our prayer unto our
God, and set a watch against them day and night,
because of them. Nehemiah 4:6, 9

Nehemiah was a builder for God, chosen to supervise the rebuilding of the walls of Jerusalem. God had laid this on the heart of Nehemiah and he was willing to assume this responsibility.

He challenged the people, "Let us build up the wall of Jerusalem" (Nehemiah 2:17). The people accepted this challenge, saying, "Let us rise up and build" (vs. 18). Nehemiah had already prayed about this. Now it was time for action.

Knowing the great magnitude of the work, Nehemiah delegated responsibility to others. The people were divided into many groups. With one vision, one purpose, they had a "mind to work," and each one worked in his assigned place.

Now the work didn't progress without opposition. Sanballat and Tobiah tried to discourage them. But they went to the one sure source of help. They went to God in prayer. "Nevertheless we made our prayer unto God." And they watched . . . "and set a watch against them day and night."

Today we are building for God. There is a needy world to be reached for Jesus Christ. To be effective builders we must first pray. But it takes more than just prayer. We must then say, "Let us rise up and build." We must have a "mind to work." It takes all of us working together to build a strong work for God.

If God's work is to be done, if a lost world is to be reached with the message of life in Christ Jesus, we must unite in one purpose, with one vision, to *build,* to *work,* to *pray* and to *watch.*

7   *There is much rubbish; so that we are not able to build the wall. Nehemiah 4:10*

Discouragement is a great tool of the enemy in any work for God. Nehemiah experienced this as they began rebuilding the walls. Sanballat and Tobiah tried to discourage him. Then discouragement came from within their own ranks. One came to Nehemiah saying, "The strength of the bearers of burdens is decayed and there is much rubbish; so that we are not able to build the wall."

Nehemiah knew that the task was not impossible — but each one must do his part! Each one would be given strength to rebuild in the spot assigned to him. But the rubbish must first be cleared away. Only then could a strong wall be rebuilt for God.

There is need for a strong work for God today. But the work for Him can only be as strong as His workers. First there must be a strong foundation in our lives. "For other foundation can no man lay than that is laid, which is Jesus Christ" (II Corinthians 3:11). On this foundation we are either building gold, silver and precious stones — or hay, wood and stubble.

Rubbish may collect in our lives preventing the building of these strong walls. There is the rubbish of indifference, materialism, self-seeking, self-pity, laziness, pride, doubt, worry. These must go. Every pile of rubbish must be cleaned out. The Holy Spirit will faithfully reveal to us all of the rubbish which has collected if we ask Him.

Take time to let God clean out all of the rubbish that is hindering your life from being the great power God wants it to be in His work of building a people for Himself. Make today housecleaning time for you.

And he ordained twelve, that they should be with   **8**
him, and that he might send them forth to preach.
Mark 3:14

Jesus was going to select a group of men to be His disciples.
They were to help Him in the ministry and carry on for Him
after He returned to heaven. It would be a training period when
He could instruct, guide and encourage them.

He spent the night in prayer before He selected them. How
important it is to pray for God's choice in selecting workers. Too
often we rush in and ask people to assume a place of service
without spending the time we should in prayer. It is also important that we pray for God's direction in our own service for Him.

Note the difference in the personalities, backgrounds and capabilities of the twelve He chose. Some were outspoken, some
were self-seeking, wanting a prominent place, one was a doubter.
Yet Jesus could see through the exterior to the potential within.

God chooses people of different personalities to work with Him
today. He chooses workers from different backgrounds. He
selects some with great talent and ability which He can use when
they are yielded to Him. He selects others with no apparent
ability but with a willingness to serve.

It is interesting to note that first He chose them to be *with*
Him; then He sent them forth in service *for* Him. Too often we
reverse this order. We become so active in our service that we
crowd prayer into any time we may have left over.

After spending time with Him first, we will carry the fragrance
of His presence with us, making our ministry more effective.

It is told that when the Mosque of Omar was first built, the
workers brought loads of incense and aromatic shrubs into the
shrine which was called Sakhrah. Anyone worshiping there carried away so much fragrance of the place that the people would
say, "He has been in the Sakhrah today."

9   *Delight thyself also in the Lord; and he shall give thee the desires of thine heart. Psalm 37:4*

As you read this promise are you tempted to say, "This is not true in my life. Instead of receiving my desires, it seems that even what I have is being taken away from me. It may work for others but not for me"?

God has promised to give us the desires of our heart, but there is a condition to be fulfilled — we are to "delight thyself in the LORD." We often hurry over the first part of this verse and concern ourselves with the promise of receiving our desires. Yet to have our desires we must be on receiving ground — "delighting in Him."

We are to delight in His Word. "Thy Word was unto me the joy and rejoicing of mine heart" (Jeremiah 15:16). And we are to delight in His will. "I delight to do thy will, O my God" (Psalm 40:8). Also, we are to delight in His presence. "In thy presence is fullness of joy; at thy right hand there are pleasures for evermore" (Psalm 16:11).

In what are we delighting today? Our homes? Our families? Our social life? Our business? God tells us to delight in Him if we want Him to give us our desires. By delighting in Him we find that our desires are to please Him. These other things can be enjoyed if we have Him in His rightful place.

Someone has said, "The more we delight in Him, the less we will desire things." The source of our delight is the secret of receiving our desires.

Blessed are the poor in spirit; for theirs is the king- **10**
dom of heaven. Matthew 5:3

In this chapter we are shown the portrait of a blessed or happy person. This is a happiness contrary to the general thinking of the world today, a happiness they do not know. The things of this world do not bring lasting or inward happiness. Andrew Carnegie once said, "There are few millionaires who laugh."

The blessed ones are not the rich, not the mighty, not the influential, but the poor in spirit. This does not refer to material poverty, not even spiritual poverty. The poor in spirit have recognized their complete dependence on the Lord. They have found that their sufficiency is in Him. "Not that we are sufficient of ourselves to think any thing as of ourselves; but our sufficiency is of God" (II Corinthians 3:5). Our insufficiency takes us to Him, receiving His all-sufficiency.

"Blessed — happy, to be envied, and spiritually prosperous [that is with life-joy and satisfaction in God's favor and salvation, regardless of their outward conditions] — are the poor in spirit [the humble, rating themselves insignificant], for theirs is the kingdom of heaven" (Amplified). The spiritually prosperous recognize their spiritual poverty.

As we come to God humbly, asking Him to empty us of self and the things that have filled our lives, we become spiritually prosperous. We who are poor in spirit are given all the riches of heaven which become available to us through Christ. We exchange the things of this life for the possession of heavenly treasures.

Weak and poor in ourselves, we now have the treasure of His presence, giving us His all-sufficiency.

"But we have this treasure in earthen vessels, that the excellency of the power may be of God and not of us" (II Corinthians 4:7).

11   *But ye are a chosen generation, a royal priesthood, an holy nation, a peculiar people; that ye should shew forth the praises of him who hath called you out of darkness into his marvellous light. I Peter 2:9*

The French have a phrase, "Noblesse Oblige," which means that because a person belongs to ranking nobility, certain obligations such as loyalty and chivalry are laid on them. We, too, belong to a nobility which places on us certain privileges of serving in His priesthood. A priest is one who stands between God and man.

We are spoken of as a holy priesthood. "An holy priesthood, to offer up spiritual sacrifices, acceptable to God by Jesus Christ" (vs. 5). As holy priests we are to worship Him, offering up spiritual sacrifices of praise and adoration. This relates to the Godward aspect of the priesthood.

Also we are a royal priesthood. We are to witness of Him the King of kings, who called us out of darkness into His marvelous light. Not only by what we say but how we live do we proclaim Him. This is the manward aspect of the priesthood.

There is a legend of three architects who brought to an oriental king their models for a temple to be built to the sun. The first was of stone, chiseled and polished. The second was of gold. Its burnished walls reflected the image of the sun from every angle. The third was of glass, so transparent that it seemed invisible at first. However, as the sunlight shone through its transparent walls, it reflected in every part the sun itself in whose honor it was dedicated. Thus it was the real temple of the sun.

As a royal priesthood, we are to shew forth His beauty and glory from the temple of our lives. We are to be so transparent that His reflection will shine through us.

And there was one Anna, a prophetess . . . . And she was a widow about fourscore and four years, which departed not from the temple, but served God with fastings and prayers night and day. Luke 2:36a, 37

12

This is the only place in the Bible where we read of Anna, a prophetess. Little is known of her. She was a widow who rose above her sorrow and bereavement. Instead of feeling sorry for herself, she found a place to serve God. For more than fifty years she had waited for the Promised One to come to redeem her people.

While she waited, she was steadfast and faithful in her service for God. "She departed not from the temple." She served Him with fastings and prayers night and day. We usually think of service for God as the activity we do. But Anna considered prayer as a part of her ministry to God.

Her patience was rewarded. She was privileged to see the face of the One for whom they had been waiting. Her heart was filled with joy, and she shared what she had seen with others. What a blessing her life was to God as she steadfastly and faithfully served Him.

Today God is in need of people who will serve Him with prayer night and day. It has been said, "Prayer is not the coating of our plans but the very foundation of God's work."

A certain bishop constantly received requests to send a certain pastor to fill their pulpits. The pastor was a man of small stature. Once the bishop said to him, "How can a man as little as you, be in such demand by all the large pulpits of our conference?" The pastor quickly replied, "I am a very little man, but I have a mighty big God."

13   *Lay not up for yourselves treasures upon the earth
. . . but lay up for yourselves treasures in heaven.*
Matthew 6:19, 20

Much of our lives are given to laying up treasures here on earth. We want to build up a large bank account and accumulate stocks, bonds and real estate. This gives us a feeling of security.

But God's Word tells us that we are not to lay up our treasures on this earth. We are not to hoard up earthly things. Our real treasure is not our bank account, our real estate, what we have in our safety deposit box, our gems and jewels.

Our treasures are to be in heaven. We are to make heavenly deposits in the Bank of Heaven. There our deposits will be safe, for God's Bank will never fail.

We may store up earthly treasures but we can't take them with us. It was said of Alexander the Great that on his deathbed he instructed that when he was taken to the grave his hands should be left outside so that all people might see that they were empty. With all the treasures he had accumulated from his conquests he could not keep even the smallest portion.

A young couple was traveling in Europe. They were planning to build a new home when they returned. So whenever they saw a vase, a picture or a piece of furniture they wanted for their new home, they purchased it and sent it back. When they returned there were many treasures awaiting them.

What treasures are you sending on ahead to await your coming? It may be souls you have pointed to Jesus Christ; it may be answers to prayer; or it may be the many helpful things you have done for others in His Name.

Where are you doing your banking? On earth? In heaven?

And the Lord, he it is that doth go before thee: he will be with thee, he will not fail thee, neither forsake thee: fear not, neither be dismayed. Deuteronomy 31:8

14

This promise was given to Joshua by Moses when Israel was camped on the east of Jordan. Their wilderness journeys were over; the Land of Promise was just across the river.

Joshua was to succeed Moses and lead the people in the conquest and settlement of Canaan. There would be danger and discouragement but the Lord would see Joshua through.

There was comfort for Joshua in these words from Moses. He was assured that God would go before him, preparing the way. Not only would He go before Joshua preparing the way but then He would go with him each step along the way. The Amplified translation reads, "He will [march] with you."

Then He told Joshua not to fear or be dismayed because He would not fail nor forsake him. What more could Joshua ask than to be confident of God's unfailing presence with him day after day?

The truth of this Scripture is for us today. We need not fear nor be dismayed for He will never fail us nor forsake us. People may fail, friends and families may fail, leaders may fail, methods may fail, but God will not. People, sometimes even our best friends, may forsake us. Even parents have been known to forsake their children but God says. ". . . I will not in any way fail you nor give you up nor leave you without support. [I will] not, [I will] not, [I will] not in any degree leave you helpless, nor forsake nor let [you] down, [relax My hold on you]. — Assuredly not!" (Hebrews 13:5, Amplified).

Most wonderful it is that He will open the way before *us* and then He will lead us along this way. Our part is to follow. The Indians have a word for "follow" which means "to put your feet in the same tracks."

15   *But we have the mind of Christ. I Corinthians 2:16*
Let this mind be in you, which was also in Christ
Jesus. Philippians 2:5

Often we are confronted in life with the need of making a rapid decision. We do not have time to search the Word for guidance, nor do we have time to pray at length about it. We must know immediately what God wants us to do.

Nehemiah was faced with such a situation. He was asked a question by the king and he had to give an immediate reply. Although he had no opportunity to go to God's Word or spend much time in prayer, he lifted his heart to God in prayer for just an instant. Immediately, he knew the mind of God and replied to the king.

David was another one who not only wanted to know God's mind but was willing to do it, assuming his responsibility in carrying out God's whole program. "He raised up David for their king, of whom he testified, I have found David, the son of Jesse, a man agreeable to my mind, who will carry out my whole program" (Acts 13:22, Berkeley).

Can we add our name to the list of those who are willing to accept responsibility in carrying out God's whole program? We must have the mind of Christ.

What a privilege is ours — that the Holy Spirit will reveal the mind of Christ to us. We must keep the channel of communication to heaven open that we will not miss it. May we be agreeable to His mind — may we be agreeable to carrying out our part in His whole program.

*For we are God's [own] handiwork (His workman-
ship) recreated in Christ Jesus [born anew] that we
may do those good works which God predestined
(planned beforehand) for us, (taking paths which He
prepared ahead of time) that we should walk in them
— living the good life which He prearranged and
made ready for us to live. Ephesians 2:10, Amplified*

The distinguished sculptor, Mr. Borglum, who carved the Rush-
more Monument in South Dakota, also did a head of Lincoln in
the capitol at Washington. He cut it from a marble block, working on it in his studio. One morning when the woman who dusted
the studio came in, she was astonished to see the face of Lincoln
on the piece of marble. She asked the secretary, "Is that really
Abraham Lincoln?" "Yes," was the reply. "Well, how did he know
that Abraham Lincoln was in that block of stone?" she said.

God has a blueprint for your life and mine — we are His work-
manship. We are, first, His possession, redeemed by Jesus Christ
through His death on the cross. Then His plan is that we be
"recreated in Christ Jesus unto good works." Have you ever
purchased an article which said, "Made in Japan," or some other
country? We are "made in Christ Jesus." ". . . Molded into the
image of His Son [and share inwardly His likeness]" (Romans
8:29, Amplified). God sees in us the potential of the likeness of
His Son. He sees in us one whom He created unto good works —
that we should walk according to His place for us on earth.

The engineer who designed Brooklyn Bridge became ill at the
time its construction was to be started. Each day his wife went
in his place, taking the blueprint along. She checked to see that
the construction was done according to the drawing. At night
she would go over all that had happened that day with her husband. He would advise and give instructions for the next day.
At last it was finished. He was sufficiently better that he could
be taken on a cot to see the bridge. As he looked at it, tears
streamed down his cheeks as he said, "Oh, it is just as I
planned it."

Can this be said of us, that we are living our lives as God
planned?

17   *Thy words were found, and I did eat them; and thy word was unto me the joy and rejoicing of mine heart. Jeremiah 15:16*

Jeremiah's life was filled with trouble. He underwent great persecution and experienced much loneliness. But even in his time of persecution his heart was filled with joy and rejoicing. The source of this joy was feeding on God's Word. God's Word was his spiritual diet; it was food and nourishment for his soul.

To grow and be strong, our bodies need food regularly. So, too, we need a spiritual diet of the Word of God to grow spiritually. "Man shall not live and be upheld and sustained by bread alone, but by every word that comes forth from the mouth of God" (Matthew 4:4, Amplified).

We are privileged to hear from God through His Word, bringing joy to our hearts. Could it be that when our joy and rejoicing are gone it is because we are not feeding on His Word?

This is not to be just a casual reading, but a real appropriating of the Word into our everyday life. As we read and assimilate it, we will grow more like the One of whom we read in it. George Mueller once wrote, "I have read the Bible through one hundred times and always with increasing delight. Each time it seems like a new Book to me."

My brethren, count it all joy when ye fall into divers temptations. James 1:2

Joy in *trials?* This is not the natural human viewpoint. Count it all joy when we are in the midst of many and various trials today? You say, "Can I count it all joy today when I am ill and there seems to be no help for me?" "Can I count it all joy today when I have lost my job and my earthly possessions?" "Can I count it all joy when I have lost a loved one?"

Yes, God says, "Count it *all* joy." We may be able to endure, but can we count it all joy? Even when our heart is broken or anxiety has crept in, "Consider it wholly joyful, my brethren, whenever you are enveloped in *or* encounter trials of any sort, *or* fall into various temptations" (vs. 2, Amplified).

There *is value* in trials — trials with a beneficial purpose. "Be assured *and* understand that the trial *and* proving of your faith bring out endurance *and* steadfastness *and* patience" (vs. 3, Amplified).

Have you ever said, "I just can't endure this any longer"? Yet, somehow, you discover that you can. How else can you learn endurance than to be placed in a position to experience the need of it?

The trial of our faith produces a steadfastness in our lives. Patience is developed in the furnace of trials. "But let endurance *and* steadfastness *and* patience have full play *and* do a thorough work, so that you may be [people] perfectly and fully developed (with no defects), lacking in nothing" (vs. 4, Amplified).

Through trials we grow in the ability to be patient. Patience helps to bring maturity and development to our lives. The occasion of testings and trials in our lives gives opportunity to show the reality of our faith. Yes, we can have *joy* in the midst of trials.

19   *If any of you lack wisdom, let him ask of God, that giveth to all men liberally, and upbraideth not; and it shall be given him. James 1:5*

It has been said that the wisest man in the world is the man who knows he doesn't know.

In the midst of trials how often we say, "If only I knew what to do"; or we may say, "I don't know which way to turn or what to do."

God has promised to give us His wisdom. "If any of you is deficient in wisdom, let him ask of the giving God [Who gives] to every one liberally and ungrudgingly, without reproaching or faultfinding, and it will be given him" Amplified).

We are to ask God for His wisdom. Wisdom is using knowledge aright. Trials can be perplexing and we need wisdom to face each one of them.

Not only are we to ask God for wisdom but we are to ask in faith. "Only it must be in faith that he asks, with no wavering — no hesitating, no doubting" (vs. 6, Amplified). *No* wavering — *no* hesitating — *no* doubting. Someone has said, "Doubt is a non-conductor of grace."

We are not to be double-minded, wanting partly our way and partly God's way. We are not to vacillate back and forth uncertain of our decision. "[For being as he is] a man of two minds — hesitating, dubious, irresolute — [he is] unstable and unreliable and uncertain about everything (he thinks, feels, decides)" (vs. 8, Amplified).

As we ask of God and ask in faith, God has promised to give liberally. We are to ask for wisdom to face serenely the trials of today, unwaveringly trusting in Him. We are to ask for wisdom to meet each trial of life and to face it triumphantly.

Blessed is the man that endureth temptation; for
when he is tried, he shall receive the crown of life
which the Lord hath promised to them that love him.
James 1:12

Certain food companies have test kitchens where their products are tested before being put on the market. When the products are released on the market, we can have confidence in purchasing them and using them. Sometimes recipes using their products are tested over and over again to determine just the right proportions of each ingredient to produce the best final result.

Life is a scene of trials and temptations, putting us through tests in order that the proportions of each ingredient in our lives are right to bring the best results. Most of the early Christians to whom James was writing were suffering persecution. They were put in prison; their goods were taken away from them. In the midst of all this they were proving their love for and faith in Jesus Christ. In this way they were becoming strong, learning patience and endurance.

One meaning of "tried" is "acceptable." We are tested to be proven acceptable. After going through these trials, we then are qualified to be acceptable and we receive God's seal of approval.

There is a reward for standing firm through trials and temptations. These give us opportunities to win the prize — the crown of life. This is a special reward for faithful endurance.

"Blessed, happy, to be envied is the man who is patient under trial *and* stands up under temptation, for when he has stood the test *and* been approved he will receive [the victor's] crown of life which God has promised to those who love Him" (James 1:12, Amplified).

It has been said that "Testing is God's vote of confidence in us."

21 *And Ruth said, Intreat me not to leave thee, or to return from following after thee: for whither thou goest, I will go; and where thou lodgest, I will lodge; thy people shall be my people, and thy God my God. Ruth 1:16*

These words are considered among the most beautiful in literature. Naomi and her husband had moved to Moab during a time of famine. There the husband died. Later her two sons, who had married Moabitish wives, died also.

Naomi, having heard that there was prosperity again in Judah, decided to return there. Her daughters-in-law decided to go with her but she urged them to remain in Moab. Orpah did as Naomi suggested — she stayed. But Ruth made a most important decision. "And Ruth said, Intreat me not to leave thee, or to return from following after thee: for whither thou goest I will go; and where thou lodgest I will lodge; thy people shall be my people, and thy God my God."

She was truly devoted to her mother-in-law. But more wonderful was her decision of faith in Naomi's God. Since Ruth had lived in Moab, a godless country, how did she know about God? The secret of it was in her words to Naomi, *"Your God* will be *my* God."

Perhaps Naomi had talked to Ruth about the true and living God. Ruth must have seen something of godliness in Naomi which caused her to make a decision for God.

What influence do our lives have on others? Do they want to be with us because they sense the presence of Christ in us? Do they want to know the God we know?

Someone has said, "One person with a glowing experience with God is worth a library full of arguments."

The Lord appeared to Abram, and said unto him,   *22*
I am the Almighty God; walk before me, and be
thou perfect. Genesis 17:1

God again appeared to Abram after a silence of many years.
He said, "I am the Almighty God." El Shaddai is the word used
and it means "The mighty-breasted One; the God who is enough."
He is the Nourisher, the Strength-giver, the Satisfier. God ap-
peared to Abram to assure Him of His power at a time of
Abram's weakness; His Almightiness for Abram's weakness.

A story is told of a poor woman who was taken to see the
ocean for the first time. As she gazed out on it, tears ran down
her cheeks. A friend said, "What do you think of it?" She
replied, "It is the first thing I have seen of which there seems
to be enough." The God who is enough, is enough for every need
we may have. His strength is enough, His wisdom is enough, His
patience is enough, His love is enough. What do you need today?
He is enough for that need.

Then He said to Abram, "Walk before *me*." Our hearts and
lives, too, are to be centered in Him, living in His will, walking
in the light of His direction.

He said, "Be thou perfect." This means to be wholehearted,
not doublehearted, not wavering back and forth. We are to be
upright and sincere. God has a right to expect loyalty and
devotion.

As God revealed Himself, Abram fell on his face in worship.

God is saying to you today, "I am the Almighty God — I am
the God who is enough for your needs. If you will in sincerity
and wholeheartedness of heart let Me take over, I will reveal
Myself to you as 'The All-Sufficient One.'"

23   *I will love thee, O Lord, my strength. Psalm 18:1*

These verses reveal the intimate relationship of the Psalmist David to his God. How God's heart must have rejoiced to hear David say, "I will love thee." God delights to have us come humbly into His presence, taking time to love Him. When was the last time you paused and told Him, "O Lord, I do love you"?

When we love someone dearly, and we know they love us, we have complete trust in them. David said, "The Lord . . . in whom I will trust" (vs. 2). Then he enumerated several things God is to the person that trusts Him:

"The Lord is my rock"; a rock is a foundation. "The Lord is my fortress"; a fortress is a place of shelter and safety. "The Lord is my deliverer"; how often we try every human source of deliverance before turning to the Lord. "The Lord is my strength"; not He gives strength — He *is* Strength — *my* strength. "The Lord is my buckler"; a shield to protect one from the enemy. "The Lord is the horn of my salvation"; in the Hebrew the word for *horn* and *shone* are the same. When David spoke of the Lord as the horn of his salvation, he recognized that the Lord was the light and glory of his life. "The Lord is my high tower"; there is safety for us in the tower. God was very personal to David; each time he said "*my.*"

First, he expressed his love to the Lord, then his trust in the One he loves. Because he trusts Him, he has confidence in calling on Him for help. "I will call upon the Lord, who is worthy to be praised; so shall I be saved from mine enemies."

He *is* worthy to be praised.

If ye then be risen with Christ, seek those things which are above, where Christ sitteth on the right hand of God. Set your affection on things above, not on things on the earth. Colossians 3:1, 2

24

What an experience it is to take off by plane on a cloudy day and, as you go through the cloud cover, to come out into the beautiful sunshine above the clouds.

This is something of the experience of the Christian — living in the atmosphere of heaven. Our citizenship is above in the heavenlies with Christ. In union with the living Christ we are raised to a new life in Him. Although the source of this life is in Christ in heaven, it is to be lived out in our daily walk in the world today. We are His representatives here on earth.

As His representatives on earth we are to ". . . aim at and seek the [rich, eternal treasures] that are above, where Christ is, seated at the right hand of God" (Amplified). We are to seek the things that will make us good representatives for Him on earth — things that will produce Christlikeness. This is not something we can work up but it comes down from above. I have heard this called the "upside down" life. As we live down here, we draw moment by moment on this life from above.

Also as His representatives on earth we are to "set our minds and keep them set on what is above — the higher things — not on the things that are on the earth" (Amplified). There are many good things on earth but they are transitory and uncertain. We are to place our affection and thinking on eternal things. The object of our affection and thinking is Jesus Christ Himself. Loving Him with all our hearts will result in one purpose — to show Him to those about us through our lives.

25   *Therefore I esteem all thy precepts concerning all things to be right. Psalm 119:128*

When an old minister was asked to give his favorite text, he replied, "When I think of a favorite verse, half a dozen dear ones come to my mind. On stormy days I want a cloak; cold days I want the sunny side of the wall; hot days I want a shady path; now I want a shower of manna; now I want a drink of cool living water; now I want a sword. I might as well try to tell which is my favorite eye. The one I might love is the one I might soon need and want."

Perhaps when asked to give a verse, you always turn to the same one. When you open the Bible to read from it, you turn to certain favorite portions.

Yet one of my richest blessings in reading the Bible through is that over and over I find some rich little gem and nugget tucked away in portions where I might least expect it.

The above verse says, "I esteem *all* thy precepts concerning *all* things to be right," not just some of them; not just the ones I especially like; not just concerning the things that are easy for me to do, but all His precepts in all things. II Timothy 3:16 says, "*All* scripture is given by inspiration of God, and is profitable for doctrine, for reproof, for correction, for instruction in righteousness."

Whose adorning let it not be that outward adorning
of plaiting the hair, and of wearing of gold or of
putting on of apparel; But let it be the hidden man
of the heart, in that which is not corruptible, even the
ornament of a meek and quiet spirit which is in the
sight of God of great price. I Peter 3:3, 4

26

Have you ever considered how much time you spend on your outward appearance? How much thought, energy and money you spend on the adorning of the body? Some spend hours before the mirror combing their hair and beautifying the face. Others take a long time shopping for just the right outfit that will be attractive. This we need to do. We should look our best for Jesus Christ.

However, we should be as diligent to adorn the inner person as the outer. Inner charm is more important than physical attractiveness.

This inner beauty is that with which the heart is adorned — a meek and quiet spirit. This is not a weak spirit but a gentle, peaceful and calm one. It comes from the indwelling Presence of the Lord Jesus Christ Himself. This calm and gentle spirit of Christ is reflected in our entire personality, our speech, in the way we perform our routine duties at home or in the office.

It is the beauty of this meek and quiet spirit that we reveal to those about us. It attracts others to the Lord.

One day I was talking with a member of the personnel staff of a large hotel. A well-known evangelist had been staying in that hotel. She said to me, "Do you know what impressed me about him? As I watched him, no matter what the pressures were he was never upset but was always calm."

In this meek and quiet spirit you have an ornament of great price.

27   *For your heavenly Father knoweth that ye have need of all these things. Matthew 6:32*

Many people are filled with fear of the future. What if they become sick and can't work? What if they lose their jobs? Often they question "what if."

It is comforting to be assured that *we* are known unto God; *our needs* are known unto Him. Jesus said in Matthew 6:25, "Therefore I tell you, stop being perpetually uneasy (anxious and worried) about your life, what you shall eat *or what you shall drink,* and about your body, what you shall put on" (vs. 25, Amplified).

We are not to worry about material things — about money to pay for the food we will need next week or the house payment next month, or the shoes little Johnny needs. "Our heavenly Father already knows what we need."

We learn a lesson of confidence, dependence and tranquility from the birds. They perch on the branches, singing their melodies of cheer without one little anxiety. God's Word says that the Heavenly Father will feed them. Even the lilies of the field are not concerned about their care. If God does this for the birds and flowers, how much more will He take care of us!

He is aware of *all* our needs — those of this present moment — and He has promised to provide not necessarily our wants but those things we have need of.

One evening a dear little girl knelt by her bed to repeat her goodnight prayer. Her mother, bending over her, prompted, "Now I lay me . . . say it darling . . . down to sleep." "To sleep . . ." she murmured as her head nodded. She fell fast asleep in the midst of her prayer. As her mother lifted her up in her arms, she roused and softly whispered, "God knows all the rest."

Brethren, I count not myself to have apprehended: but this one thing I do, forgetting those things which are behind, and reaching forth unto those things which are before, I press toward the mark for the prize of the high calling of God in Christ Jesus. Philippians 3:13, 14

28

Paul's great desire was to know Christ. He was not satisfied with his present attainment — he wanted to know Him better each day. He was willing to put anything out of his life that would detract from this desire.

His sight was set on the goal before him. His life was dedicated to attaining it. To reach this goal, he knew his eye must be single to it. "But this one thing I do — it is my aspiration." Someone has said, "Singleness of aim avoids many a traffic jam of secondary considerations."

The past must be forgotten — its successes, failures, sorrows, joys, hardships, casc. Paul had to forget any regrets he may have had for his past life. He must forget any successes he had. And he must be satisfied with neither the past nor the present. Thorwaldsen, the great sculptor, was once asked, "What is your greatest statue?" He quickly replied, "My next one."

Paul realized that he must reach forth as a runner with his eyes fixed on the goal. There must be no diversions to keep from attaining the prize of the high calling in Christ Jesus.

The Swedish Nightingale, Jenny Lind, won fame and fortune as an operatic singer. At the height of her career she left the stage. One day a friend found her sitting on the seashore, her Bible on her knee. She was looking at the glory of a sunset. The friend asked how she could abandon her career. She replied, "When it made me think less of the Bible, and nothing of God's glory about me, what else could I do?"

29

Lord, thou hast been our dwelling place in all genera-
tions. Before the mountains were brought forth, or
ever thou hadst formed the earth and the world,
even from everlasting to everlasting, thou art God.
Psalm 90:1, 2

What grandeur and majesty is expressed in this Psalm. Moses acknowledged God as the Self-Existent One, "even from ever-lasting to everlasting *thou art God.*"

This was written of the wanderings of the Children of Israel through the wilderness. As they roamed about in the desert country, they must have longed for a permanent home. Often they must have wished they could settle down and have a feel-ing of security.

Moses, experiencing the day-by-day change of their desert life, looked beyond the changeableness of life on earth and wrote of the dwelling place that is lasting and permanent, that is unchang-ing. This dwelling place is God Himself.

God is a living God. He always was — and He always will be. He will never change. "For I am the Lord, I change not" (Malachi 3:6). And He is the same today as He was yesterday. He will not change tomorrow. Kingdoms have come and gone — people have come and gone, but God remains steadfast, unmove-able and unchanging. Through all the generations He has re-mained the same. Through all the generations He has been the dwelling place of His own.

Today our own dwelling place can be in this same God of the generations. God has made this possible through acceptance of Jesus Christ as Saviour. Knowing Him in this personal relation-ship we experience the security of dwelling in the very God of the ages. What need have we to fear when He is our dwelling place?

"Lord, You have been our dwelling place *and* our *refuge* in all generations [says Moses]" (Amplified).

So teach us to number our days that we may apply our hearts unto wisdom. Psalm 90:12

30

God has allotted time to each of us. However, the time span of life is not the same for all of us. For some it is longer, others shorter. Yet even the longest length of life is so short in the light of eternity. "We spend our years as a tale that is told." A tale is a story. In the Hebrew "tale" gives the idea of a single thought. We spend our years as a thought. Yet how much more time we spend planning to live here than for eternity.

As Moses recognizes this He asks God to teach us to make good use of our time. Every day is a special trust from God to be used to the greatest advantage for His glory. Our days are numbered to us by the Lord and we are to make them count. David said, "Lord, make me to know how frail I am" (Psalm 39:4).

Moses asked God to teach him the value of time and its use. So God will teach us. We are to make our days count by applying our hearts unto wisdom; not just wisdom of the mind but of the heart. He will teach us to make our time count in our business, in our office, in our home, in our neighborhood. Are we letting Him make our time count for Him?

Time is short. If we don't learn God's method of counting, life will soon be gone before we can make full use of it. Every moment should be wisely spent. This motto is a reminder and a challenge to each of us: "Only one life, 'twill soon be past. Only what's done for Christ will last."

31 *I beseech you therefore, brethren, by the mercies of God, that ye present your bodies a living sacrifice, holy, acceptable unto God, which is your reasonable service. Romans 12:1*

This Scripture pictures a life consecrated to God. We are to present our bodies to Him. Is it possible that we are willing to give God everything but the one thing He wants most of all — our own selves?

We give Him our talents, our time, our treasure. This is right, but before they can be effective we must give Him our lives. A gift must be given to a person before he can use the gift. So we must give our lives to God before He can use us. He wants a total commitment of ourselves to Him.

He wants our bodies — our hands, feet, eyes, ears, lips, will, heart. Someone has said, "Unless He has our yielded bodies He has nothing." "But first gave their own selves to the Lord, and unto us by the will of God" (II Corinthians 8:5).

When we present ourselves to Him, self comes off the Throne of our lives and we give the Lord this honored place. As we look back at Calvary, we see how God showed His great mercy toward us. "While we were yet sinners, Christ died for us" (Romans 5:8b). We not only recognize this as our reasonable service but our response to such love as His will be the giving of ourselves to Him.

After a challenging missionary service in a church in Scotland, the people gave generously to send out additional missionaries. Ten-year-old Alexander Duff had nothing to give. He slipped out of his seat, going to the ushers in the rear of the church. "Please put the plate down low," he said to an usher. Thinking it a childish whim, the man did so. Stepping on the plate the boy said, "Dear God, I have no money to give but I give myself." Later he went as a missionary to India.

I beseech you therefore, brethren, by the mercies of God, that ye present your bodies a living sacrifice, holy, acceptable unto God, which is your reasonable service. Romans 12:1

1

Frances Havergal wrote the hymn, "Take my life and let it be, consecrated, Lord, to Thee," from the experience of her own life which was yielded to the Lord.

One day as she re-read the verse of the hymn, "Take my silver and my gold, not a mite would I withhold", she was convicted that she had not really done that. There was her collection of jewelry. She decided to send it to her church missionary society as an offering, saving a few pieces given her by her family. Then she included a check for the value of the jewels she kept. She said, "I never packed a box with such pleasure."

Do we sing, "Take my life and let it be, consecrated, Lord, to Thee," without having experienced such a commitment of *our* life to the Lord?

In the Old Testament times an animal was killed as a sacrifice and placed on the altar. Now through Christ our lives can be living sacrifices to God, holy, clean, free from blemish, set apart for God. Such a sacrifice is acceptable, well-pleasing to Him, consistent to His will.

This is our reasonable service, the least we can possibly do in return for all He has done for us. This we do because of our devotion for Him. Have we presented ourselves to Him? The use of the tense here indicates that the word "present" means complete. Has our presentation of ourselves been complete?

We hear people say, "I would die for Him." There have been some who have been called upon to do just that. But today can you say, "I present *myself* a *living* sacrifice to *live* for Him"?

2

And be not conformed to this world; but be ye transformed by the renewing of your mind, that ye may prove what is that good, and acceptable, and perfect will of God. Romans 12:2

In verse one our bodies are to be yielded to God. In this verse our minds are to be renewed.

We often hear and use the expression, "When in Rome do as the Romans do." But God says, "Do not be conformed to this world." Phillips writes, "Don't let the world around you squeeze you into its own mold, but let God remold your minds from within, so that you may prove in practice that the Plan of God for you is good, meets all His demands and moves toward the goal of true maturity."

Someone has said, "Do not cut your pattern from this world. Do not get your styles from this world. Christ is our Master Stylist." Conformed or transformed — this is our challenge. Instead of being conformed we are to be transformed. This transformation within will prevent our being conformed without. It comes from a renewed mind. "Let this mind be in you which was also in Christ Jesus" (Philippians 2:5). This is adjusting our life to the mind of the Lord. It is occupying our minds with Him.

With the renewing of our minds we will prove to ourselves in our own experience that His will for us is always good, acceptable and perfect.

"Do not be conformed to this world — this age, fashioned after and adapted to its external, superficial customs. But be transformed (changed) by the [entire] renewal of your mind — by its new ideals and its new attitude — so that you may prove [for yourselves] what is the good and acceptable and perfect will of God, even the thing which is good and acceptable and perfect [in His sight for you]" (Amplified).

That in all things he might have the pre-eminence.
Colossians 1:18

3

Summer has a way of disrupting our schedules. Vacations come, company comes, the children are home, activities increase. This seems to work havoc with our quiet time with God.

In the fall when things begin to settle down into the regular routine again, it is good to pause and check our spiritual schedule.

What place does God's Word have in our daily schedule? A little girl once found a book in her home and asked her mother what it was. She said, "It is God's Book — the Bible." The daughter replied, "Why don't we send it back to Him? We aren't using it." Not only should we read the Word, but we should meditate on it. "This book of the law shall not depart out of thy mouth; but thou shalt meditate therein day and night" (Joshua 1:8). Do we really meditate on the Word? One definition is "to think in view of doing." It has been said, "We only know as much of God's Word as we put into practice." Let us meditate on God's Word daily.

What place does prayer have in our schedule each day? Is it a regular habit with us? Prayer had an important place in Daniel's schedule. "He kneeled upon his knees three times a day and prayed" (Daniel 6:10). The Psalmist said, "Evening and morning, and at noon, will I pray, and cry aloud; and he shall hear my voice" (Psalm 55:17). Time for prayer should be included each day.

What place does Christ Himself have in our schedule? Is our life built around him? "That in *all* things he might have the pre-eminence." Let us be sure He is in the center of our daily life.

Take time out to check the place God's Word, prayer and Christ Himself have in your life. "The good is evil if it keeps us from the best."

4   *And all of us, as with unveiled face, [because we]*
continued to behold [in the word of God] as in a
mirror the glory of the Lord, are constantly being
transformed into His very own image in ever increas-
ing splendor and from one degree of glory to an-
other; [for this comes] from the Lord [Who is] the
Spirit. II Corinthians 3:18, Amplified

In the story of "The Great Stone Face" by Hawthorne, Ernest
lived in a valley surrounded by high mountains. The rocks on
the side of one of the mountains were in such a position as to
resemble a face. It was a tradition that some day a native son
would become a very noble man, resembling the Stone Face.
Ernest loved to look at the face. He would spend hours gazing
on it. As he grew to manhood, he constantly watched for someone to return to the valley who would look like it.

From time to time native sons returned — a man of wealth, a
great general, a philosopher. Each time Ernest was disappointed
that there was no resemblance to the Great Stone Face. Years
later, when Ernest was an old man, a poet came. Surely he must
be the one. But as the poet heard Ernest talking, he raised his
arms suddenly and said, "Ernest is the image of the Great Stone
Face." And it was true. He had gazed at the face for so long
it had become a part of him and he now resembled it.

This is true of the Christian life. Our purpose is to become
like Jesus Christ. God's Word, itself, reveals Him to us. Someone has said, "We must behold in order to reflect the beauty of
Jesus." As we look at Him in the Word, we are transformed and
become a mirror to reflect His image. Then we reflect Him from
our lives to those about us.

As Jesus landed He saw a great crowd waiting, and **5**
He was moved with compassion for them, because
they were like sheep without a shepherd; and He
began to teach them many things. Mark 6:34,
Amplified

Vacation time is nearly ended for this year. Many of you have
been sight-seeing in our beautiful United States. Some have been
traveling in other countries. However, some of you may be
saying, "I haven't had a trip all summer. I, too, would like to
see some wonderful sights." You can do some wonderful sight-
seeing at home, sight-seeing with an eternal purpose. This was
the kind of sight-seeing Jesus did as He went about. He saw the
people about Him and recognized their needs.

Our first sight-seeing trip must be to Jesus, the Saviour of the
world. We must see our need of Him, believe on Him and invite
Him into our heart. "Look unto me and ye shall be saved"
(Isaiah 45:22a). Have you met Him personally as your Saviour?
If not, why not today?

Then each day our life can be a sight-seeing trip for Him. "Lift
up your eyes, and look on the fields; for they are white already to
harvest" (John 4:35). We need to see those about us with
spiritual needs. When was the last time you took a sight-seeing
trip around your neighborhood, your community, or place of
business? Are you sight-seeing for God as you ride a bus, a
plane or a train?

If we are to see as He sees, our vision must be filled with Him.
The disciples went on a sight-seeing trip with Him. He took
three of them to the top of the mountain one day. There He was
transfigured. "And when they had lifted up their eyes, they saw
no man save Jesus only" (Matthew 17:8).

Have you taken a sight-seeing trip into His Presence? Have
you so focused your spiritual eyes on Him that He can set the
direction of your life? May we see Him so clearly, that we may
see the world and its needs through His eyes.

6   *And whatsoever we ask, we receive of him, because we keep his commandments, and do those things that are pleasing in his sight. I John 3:22*

John writes of the great assurance of answered prayer we can have. We can receive what we ask for. But there is a double condition for prevailing prayer. In other words, if we expect God to hear us, we must hear Him. We must be in such a relationship with God that He can answer our prayer.

We are told here that we can have whatever we ask for — because: we keep His commandments and do the things that please Him. This is the result of a life yielded to God. We are to do His will as revealed in His Word and do the things pleasing in His sight. The secret of prevailing prayer is a life *wholly* at God's disposal.

George Mueller was one of the great giants in prayer. The secret of his power in prayer, of asking and receiving, was that God had all of George Mueller. He was completely dedicated to doing God's will and desiring to please Him.

"And we receive from Him whatever we ask for, because we (watchfully) obey His orders — observe His suggestions and injunctions, follow His plan for us — *and* (habitually) practice what is pleasing to Him" (I John 3:22, Amplified).

You have not chosen Me, but I have chosen you — I have appointed you, I have planted you — that you might go and bear fruit and keep on bearing; that your fruit may be lasting (that it may remain, abide); so that whatever you ask the Father in My name [as presenting all that I AM] he may give it to you. John 15:16, Amplified

Jesus reminded His disciples that He had chosen them for His work. They were not selected because of their educational training or their natural ability. Some of them were ordinary men, some uneducated, self-seeking and even quarrelsome at times. But the Lord had picked each of them for the work He wanted them to do.

So, too, God selected us to serve Him. It is not important whether we feel capable or not, but it is important whether we respond or not. We have been appointed for a certain position. It may be a place of leadership or it may be a secluded place. We must be willing to serve in the place of His choosing.

Then He plants us where we are to serve Him. Some of us are planted in certain neighborhoods; some of us in certain offices or places of business. Blessing comes if we are in God's selected place for us.

God's purpose for us is to bear fruit and keep on bearing fruit. We are to reproduce the Fruit of the Spirit in our lives; we are to bear fruit as we bring others to know Jesus Christ.

Also we are chosen for the ministry of prayer. One of the conditions for answered prayer is to ask in His Name. We might illustrate it thus. Someone may bring a letter to us from a friend of ours which reads, "This will introduce so-and-so, a friend of mine. Do what you can for her. I will consider that you are doing it for me." So "asking in Jesus' name," means going to the Father with our needs. He has promised to answer our prayer, for He does it for His Son.

The secret of such a fruitful and prayerful life is a life of abiding — "Abide in me and I in you" (John 15:4).

8   *Let your light so shine before men, that they may see your good works, and glorify your Father which is in heaven. Matthew 5:16*

How much we appreciate light. We enjoy the bright sunshine, especially after we have had some dark, cloudy days. How thankful we are to see the moon and stars shine brightly in the night sky when we go out at night. I even notice that my plants always turn toward the light.

We read of the old lamplighters who went up and down the streets at dark lighting the street lamps. They carried a light on a long pole to light the old gas lamps along the street. The lamplighter himself couldn't be seen, but as you looked down the street and saw the lights burning, you could see where he had been.

In the darkness of this world today we have the privilege of being lamplighters for Him. We are just the carriers of His Light, those through whom He can shine forth.

A Sunday school teacher asked for a definition of a saint. One youngster eagerly raised her hand and said, "A saint is a person that the light shines through."

"Arise, shine; for thy light is come, and the glory of the Lord is risen upon thee" (Isaiah 60:1). It has been said, "The Living Christ within makes a steady light without." God is saying, "*You* are the Light of the World today." *Arise — now — shine.*

But Peter said, Not so, Lord. Acts 10:14

A young lady once had a conference with her pastor. She told him she was having difficulty in yielding her life completely to the Lord. A fine pianist, she feared that in yielding her life she would have to give up her music. Also she was afraid He would send her to some other land as a missionary and she did not wish to leave her home.

The pastor turned to Acts 10:14 and read the three words which Peter said, "Not so, Lord." He mentioned that this was really a contradiction. If Christ was Peter's Lord then Peter had no right to say, "Not so." If he could say, "Not so," then Christ was not his Lord.

Then he wrote the three words on a piece of paper and told her that she had to choose. Either the "Not so" must be crossed out, or "Lord" must be crossed out. He left her alone for a while. When he returned, he saw that the paper read "Lord." She had made her choice.

Peter, being a Jew, did not have fellowship with the Gentiles. God was revealing to Peter that He was no respecter of persons. The Gospel must cross all barriers — salvation is for *all* people.

When God told Peter to kill and eat the animals considered unclean, Peter answered, "Not so, Lord." If He was Peter's Lord, he had no right to say, "Not so."

We cannot honestly and consistently say, "Not so" and "Lord" at the same time. He cannot really be the Lord of our lives unless we are willing to say, "Yes, Lord" to His will for us. If we say, "Not so," we cannot say, "Lord." He must be Lord *of* all or He is not Lord *at* all.

What is your choice? Not so? Lord?

10 *Till I come give attendance to reading, to exhortation, to doctrine. I Timothy 4:13*

Paul wrote to Timothy setting forth certain standards for him to follow. He reminds Timothy of the importance of the Word of God in his ministry. If he was effectively to use the Word with others, it must have a vital part in his own personal life.

Timothy was to devote himself to private as well as public reading of the Word. It was his duty to challenge the people to action through the Word and to teach them from the Word that they might be grounded in doctrine. He was not to just read the Word but to meditate on these things (vs. 15) and to continue in them (vs. 16).

Each day most of us do some reading. We read the newspaper, a magazine and perhaps even a book. But are we as careful to devote some time each day to reading God's Word? Do we give "attendance" to reading?

Have you ever read a chapter of the Bible through and after you have finished you cannot tell what you had read? Another time God may have spoken to your heart from the very first verse you read. We need to read the Word more than casually. We should meditate in it, appropriating it into our lives. It should be a continual day-by-day experience, not just an occasional one.

One day a woman could not locate her Bible. Finally she asked her cleaning woman if she had seen it. The cleaning woman said, "Praise the Lord!" She went on to say, "When I begin to work in a new place, I hide the Bible if they have one." "Why?" asked her employer. "To see how long it is before they miss it," replied the cleaning woman.

How soon would you miss your Bible if it were hidden?

Be careful for nothing. Philippians 4:6a   *11*

Do you know people who are constantly worrying? They do not seem to be happy unless they are worrying about something. They almost seem to take pride in their capacity for worry. In these days of uncertainty and insecurity it is easy to become so burdened with anxious cares that we begin to worry.

God's Word says, "Be careful for *nothing*." That means not even one thing. Phillips reads, "Don't worry over anything whatever." Berkeley reads, "Entertain *no* worry." It is easy to tell others not to worry, but not so easy to take this advice for ourselves.

Worry exhausts the mind, depresses the spirit and wearies the body. It leaves the cares exactly as they were. Worry implies that God cannot handle our burdens. We are not to be "full of care" about anything.

But we can be free from every worry, every care, every anxiety. Not one is too great for God, and He is in control. Worry and trust do not go together. "Which of you by taking thought can add one cubit unto his stature?" (Matthew 6:27).

The secret of a life free from worry in *all* things is to commit them to God.

A man came into the telegraph office to send a message into a rather remote area. After he left, a man sitting near by said to the operator, "According to the news there is a heavy snowstorm up there — the roads are all blocked. Probably the message will not get through even after you send it." The operator replied, "I'm only responsible for this end. There's someone at the other end who knows his business without my trying to carry his worries for him."

How many worries do we have because we try to carry both ends of the line — our own and God's?

12   *But in everything by prayer and supplication with thanksgiving let your requests be made known unto God. Philippians 4:6b*

We are given a prescription to cure worry, giving us instead the peace of God. This prescription is prayer. "In everything by prayer and supplication." So often we try to work things out ourselves before we take them to God in prayer. But prayer can do what care cannot.

Prayer is our whole approach to God. It covers every aspect of our prayer life, our worship, adoration and confession. Supplication covers the specific petitions for our needs. "In every circumstance and in everything by prayers and petitions [definite requests] with thanksgiving continue to make your wants known to God" (Amplified).

Not only are we to be prayerful but we are to be thankful. Our prayer is to be accompanied by thanksgiving. Often we ask God for something and then fail to thank Him for the answer. We take so many things just for granted and never pause to thank Him. Have you ever thanked Him for such things as your eyesight, your voice, your sense of humor and many other things? As we thank Him for answered prayer, our faith is increased to pray for our present needs.

The antidote for care is prayer. It has been said, "Worry depreciates the value of our past blessings." In everything — we are to make our requests known to God. One by one we are to bring to Him our requests. Sometimes we take our needs to people instead of to the Lord.

Daily prayer lessens care. Someone has said that we need to take our baggage of care to the check room and check it there so we won't have to carry it about. Then "Pray your way through the day."

And the peace of God, which passeth all understanding, shall keep your hearts and minds through Christ Jesus. Philippians 4:7

13

When we are free from anxiety, when we are prayerful and thankful, we can be peaceful. Today hearts around the world are failing for fear. Yet God's peace can mount guard over our hearts and minds. Many may be our foes, the enemy may come in like a flood, yet God's peace can mount guard over us. The anxiety of the world need not affect the child of God.

This peace of heart and mind is more than passive resignation to unpleasant circumstances — it is a peace that passeth all understanding. It may not be explained but it can be experienced, this serenity in the midst of turmoil and confusion.

Someone has said, "A consistent Christian may not always have rapture, but he does have that which is much better, the calmness and serenity of God's perpetual presence."

God's peace is really the Lord Jesus Christ, Himself. Ephesians 2:14 says, "*He* is *our* peace." He, our very Peace, is ready to mount guard over our lives, giving us not only peace of heart but peace of mind, too. This is a peace the world doesn't give, neither can it take it away.

It has been said, "He who takes all to God in holy interview finds that the Divine Presence throws such a defense around the citadel of His soul that He is kept by the power of God from *all* anxiety and care."

"And God's peace [be yours, that tranquil state of a soul assured of its salvation through Christ, and so fearing nothing from God and content with its earthly lot of whatever sort, that is, that peace] which transcends all understanding, shall garrison *and* mount guard over your hearts and minds in Christ Jesus" (Philippians 4:7, Amplified).

14

You are the salt of the earth, but if salt has lost its taste — its strength, its quality — how can its saltness be restored? It is not good for anything any longer but to be thrown out and trodden under foot by men. Matthew 5:13, Amplified

Salt was a commodity familiar to the people of Jesus' time. It was used as a bond of hospitality. Since it was scarce, it was valuable and very precious. Sometimes soldiers were paid in salt.

Salt is used as a seasoning, a preservative and an antiseptic. As a seasoning salt, it adds flavor and zest to the food. It also prevents decay. And it has a healing quality. Salt has an important work to do but does it inconspicuously.

Jesus called His disciples the salt of the earth. We are a savoring influence, a preservative in the world against evil. We are the salt of the *earth*. Our influence should have an effect for Jesus Christ on those about us. Salt also makes people thirsty. Are we salty Christians, making others thirsty for Jesus Christ?

The slogan of a well known salt company is "When it rains it pours." It shows a little girl with an umbrella in the rain. Salt is *pouring* out on the earth from the box she is carrying in her arms.

God poured out Himself for mankind when in love beyond measure He sent His Son to become the Saviour of the world. Jesus poured out Himself for a sinsick world when He died on the cross. "Who loved me and gave himself for me" (Galatians 2:20).

Salt is not effective unless it is applied. So, too, we are not effective for the Lord unless the love of Christ so constrains us that we are willing to be poured out in service for a world in need of Jesus Christ.

It is better to trust in the Lord than to put confidence in man. Psalm 118:8

15

A pair of scientists and botanists were exploring in the Alps for some special kinds of flowers. One day they spied through their field glass a flower of rare beauty. But it was in a ravine with perpendicular cliffs on both sides. Someone must be lowered over the cliff to get it.

A native boy was watching. They said to him, "We will give you five pounds if you will let us lower you into the valley to get the flower." The boy looked into the valley and said, "Just a moment. I'll be back." He soon returned with a man. "I'll go over the cliff," he said, "and get the flower for you if this man holds the rope. He's my dad." Have we learned to trust the Lord as this little boy did his father?

Sometimes we find ourselves putting our confidence in man and what we think he can do for us. But man can let us down. Man can disappoint us. Not so the Lord. Needs may be pressing in but we can look up, trusting an all-wise, all-loving God to do all for our good and His glory.

We can trust the rope of our circumstances to Him. Man may become weary and let the rope drop; or he may be distracted or become impatient. But God never wearies of holding the rope. We can confidently leave it in His strong hand.

John Calvin said of this verse, "All make this acknowledgment and yet there is scarcely one in a hundred who is fully persuaded that God can alone afford him sufficient help."

Was he right? Do we really believe God can handle any situation? Are we willing to trust the ropes of our lives into His unfailing hands?

16   *Cast thy bread upon the waters: for thou shalt find it after many days. Ecclesiastes 11:1*

The farmers in Egypt had the custom of sowing their crops in the rich deltas of the Nile River. In the spring the fields were flooded by the overflowing waters of the river. Then the farmers scattered their seed on the waters which carried it out over their fields. As the waters receded, the seed settled down in the fertile loam. Later on an abundant harvest was reaped.

We are sowers, going forth to sow the seed of God's Word. As we scatter it and it is planted in the human heart, we have God's promise, "So shall my word be that goeth forth out of my mouth; it shall not return unto me void, but it shall accomplish that which I please, and it shall prosper in the thing whereunto I sent it" (Isaiah 55:11).

Sometimes the seed produces life right away — but not always. It may take years. Once a man tore down an old building that had stood for many years in his yard. He smoothed over the ground and left it. The rains fell upon it. The sunshine warmed it. Soon many flowers sprang up but they were unlike any growing in that area. It was discovered that a garden had once been on that spot. The seeds had lain in the soil during the years. When the sun and rain reached the seeds, they began to grow.

How important it is for us to sow God's Word. It may be years before we see the results — and we may never see any. But as we sow and water the seed with our prayers, we can trust the results with God. Have you been sowing today? Where?

Great is our Lord, and of great power: his under- **17**
standing is infinite. Psalm 147:5

It has been said, "God is great in great things, but very great in little things."

A group of people stood on the Matterhorn admiring the sublimity of the scene when a gentleman produced a pocked microscope and having caught a fly, placed it under the glass. He reminded them that the legs of a fly in England were naked. Then he called attention to the legs of this little fly which were thickly covered with hair, thus showing that the same God who made the lofty Swiss mountains, attended to the comforts of the tiniest of His creatures, even providing socks and mittens for the little fly whose home was in these mountains.

In the first few verses of this Psalm we read of the God who is great enough to number the stars and call them by name. Although the scientist has studied the wonderful things of the universe with his telescope, he has never been able accurately to count all the stars. But God has.

Yet the God who can count and name the stars has a heart of love for the individual — for you and me. He who is great enough to do all this is also great enough to heal the broken hearted and bind up their wounds, (vs. 3) and to lift up the meek (vs. 6). He has a loving concern for all His dear children.

Are you broken hearted today? He will pour the Balm of Gilead into your heart bringing healing to it. Have you been wounded? He has promised to bind tenderly and lovingly each of your wounds. Are you bowed down by grief or trouble? The Lord Himself will lift up the meek.

Place yourselves with all of your needs in His all-wise care and keeping.

18   *But the God of all grace who hath called us unto his eternal glory by Christ Jesus, after that ye have suffered a while, make you perfect, stablish, strengthen, settle you. I Peter 5:10*

We are in a conflict but the God of *all* grace is our Helper. Peter who had denied the Lord could speak from experience of this grace. In every trial God is there supplying us with the grace we need; grace for sickness, grace for sorrow, grace for trouble. He said, "My grace is sufficient for thee" (II Corinthians 12:9). The God of all grace delights to show mercy to all those who trust in Him.

God is working in our lives 1) to perfect us. He wants to complete the work He has begun in us and mature us; 2) to establish us. He will establish us firmly in the faith. "And set my feet upon a rock and established my goings" (Psalm 40:2); 3) strengthen us. Our own strength is limited but God's Word says, "I have strength for all things in Christ who empowers me — I am ready for anything and equal to anything through Him Who infuses inner strength into me [that is, I am self-sufficient in Christ's sufficiency]" (Philippians 4:13, Amplified); 4) settle us. We are to rest on our strong, firm foundation, Christ Jesus.

One of God's processes for accomplishing this in our lives is suffering. We wonder sometimes why we have suffering, but God uses it to complete His perfect work in our lives.

Someone has said, "Suffering helps to repair our defects, strengthen our weaknesses, and cure our instability." And it is only for a while.

"After you have suffered a little while, our God Who is full of kindness through Christ will give you His eternal glory. He personally will come and pick you up, and set you firmly in place, and make you stronger than ever" (Living Letters).

What have they seen in thine house? Isaiah 39:4   *19*

Painters were to come in and paint our apartment in a couple of days. We moved some of the furniture out but most of our things were piled in the center of the rooms. The first morning as my husband and I looked at the daily Scripture on our calendar, we read the above verse. We had a good laugh over it, for all we could see was "junk" about us. But when we started putting the things back, neither of us could find any junk. All of my things seemed necessary and my husband was sure that his things were.

Hezekiah had a serious illness in which his life was given up as lost. The Lord sent him word, "Set thine house in order." In answer to Hezekiah's desperate petition God spared his life, giving him fifteen more years.

When a delegation came from Babylon to visit him, he had a wonderful opportunity to tell what God had done for him. Instead of talking about the Lord, we read that he showed his gold, silver, spices, and armour. Isaiah then brought him this message from the Lord, "What have they seen in thine house?"

Is your house set in order? What does God see within? Things that are useful to Him — or junk? Treasure or trash? Does it reflect His presence?

Perhaps some setting in order is necessary. Our first preparation is to have a personal relationship to Jesus Christ. He must indwell our lives. "He that hath the Son hath life, and he that hath not the Son of God hath not life" (I John 5:12).

Some housecleaning may be necessary. Let the Holy Spirit remove all that does not glorify Him.

"What have they seen in *thine* house?" "Set *thine* house in order."

20 *Call unto me, and I will answer thee, and shew thee great and mighty things, which thou knowest not.*
Jeremiah 33:3

Calling out implies a need, a cry for help, doesn't it? As we call to God, He promises that He will do three things. He will answer; He will show us great and mighty things; and He will show us things which we know not.

A more literal translation of the word "mighty" is "fenced-in," or "hidden" things. These are the things that, humanly speaking, are impossible to reach.

The condition for receiving these great and mighty or "fenced-in" things is calling on God in prayer. How willing He is to answer when we call. He gives us His promises to encourage prayer. Keith Brooks has said, "Those who pray and take His promises for their pillow will find that their Father above will do for them things which humanly they could not understand. But He cannot bestow His choicest gifts upon hasty comers and goers." It has been said, "Faith honors God by counting upon His infinite resources."

Parmento, a favorite with Alexander, asked him for something almost worth a kingdom. This he did with fear and trembling. The emperor replied, "It may be too much for Parmento to ask, but it is not too much for Alexander to give."

Daily our life can be one of answered prayer. As we fulfill our part in calling, God will fulfill His in answering and doing the impossible for us.

"Call to Me and I will answer you and show you great and mighty things, fenced in and hidden, which you do not know — do not distinguish *and* recognize, have knowledge of *and* understand" (Amplified).

"Great and mighty needs" bring "great and mighty answers."

Let us go on to perfection. Hebrews 6:1   *21*

It is interesting to watch the growth and development of an infant through childhood, teen years and finally to adulthood.

We are desirous of growing and developing, aren't we? We did not want to stay in the same grade at school year after year, did we? But before we could be promoted we had to take final exams, pass some tests, or in some way give evidence that we had satisfactorily completed the prescribed work.

God's Word sets a goal before us. We are to go on to perfection or "full growth"; from spiritual infancy to spiritual maturity. "That (we might arrive) at really mature manhood — the completeness of personality which is nothing less than the standard height of Christ's own perfection — the measure of the stature of the fullness of Christ, and completeness found in Him" (Ephesians 4:13, Amplified). Our goal is maturity in Jesus Christ. Of course we will never reach all that there is in Christ, so we must not become discouraged.

God wants us to continue to grow and mature in Christ. Too often we stop too soon, satisfied to stay just where we are. But God's Word says, "Let us go on instead to other things and become mature in our understanding, as strong Christians ought to be" (Living Letters).

Bishop Wescott, in his commentary on Hebrews, gives this meaning, "Let us be borne or carried on." Sometimes we feel that we are all alone and don't make the effort we could. But there is One, Jesus Christ, who is ready to carry us on to full growth. We are to go on, showing progress in our spiritual growth; we are to press on with perseverance; we are to be borne on toward our goal of the full stature of Christ.

In which grade are we spiritually?

22   *Ye also helping together by prayer for us. II Corinthians 1:11*

Paul, the great missionary, asked others to pray for him, feeling the need of their strong prayer support. He was a mighty man of God, a blessing wherever he went, but he recognized that apart from prayer his ministry would not be fruitful. He knew the importance of praying for one another.

How often people will say, "All I can do is pray for you." That is the greatest thing they can do. Workers for God need prayer more than anything else.

The Amplified New Testament reads, "While you also co-operate by your prayers for us — helping and laboring together with us." Through your co-operating, helping and laboring in prayer for those serving in Christian work, you are sharing in what God is doing in His work today.

There is power in united prayer. Your prayer for God's work added to the prayers of others brings power into His work. The power of the enemy is broken through united prayer. A little girl once heard someone say, "Satan trembles when he sees the weakest saint upon his knees." Later one day she spent a longer time than usual in her prayers. When her mother asked her why, she said, "I wanted to keep Satan trembling longer."

In reading of the early Christians, we find that they were bold in their witness and as a result, many believed in God. One of the secrets of power in this early ministry was the fact that "They lifted up their voice to God with one accord" (Acts 4:24). There was unity as they lifted their "voice" (not voices) to God in prayer. They prayed as one voice. Such united prayer brought results.

Such united prayer still brings results today. You are a "helper" in prayer today as you lift your voice with others as one, praying for God's work and for those serving Him.

Elias was a man subject to like passions as we are **23**
and he prayed earnestly that it might not rain: and
it rained not on the earth by the space of three years
and six months, and he prayed again, and the heaven
gave rain, and the earth brought forth her fruit.
James 5:17, 18

Elijah was a prophet of God. He was a man of great power with God, a man God used during a time of idolatry and apostasy in the land of Israel. He knew the power of the *living God* in his life. "As the Lord God of Israel liveth" (I Kings 17:1). He knew the power of prayer. "Before whom I stand" (vs. 1). He recognized that the Living God was the God of the Impossible, because there was nothing beyond the reach of God through prayer.

Elijah prayed earnestly that it might not rain and it did not. His request was definite and God answered. Then later he prayed for rain and again his prayer was answered.

We, too, can have power in prayer such as Elijah did. We, too, can stand before the Living God in prayer, making our requests known and receiving His answer to them.

A man was hurrying to get to the bank before it closed. He had to stop for a traffic light. He said to his son, "By the time I park the car, the bank will be closed." "Why don't they keep the bank open as long as the stores?" asked his son. "They don't work very long." The father answered, "But the employees in the bank work long after the doors are closed. Much of their work is done behind closed doors."

Behind the closed door of prayer we can do our greatest work for God.

24 *Get thee hence and turn thee eastward, and hide thyself by the brook Cherith, that is before Jordan. I Kings 17:3*

After Elijah had appeared before King Ahab, telling of the three and a half year drought to come, his life was in danger. But God was guiding the course of Elijah so that he need not have a fear. God told him to go and hide himself by the brook Cherith. This place would be a safe refuge from danger for him. Though Ahab sought for him throughout the entire kingdom, he couldn't find him.

In his place of hiding Elijah was to learn deeper lessons of complete trust in God. God said, "And it shall be, that thou shalt drink of the brook; and I have commanded the ravens to feed thee *there*" (vs. 4). "God controlled the supplies, the supply route, and the suppliers of his necessities."

There in this hidden place Elijah was to experience the providential love and care of God. God would not forget him. *"There"* in the place where God sent him, he would be provided for day by day. He promised that Elijah would be able to drink from the brook. The ravens would bring food for him to eat. Someone has said, "God fed Elijah at the Black Raven Cafe."

There is a place today where God has placed us or wants us to be. It may be a hidden place away from the crowds. We may not understand why. But there are lessons of trust for us to learn there. If God has put us there, He has a purpose to be accomplished. We can trust Him to provide every need for us *there* in the place of His choosing. God's ravens will always find us there.

Trust Him *there* wherever you are.

Let us therefore come boldly unto the throne of grace, that we may obtain mercy and find grace to help in time of need. Hebrews 4:16

25

We have a High Priest, Jesus Christ, seated at the right hand of God, the Father, in heaven. There He intercedes for us, ministering to our needs. "Seeing he ever liveth to make intercession for them" (Hebrews 7:25b). Through Him we have access into God's Presence.

We are to come to God's Throne of Grace (unmerited favor) to obtain His mercy or pardon for sin. "Let us then fearlessly and confidently and boldly draw near to the throne of grace — the throne of God's unmerited favor [to us sinners]; that we may receive mercy [for our failures] . . ." (Amplified).

At His throne we receive help for every need; help to face all the tensions, trials and temptations of life. "And find grace to help in good time for every need — appropriate help and well-timed help, coming just when we need it" (Amplified). "Help" can be translated from the Greek as "in the nick of time." It is just for the time we need it.

We have an open line of communication to heaven always. We are to come that we may obtain. This indicates that He is already there waiting for us. We are to come boldly into His presence.

"My little boy," said a mother, "is getting to the age he wants to go his way instead of mine. Consequently he often gets into difficulty and comes to me to smooth things out." One day when he came to her she scolded him a little and then said, "Why did you come to me when you got hurt disobeying me?" With eyes filled with tears, he looked up and said, "Where else would I go?"

26 *When thou passest through the waters, I will be with thee; and through the rivers they shall not overflow thee; when thou walkest through the fire thou shalt not be burned; neither shall the flame kindle upon thee. Isaiah 43:2*

During the time of a major flood in our city I watched on television the destructive power of the flood waters. As I watched, I was reminded of the flood waters of trouble that sometimes come into our lives.

Are you experiencing these flood tides of trouble rising higher and higher in your life until you feel that you are sinking beneath them? Are you almost overwhelmed as trouble and affliction sweep over you? David cried, "Save me, O God; for the waters are come in unto my soul" (Psalm 69:1). In your time of trouble you can cry out to God.

As we call to God for help, He draws near in a special way, saying, "Just remember that even though you are in the flood waters now, I am right there with you. I promise that they will never overflow you."

As we watch the tide of the ocean coming in, breaking and then receding, we realize that it is subject to God's power. So, too, the waters that sweep over our lives are in His control so we need not fear. He has promised that they will not overflow us. He is right there with us as we go through the deep waters. He hasn't assured us that this help will come ahead of time, but *"when* thou passest through."

Whatever trouble we may be passing through just now, His eye is upon us, His loving arms upholding us moment by moment. We can rest in Him, assured of His presence. "My presence shall go with thee, and I will give thee rest" (Exodus 33:14).

A merry heart maketh a cheerful countenance. Proverbs 15:13

Have you ever sat where you could watch crowds of people and study their faces? Often as I do this, I note that many of them do not register a look of joy or cheer on their faces. Yet it takes less effort, fewer muscles, to smile than to frown.

The television industry has produced a show which induces smiling — "Smile — You're on Candid Camera." In one of my places of employment we were reminded from time to time that we were to give service with a *smile.*

A sunny, happy countenance should characterize the life of Christians. God's Word gives us the recipe for a cheerful countenance. "A *happy* heart makes the face look sunny" (Berkeley). This is an inner cheerfulness which is not affected by circumstances. "A cheerful heart makes a good cure" (Proverbs 17:22, Berkeley).

A smile can be an artificial expression put on the face. But there is the reality of a cheerful countenance that comes from the heart at peace with God. An inner joy and radiance that glows in a heart resting in God is reflected on the face. Often when a cheery person with a bright smile on his face enters a room, the entire atmosphere is changed. Spirits are lifted. Such a cheery disposition reacts like a tonic. A smile is contagious.

The world today is full of tension and trouble. How we need "smilers." When I am going out, before I leave I not only check to be sure that I have such articles as my gloves and purse, but also my smile.

It has been said, "A smile is a light in the window of the face that shows that a happy heart is at home." Be sure you have your brightest and cheeriest smile with you today.

28 *If God be for us, who can be against us?* Romans 8:31

Sometimes I have heard a person express this feeling: "Everything and everyone is against me." Perhaps it may seem so. Yet from God's Word we can be assured that *God* is for *us* — for you and for me. The One who created the Universe, the One who upholds the earth is for us.

In the most wonderful way God has proved His love for us. He has shown that He is for us by sending His Son to earth to redeem mankind. "He that spared not his own Son, but delivered him up for us all" (vs. 32). Who then could ever doubt that God is interested in him?

Since God is for us, who can be against us? No one. What difference does it make who opposes us when *God* is for us? "Who can be our foe if God is on our side?" (Amplified). Since God is for us why should we fear man or what man can do?

During World War II a liner sailed from an English port for America. The crossing was dangerous because of enemy subs and cruisers. The Captain was given these orders, "Keep straight on this course. Turn aside for nothing." He was given a special code and told, "If you need help, send a wireless message in this code."

After a few days an enemy cruiser was sighted. The Captain sent the message in the code given, "Enemy cruiser sighted. What shall I do?" The reply came back, "Keep straight on. I'm standing by." No help could be seen but they kept on, reaching port safely. In a short time the protecting vessel, the one standing by, came into the harbor.

Amid the dangers and trials of life God is saying, "Keep straight on. I'm standing by."

In the world ye shall have tribulation: but be of good cheer; I have overcome the world. John 16:33

29

Our Lord *is* victorious. He has overcome the world. What joy! What comfort.

When Jesus Christ, the Son of God, came to earth, He lived among mankind as one of us. He went about doing good — He was touched with the needs of the people about Him. Yet He overcame the world as He triumphed over death — as He rose from the dead to become the Living Saviour.

This doesn't mean a life without trials and trouble. Such are inevitable to all of us. He said, "In the world ye *shall* have tribulation." Tribulation means "pressure" or "anguish." As I travel across the country many people tell me of their pressures. Many are anguished, heartbroken and disappointed.

Paul experienced tribulation in his life. He was beaten, he was put in prison. Yet he could say, ". . . but we glory in tribulations also: knowing that tribulation worketh patience" (Romans 5:3).

But Jesus said, "Be of *good cheer.*" You mean we are to be of good cheer when we have lost all earthly possessions? Can we be cheerful when sickness has laid us low? How can we be cheerful when loved ones have failed us and broken our hearts?

As the pressures of life come, Jesus draws near to us lovingly whispering, "You *can* be cheerful, not in your circumstances, but in *me.*" Your deliverance may not be *from* trouble, but *in* trouble. He will give you moment by moment grace to bear trouble and strength to endure. Every experience that comes to us while we are in the world has been conquered by Him. We are refined in the midst of the pressures. The dross is removed.

Cheer up! Victory is yours! You can be triumphant in Him! He has overcome the world.

30

Come to Me, all you who labor and are heavy-laden and over burdened, and I will cause you to rest — I will ease and relieve and refresh your souls. Matthew 11:28, Amplified

Today people everywhere are seeking peace and rest. One day Jesus stood before the people and spoke the above words that have brought comfort through the ages. He could see the weary, toiling and heavy-hearted ones. His heart went out to them. He said, "Come to Me you who are overburdened, *every one* of you and I will give you rest."

The Aramaic reads, "Come unto me, all you who are tired and carrying burdens and I will give you rest." Come to me, busy, toiling ones, and I will *give* you rest — it is a gift. Come to me, crushed and burdened ones, and I *will* give you rest — it is My promise to you.

F. B. Meyer interpreted Jesus' words thus, "On this breast of Mine is a pillow for every heart — My breast is broad enough — My heart is deep enough. I offer Myself to all weary ones in every clime and age as the *rest giver*."

In Him we can have rest from the guilt of sin, rest from its penalty, rest from an accusing conscience. But before we can experience His rest in our lives we must know personally the Rest Giver, Jesus Christ. "For we which have *believed* do enter into rest . . . " (Hebrews 4:3a).

A man was looking at Thorwaldsen's statue, "The Christus Consolator." A child overheard him express his disappointment in it. She said, "You must go close, kneel down and look up into His face."

Take all your burdens and cares today, and kneel before Him who said, "Come unto me." As you *give* Him *all* your needs, your problems, and your sorrows, He will give *you* His rest.

Take My yoke upon you, and learn of Me; for I am gentle (meek) and humble (lowly) in heart, and you will find rest — relief, ease and refreshment and recreation and blessed quiet — for your souls. Matthew 11:29, Amplified

1

Not only does He say, "Come unto Me and I will *give* you rest," (vs. 28) but He says, "Ye shall *find* rest" (vs. 29). Many have received rest for their souls but never found the rest necessary for daily living, rest in time of sorrow, pain, bereavement and trial.

"Ye shall *find* rest for your souls." How? He says, "Take *My* yoke upon you and learn of *Me* . . . and you will find rest."

A friend once visited Mr. Moody at his boys' school in Massachusetts. The school owned a team of white oxen. Showing them to a friend, Mr. Moody said, "It is always interesting to watch these oxen. When one is brought out to be yoked up, no matter where the other may be, he always comes and stands by the other oxen that he might be yoked with him." Jesus is saying to us, "Come and share my yoke with me and we will plow the field of life together."

Yoked with Him we learn of Him. We take Him for our pattern. We learn of His meekness and His lowliness. We learn that He is the Strong One, the All-sufficient One. As we rest in His strength and His all-sufficiency, the stress and strain of our lives is gone. Yoked with Him we are delivered from the unrest of self-effort and self-will. Rest comes in yielding ourselves to Him and taking His yoke upon us. So we *find* rest yoked together with Him.

Our world may seem to fall apart, disappointments may come, problems may arise. Yet yoked with Him who knows what is best for us, we walk step by step, resting in His love, trusting Him with the working out of His plan.

2 *For my yoke is wholesome (useful, good) — not harsh, hard, sharp, or pressing, but comfortable, gracious and pleasant; and My burden is light and easy to be borne. Matthew 11:30, Amplified*

There is rest for us as we are yoked with our Rest Giver. This does not give us a life of inactivity, however. It is a rest "full of work," a life of restful activity.

"My yoke is easy and my burden is light." A son offered to help his father carry a heavy basket. The father cut a stick, placing it through the handle of the basket. The end toward him was short. The end toward the boy was three or four times as long. Each one took hold of his end of the stick. The basket was lifted and carried easily. The boy was bearing the burden with the father but he found his work easy and light because his father bore the heavy end of the stick.

So it is when we are yoked with Christ. Because He carries the heavy end of the burden, the part laid on us is light. Someone has said, "Jesus was saying in effect, 'Look at life from my viewpoint; yoke yourself to me and learn of me, my meekness, lowliness and you will have rest. Then you will find my yoke is easy and my burden is light, for I am carrying the heavy end of it for you.'"

Is there frustration, turmoil, anxiety and worry in our lives? It may be the result of pulling in the opposite direction from Him. Instead of walking in harmony with Him and His will we seek our own desires and ambitions. This prevents heart rest.

If we are yoked with Jesus Christ, He takes the heaviness of our burden. Thus the burden becomes His, making it light and easily borne.

Not slothful in business; fervent in spirit; serving the Lord. Romans 12:11   **3**

There are people who conduct their business so efficiently that we often remark that they seem to have "an eye for business." Others are so haphazard you wonder how they are able to remain in business.

As Christians we are "in business" for the Lord serving Him, whether in Christian or secular fields of activity. Regardless of our "business" we should do it as unto Him. We should have His interest and His glory as our object.

In our service for Him we are not to be slothful, or careless. He does not want us to be half-hearted, lukewarm, lacking zeal. We hear occasionally of epidemics of sleeping sickness. Is it possible that any of us might have "spiritual sleeping sickness"?

We are to be fervent in spirit, full of enthusiasm. Those who are interested in sports are enthusiastic, often showing it outwardly. Why shouldn't we be just as zealous in whatever we do for the Lord? One day after I had finished speaking, a girl came to me saying, "I am so glad to hear someone excited about Jesus Christ."

It has been said, "As a bond slave, whose heart is captivated by the loving kindness of his master, will perform devoted service far beyond the call of duty, so the Christian with fervency of spirit will serve the Lord." Have we become apathetic in our service for the Lord? Have we lost the enthusiasm and love we used to have in serving Him? We can ask God to give us again the joy and fervency we need to make our time really count for Him. It is time to awake, time to avail ourselves of the opportunities that are before us to serve the Lord with great earnestness and enthusiasm of spirit.

"All of us must quickly carry out the tasks assigned us by the One who sent Me, for there is little time left before the night falls and all work comes to an end" (John 9:4, Living Gospels).

4   *Let the beauty of the Lord our God be upon us.*
     Psalm 90:17

Women spend much time and money on making themselves attractive. More important than outer beauty, however, is the inner beauty of life. This inner beauty of life is found in the person of our lovely Lord, Jesus Christ, Himself. He is spoken of as the One Altogether Lovely. His presence in our lives gives us this inner radiance. God desires that we be conformed to the image of the Lord.

This beauty of Jesus Christ is something we can ask for. *"Let the beauty of the Lord our God be upon me."* The transformation takes place in the secret place of His presence. "Strength and beauty are in his sanctuary" (Psalm 96:6b). As we behold Him we are transformed into His beauty and loveliness.

In St. Peter's Church, Cologne, hanging side by side, there are two pictures of the crucifixion of Peter. Early in the nineteenth century, when Napoleon ransacked the city, he took the original of the picture away. The artist painted another one to take its place. In time the original was restored and the two were then hung side by side. There is so little difference in them that one can hardly tell which is the original.

The Holy Spirit will do this in our lives. Christ, the Original, is absent, but the Holy Spirit will work in our lives conforming us to His likeness. Are we so nearly like the Original that people cannot see much difference?

*And I said, Oh that I had wings like a dove! for
then would I fly away, and be at rest. Psalm 55:6*

5

This cry which came from the heart of David the Psalmist is duplicated in the hearts of many in the present day. This is a day of tranquilizers and sleeping pills. To escape the pressures of life and to experience rest is the great quest of people today.

Man was made for God's pleasure and only as God fills His rightful place is a person at rest.

David endured great misunderstandings. Friends and family became his enemies. Into his heart crept a longing to rise up on wings as a dove and fly away from all his troubles and find rest.

Perhaps today you, too, may desire to fly away from your circumstances. Even though the dove is swift in its flight, its wings could never bear us away from life. Though we might be able to leave some situations, we can never get away from ourselves. We are to use our wings not to fly away, but up. The wings of faith will carry us up into the very presence of God where the soul is at rest. Our rest comes only as we are resting in God Himself.

One day someone was watching two birds. One bird was flapping its wings energetically, working hard at it. The other flapped its wings a bit as it rose into the air current, stretched its wings and sailed along with the current.

On wings of faith we can stretch our wings and rise above the problems of life. Instead of working so hard against the wind currents, we can turn and sail along on the current of His will. Rest then will be ours, rest *in the Lord.*

"Rest in the Lord, and wait patiently for him" (Psalm 37:7).

6   *Unto you therefore which believe he is precious.*
     I Peter 2:7a

Webster defines precious as "something highly prized; valuable; choice; rare." Gems are spoken of as being precious. Precious gems have great beauty and are costly. In this verse we read of *Someone* very precious, the Lord Jesus Christ.

He is precious because of who He is. He is the very Son of God. "For in Him the whole fulness of Deity (the Godhead), continues to dwell in bodily form . . . giving complete expression of the divine nature" (Colossians 2:9, Amplified). He is precious, as through eyes of faith, we see Him in His loveliness and beauty. He is the One "Altogether Lovely" (Song of Solomon 5:16). "Thine eyes shall see the king in his beauty" (Isaiah 33:17a).

Then He is precious because of the great price He paid for our salvation. "As Christ also loved the church, and gave *himself* for it" (Ephesians 5:25). He gave the greatest price anyone could give, His very life for our redemption.

He is precious to us for what He does for us. He sustains, guides and comforts. He is precious because He provides our every need. If we need strength, He gives it; if we need peace, He gives it. He can even do the impossible for us. He is precious because He gives purpose to our lives. He makes us like Himself.

A Spanish artist painted "The Last Supper." He put his whole soul into the figure and countenance of the Saviour. Without thinking, he painted some beautiful cups in the foreground. When friends saw the picture they said, "What beautiful cups!" "Ah," he said, "I have made a mistake. These have diverted the eyes from the Master and that cannot be." He quickly painted the cups out of the picture.

When we have found Him precious, we, too, will want to paint out of our lives all that would detract from His preciousness and loveliness.

There was a man sent from God whose name was **7**
John. John 1:6

John the Baptist was chosen of God for a particular ministry. He was sent to be a "voice" for God. When the priests and Levites came to him asking who he was, he replied, "I am the voice of one crying aloud in the wilderness — the voice of one shouting in the desert — Prepare the way of the Lord (level, straighten out, the path of the Lord), as the prophet Isaiah said" (vs. 23, Amplified).

One day John was with two disciples when Jesus appeared on the scene. John "looked upon Jesus" (vs. 36). His eyes were focused in the right direction. We, too, can see "Him," our Lovely Lord, with eyes of faith. We need to take time to pause and look into His face that our vision might be filled with Him.

John's conversation pointed to the Saviour. He said, "Behold the Lamb of God." He didn't give a long doctrinal discussion about Him but in a few simple words he spoke of who Jesus was.

Today there are many who are seeking reality — something to satisfy. We may feel incapable of talking to such people. However, we need not give a technical talk on theology. We, too, can talk of Jesus Christ as John did — tell what He has done for us, what He means to us.

The two disciples heard and as a result "they followed Jesus." John had to speak before they could hear. "How then shall they call on Him in whom they have not believed? and how shall they believe in him of whom they have not heard? and how shall they hear without a preacher?" (Romans 10:14). How many are waiting for you to speak that they might hear?

Today God is in need of people to be "His voice" that others might hear and follow Him.

8 *The Lord seeth not as man seeth for man looketh on the outward appearance but God looks on the heart. I Samuel 16:7*

Today much emphasis is put on the outward physical appearance of people. And this is important. We should desire to make the most of our physical make up. Yet God looks through all the outward adorning — He sees within. He looks for the inner beauty of the heart.

The above Scripture is the story of Samuel anointing David as King at the time of Saul's rejection. Samuel was to take a horn of oil and anoint one of Jesse's sons as king. One by one they passed before him, all of them fine specimens of manhood. But God didn't reveal any of them to Samuel as the King. He asked if all of Jesse's sons were there and was told that the youngest, David, was out taking care of the sheep. David was called and when he came in, the Lord said to Samuel, "Arise, anoint him for this is he." David was a handsome young man, a handsomeness that came from a heart right with God. God saw David as a "man after His own heart."

Physical qualities do not indicate the inner value of a person. It is the heart that God sees and we cannot fool Him. Nothing in the heart is hidden from God. He sees our thoughts, our desires, our attitudes — whether they are right toward Him.

Sometimes it becomes discouraging to us to know that God can see all our weaknesses and failures. Yet He sees more than this, He sees our motives and our efforts. He recognizes our love for Him and knows our desire to please Him.

People may see our failure. They may not understand. But God can see in us what no one else sees. He sees *us* through *His Son.*

Thy Word is a lamp unto my feet, and a light unto my path. Psalm 119:105

9

My husband and I traveled a great deal. Before we took a trip, we always secured maps and studied them thoroughly to know the best route to take. In fact, we gathered all the information we could possibly obtain to make the trip easier and safer.

On one trip I had been informed that a certain highway was the best route. We came to a turn-off which I thought was the highway we were to take. However, I didn't check the map. Soon we discovered we were not on the right road. Instead of a wide paved road we were on a narrow, dusty road winding through the mountains. Not only did it take us longer, but it was a rough road. I should have checked the map. Official maps are wonderful guides, saving time and gasoline, if we use them and follow them.

We need spiritual illumination for our walk through life and God has provided it. The Bible is God's "official map" for our daily travel to show us the right way.

Foot lamps used to be worn at night. They were fastened on the toes and as the person walked, the lamp cast a light on the next step ahead. So God's Word is a lamp for our way, lighting our feet step by step for our immediate needs just ahead. We can be assured of its light on our path through life.

In planning a trip we plot our entire trip. Then we take it mile by mile. So with our trip through life. The light of God's Word gives the general knowledge of God's will for our way. Then the "foot" lamp of His Word lights up the next step ahead for our immediate needs.

Spurgeon said, "The Word of God is a lamp by night, a light by day and a delight at all times."

10

When he giveth quietness, who then can make trouble? Job 34:29

Most of us have experienced being in a severe wind storm at some time. Perhaps it blew all day and as we watched the trees bent over by the fury of the storm, a little fear crept into our hearts, wondering if even our home might be shaken off its foundation. How thankful we were to feel the security of a strong building which remained unshaken, a place of quietness from the stormy elements.

Sometimes the winds of adversity blow on our lives, reaching almost hurricane proportions. Regardless of the severity of the storm, no matter how strong the gale about us, at the very center of our lives we can experience this quietness that God gives to us. We are told that in the midst of the raging hurricane, in its very "eye," there is a calm.

Jesus was once in a boat with His disciples when a storm came up quickly on the Sea of Galilee. As the waves swept over the boat filling it with water, it seemed inevitable that the boat would sink and they would drown.

As Jesus stood up, saying, "Peace be still," the wind ceased, and there was a great calm.

This experience of inner calm and quietness in the storms of life is for us. He draws near and lovingly whispers to us, "Peace be still." This quietness comes from His presence within. Then no storm can overwhelm us nor trouble defeat us.

Reach out today and take His quietness for your present need.

Behold the handmaid of the Lord; be it unto me according to thy word. Luke 1:38

11

Mary, an obscure maiden of Nazareth, was chosen by God to be the vessel through whom His Son, Jesus Christ, would enter this world in human form as the Saviour of the world.

Very humbly, she was *submissive* to God's will. Her faith in God was so strong that she was willing for His plan for her life. Are we as submissive, ready to say, "be it unto me according to *thy* word"?

Mary went to visit her cousin Elisabeth who was also expecting a baby. Elisabeth said, ". . . And blessed is she that believed: for there shall be a performance of those things which were told her from the Lord" (vs. 45).

Then Mary broke forth in singing the beautiful Magnificat. Out of her life of quiet *submission* burst forth this *song* of *praise* to God. Her deep love for God overflowed from her heart in praise and worship. "My soul doth magnify the Lord" (vs. 46).

Magnify means to enlarge, to make larger. Sometimes we carry a magnifying glass to use in reading maps, telephone numbers or other small print. By its use, fine print appears large enough to be read easily. Not only did Mary magnify the Lord but she said, "My spirit hath rejoiced in God my Saviour" (vs. 47).

Can we say as Mary did, "My Saviour," because we have received Him into our lives? Can we say as Mary did, "My soul doth magnify the Lord"? Do we magnify Him in our daily living — in our prayer life — in our service?

Christ was willing to leave His home in glory that He might enter our lives and turn them into symphonies of song. "My spirit hath rejoiced in God my Saviour."

"O magnify the Lord with me, and let us exalt his name together" (Psalm 34:3).

12   *Likewise the spirit also helpeth our infirmities: for we know not what we should pray for as we ought: but the spirit itself maketh intercession for us with groanings which cannot be uttered. Romans 8:26*

Have you ever knelt in prayer and felt you didn't know how to pray? You just couldn't seem to find the words to voice the need of your heart? Have you ever felt that you were a failure when it came to prayer?

Should we stop praying? No, we still have the need for prayer. R. A. Torrey has said that at such a time, "Be silent and look up to God and let His Holy Spirit, according to His promise, move your heart to prayer and to awaken and create real earnestness in your heart in prayer."

God, knowing our feeling of weakness in prayer, has provided a helper for us — the Holy Spirit Himself. A member of the Holy Trinity, the Holy Spirit prays in us and for us. Thus prayer is God's work in us through His Spirit.

Andrew Murray said, "Prayer is the work of the Triune God; the Father, who wakens the desire and will give all we need; the Son, who through His intercession, teaches us to pray in His Name; and the Holy Spirit, who in secret will strengthen our feeble desires."

At times we become so burdened as we pray that we cannot pray audible words, until we almost despair of praying at all. But we need not become discouraged. The Holy Spirit is our prayer helper. He understands our groanings and knows how to pray our "groanings" aright before the throne of God.

Through the Spirit of prayer, our life may be one of continual prayer. The Spirit of prayer will help you become an Intercessor, asking great things of God for those around you.

Say not ye, There are yet four months, and then **13**
cometh harvest? behold, I say unto you, Lift up
your eyes, and look on the fields; for they are white
already to harvest. John 4:35

Very likely Jesus was looking out on the harvest fields around Him. Yet He was not speaking merely of the fields of ripened grain He saw. He was thinking of a greater harvest — a spiritual harvest.

The harvest is ready now. There are people all about us in need of Jesus Christ. Now is the time to reap the harvest of those whom the Holy Spirit has prepared.

When the harvest is ripe, the reaping must be done quickly. But a harvest needs reapers. The laborers are few. The Lord told us to pray for reapers. "So pray the Lord of the harvest to force out and thrust laborers into His harvest" (Matthew 9:38, Amplified).

As we pray for laborers, we must be willing to be in the God-chosen place for us to reap. He has a place for each of us — not the same place, not the same work, but a specially prepared field. Sometimes God has to use forceful methods to thrust us out into this field.

The dandelion has been used to illustrate this thought. The seeds are ripened and loosened. Then comes a puff of wind which releases them from the spot where they have browned and ripened. Someone has called these "winds of severance." The seeds will be carried to new spots where they, too, will eventually bring forth a harvest.

Sometimes, not understanding why, we are removed from a place and we may even rebel against the move. But God wants our lives to bring forth a new harvest in a new place.

You can reap for Him *now* wherever you are.

14   *We make it our ambition to please Him. II Corinthians 5:9, Weymouth*

Red has long been one of my favorite colors. However neither my mother nor my husband liked it. Consequently I have worn very little red. One Christmas I casually suggested that I might get a new red dress. Many of my friends would be wearing lovely dresses of this color during the holiday season. My husband proceeded to tell me at length why he didn't think I should get a red dress. Then he told me to get what I wanted.

Later I told him I had my new "red" dress to show him. Do you know what color it was? I had bought a blue dress, his favorite color. To me the color of the dress was not important. I wanted to please him much more than to have something that I desired.

To please *Him!* What more wonderful ambition or desire could one have? Enoch had such a life. "He (Enoch) had this testimony, that he pleased God" (Hebrews 11:5). Jesus Christ Himself gave us the most perfect example of this. "For I do always those things that please him" (John 8:29). "My meat is to do the will of him that sent me and to finish his work" (John 4:34).

We need to ask ourselves, "Are the words I speak pleasing to Him? Are the plans for my life pleasing? My friends? My thoughts? My habits? My actions?" Do you want your life really to count for Him? Make it your daily ambition then to please Him.

There may be difficult days ahead, problems to solve, decisions to make, times of discouragement, and much work to be done for Him. If we make it our ambition to please Him moment by moment, it will give the right direction not only to our daily lives and their needs, but to our service for Him.

However we possess this precious treasure [the di-
vine Light of the Gospel] in [frail, human] vessels
of earth, that the grandeur and exceeding greatness
of the power may be shown to be of God and not
from ourselves. II Corinthians 4:7, Amplified

15

Not long ago I saw a delightful demonstration of the arranging of artificial flowers. My eye was taken with the beauty of the flowers and the symmetry of their arrangement. Later I noted that the containers used were ordinary and plain. My interest had been in the flowers, not the vases.

Paul here contrasts the majesty of the message with the weakness of the messenger. The precious treasure of the Light of the Gospel is contained in frail vessels of earth.

In Bible times earthen jars were often used to put coins in, then hidden in the earth. Archeologists have dug up some of them. Earthen vessels were cheap and easily obtained. Their only value was in what they contained.

The earthen vessels of our lives are only containers for the most precious treasure, the person of Jesus Christ. We are to reflect and enhance the beauty of the Lord, the Lily of the Valley, the Rose of Sharon. As we are hidden from view, those about us will see the precious treasure contained within.

When Gideon and his small army went forth to battle against the mighty Midianites, they were instructed to carry pitchers containing lamps. At a given signal they were to break the pitchers, letting the light shine forth, and to shout, "The sword of the Lord, and of Gideon." As they obeyed, the Midianites were put to rout.

Today our human, frail vessels need to be broken of self that the Light of the World might shine forth; that people might know that the power is of God and not of ourselves.

"This priceless treasure we hold, so to speak, in a common earthenware jar — to show that the splendid power of it belongs to God and not to us" (II Corinthians 4:7, Phillips).

16 *For we which have believed do enter into rest.*
Hebrews 4:3

Not long ago I listened to a program telling of a company that is now retiring its employees in their forties. Several men were interviewed who had already been retired. With enthusiasm they were telling how they enjoyed it.

Sometimes when we become weary, we think how wonderful it will be when we can retire and rest. The rest we read of in God's Word does not mean retirement from activity. It is God's rest. The one requirement is faith. This rest is made available to us by the work of redemption. We are to rest in the finished work of Christ on Calvary.

God has put some "resting places" along the way for us. Mary found a resting place at the feet of Jesus (Luke 10:39). We find another resting place as we mount up on the wings of the eagles above the storms and circumstances of life. Sometimes the resting place is a time of fellowship with a dear Christian. It may even be in a sick room.

We have a *place* of rest. "Rest in *the Lord*" (Psalm 37:7). He invites us to rest in Him. "Come unto *me*" (Matthew 11:28). He does not say "go" but "come." Resting is always *in* Him.

His rest is a *gift* to us. "I will *give* you rest" (Matthew 11:28). Too often we struggle along in our own weariness when He is entreating us to come unto Him and receive His rest.

Do you have the habit of faith that keeps your heart open toward God? Are you abiding right now in *His* rest?

Come now and I will send thee. Exodus 3:10a   **17**

Moses was chosen of God to deliver his people. He had a deep concern for them. "He went out unto his brethren, and looked on their burdens." He undertook to help them but as we so often do, he tried to do it in his own way and failed. "He looked this way and that way" (vs. 12), instead of waiting for God to lead him.

Moses had been "learned in all the wisdom of the Egyptians, and was mighty in words and in deeds" (Acts 7:22). Now he must be trained in the School of God. Someone has said, "Moses needed the Seminary of the desert to fashion him into a vessel for use." He had his degree in the School of Men but he had yet to learn his alphabet in the School of God. "God equips those He calls instead of calling those who seem to be equipped."

God took Moses away from the hustle and the bustle of people, away from the life in an Egyptian court, into the desert to prepare him for this work. There are courses in God's University which we, too, must take alone with Him. But we become so busy we fail to spend the time we should with Him.

Out on the desert Moses was prepared to be the leader of the Israelites as they left Egypt. God called Moses aside into His presence at the burning bush. It was then that He commissioned Moses. God said to him, "Come now therefore, and I will send thee" (vs. 10).

Moses still had many lessons to learn. He made many excuses. Yet he learned that it was not a question of who he was but who *God is*. "Certainly I will be with thee" (vs. 12) is sufficient assurance for anyone to be obedient to God's call.

18   *And Jesus replying said to them, Have faith in God (constantly). Mark 11:22, Amplified*

Prayer is the key that unlocks the storehouse of heaven. Hallesby said, "To pray is to let Jesus come into our needs — to open the door, giving Him access to our needs. Jesus sees our helplessness; He recognizes our complete dependence on Him. It is our helplessness that opens the door to Him and gives Him access to our needs. Hallesby also said, "Helplessness united with faith produces prayer."

In the story of the wedding of Cana in John 2 a need arose. It was a desperate situation, a need which the family could not meet. Mary, the mother of Jesus, was there. She was aware of the need and went to the one source from which help could come, the Lord Jesus. As she told Him of the need, He answered the request and performed a miracle.

Psalm 37:5 reads, "Commit thy way unto the Lord; trust also in him; and he shall bring it to pass." Mary did this. She voiced the need and He answered it. She committed the need to Him and trusted, and He brought it to pass.

Do you have a need which you cannot meet and you do not know to whom to go for help? Do you have a problem you can't solve? In your helplessness let Jesus enter into your need. The very fact that you call on Him in your helplessness indicates your faith in Him that He can meet your need. It may be a material need or it may be a spiritual need, but as you give Him access to it, it is His responsibility to answer. As you commit and trust, He will bring it to pass for you.

"You have only proved the sufficiency of God when you have asked of Him the impossible."

Simon Peter saith unto them, I go a fishing. They say unto him, We also go with thee. They went forth, and entered into a ship immediately; and that night they caught nothing. John 21:3

19

One day after Jesus' death and resurrection, the disciples were together at the Sea of Galilee. They didn't fully understand all that had happened. Their life was not the same now. As they looked at some of the fishing boats on the lake, their old fishing instinct returned. Suddenly in his usual impulsive way Peter said, "I go a fishing." The sad thing was that not only did he forget his call to be a fisher of men but he took others with him. "We also go with thee." Quickly they got into a boat and pushed out on the lake.

Eagerly they cast their nets but caught no fish. Again and again they cast their nets but caught not one single fish. Although experienced fishermen, they had no fish to show for their night's labor. Their secret of failure was in doing it without being directed by the Lord. He has said, "Without me ye can do nothing."

Disappointment and defeat followed their human efforts. Lack of success followed their self-willed efforts. Failure teaches us our own helplessness, causing us to commit our all to the Lord and rely on Him.

By morning the men were weary and defeated. Then Jesus appeared. Always He is waiting for us to come to the end of ourselves before He can use us. He instructed the men to cast their nets into the sea and this time they had many fish.

He will use us as fishers of men. If we try to serve in our own strength and efforts, the result will be failure. But directed by Him, our fishing will be productive for Him.

20 *For ye have not passed this way heretofore. Joshua 3:4b*

Today is a brand new day coming to us from the hand of God. We have not passed through it before. Berkeley translates the above verse, "When you see the ark — leave your places and follow it; so that you may know the way to go, because you have never walked this path before."

Our way or path is made up of our todays. I have personalized this verse to myself this way, "*You* have never walked this today before." Today is an "unknown day." It will have problems we have never met before. There will be new needs to be met. Today will have new trials we have not experienced. Yet today will be filled with new blessings and new joys to be received.

With what anticipation we can look forward to our days — not to the problems, trials and difficulties — but with expectation to God who has promised to be with us in the midst of our problems. He has promised, "I will never leave thee nor forsake thee" (Hebrews 13:5).

He knows and understands each moment of each day. "For we have not an high priest which cannot be touched with the feeling of our infirmities; but was in all points tempted like as we are, yet without sin" (Hebrews 4:15). He knows the steep paths, the stony places, the hot sandy stretches, the cool shady places. He will lead us according to what we are able to endure.

Each day is a new day. It is an unknown day — one through which you have not passed. But He knows the day; He has prepared it for you. This unknown day to you is known to God. He not only knows the problems but He has the solution.

Not only does He know *your* needs today, but He can meet *them*.

But with God all things are possible. Matthew 19:26a

Have you visited Heaven's Workshop? This is a "Specialty" shop, specializing in the impossible. There is nothing too small or too large to bring to this shop, for God is the "Specialist" who can do the impossible.

In Mark 10:27 we read, "And Jesus looking upon them saith, With men it is impossible, but not with God: for with God all things are possible"; man's inability, "with men it is impossible"; God's ability, "with God all things are possible."

At one place where I worked, there was a customer whose place of business was called "The Fix-it" Shop. God is the One who can "fix up" our problems and needs for us — He has not failed yet. This shop never closes; we have twenty-four hour-a-day service, seven days a week.

When we take our car to a garage for repairs, we may have to wait for service. Another job may have to be finished before beginning ours. Perhaps a part is needed and must be sent for. So in God's Workshop, sometimes we have to wait. God may have to do something in our life before He can work out the problem. Perhaps He may have to work in the life of someone else before He can complete our need. It may take time to work our problems out for us. But "God's delays are not denials." He may delay in answering in order to enlarge our capacity to receive. We look at the problem from "right now." God looks at it from Heaven — and He does the impossible for us.

Visit God's Specialty Shop today with all your needs. "God is the One who delights to do the *impossible.*"

22   *Blessed are ye that sow beside all waters.* Isaiah *32:20a*

We are engaged in a seed-sowing ministry. God's Word tells us that the seed is the Word of God. There is a blessing that comes from sowing this seed — "Blessed are *ye* that sow."

The scope of the sowing is "Beside *all* waters." "The field is the world" (Matthew 13:38). What an extensive ministry this is, one we couldn't possibly accomplish alone or even with a few helpers. We are not even beginning to keep up with the increase of population in the increase of our Gospel ministry, we are told. God needs *each one of us* today to help Him in sowing the seed that there may be a harvest of transformed lives.

We might think of it in this way. God's field is subdivided into smaller plots. He assigns a particular plot to us. We need not all serve in the same place or in the same way. To each of us is given a particular place to serve — a particular work to do. Blessed are we as we do the work He has called us to do in the place He has assigned to us.

Our field may include our homes, our families, our neighborhoods, our offices, our churches. We share in sowing the seed of the Word of God in these fields. Regardless of our particular responsibility, the purpose of our labor is to have a harvest of souls for Him.

The abundance of the harvest depends on the abundance of seed sowing. "But this I say, he which soweth sparingly shall reap also sparingly; and he which soweth bountifully shall reap also bountifully" (II Corinthians 9:6).

What about your particular plot? Have you been sowing the seed for an abundant harvest?

In the year that King Uzziah died, I saw also the **23**
Lord sitting upon a throne high and lifted up and
his train filled the temple. Isaiah 6:1

Isaiah the prophet was in the temple when he had a vision. He was allowed to look beyond the limits of his eyesight to see the Lord in all His holiness.

This happened at the time of King Uzziah's death. Uzziah had been one of Judah's great kings. At the height of his power he sinned and was smitten with leprosy from which he died. Isaiah was deeply affected by his death. It seemed that Uzziah had been a hero to him.

At the time the king died, Isaiah saw the Lord. Perhaps at the death of a loved one when our hearts are bowed down with grief, we have a fresh and deeper revelation of the Lord in His holiness. We realize that God will at such a time more completely fill our lives with His own presence.

Perhaps our vision is too filled with material things of this earth. They may have to be removed before we can see God in all His beauty.

In the midst of Isaiah's sorrow his eyes were lifted up and he saw the Lord. "For mine eyes have seen the King, the Lord of hosts" (vs. 5).

Today you may be experiencing trouble and sorrow in your life. You have a great heartache. In the midst of it right now God wants you to lift your eyes and see *Him.*

There was once a man whose eyes had been blinded for a long time. He underwent surgery in an attempt to restore his eyesight. When the bandages were being removed, it was evident that he would be able to see. He said, "Have the surgeon right here by my side. The first one I want to see is the one who has restored sight to my eyes."

What is filling our vision today? The things of earth? Or the Lord? May a new vision of God Himself be ours today.

24   *Then said I, Woe is me! for I am undone, because I am a man of unclean lips; and I dwell in the midst of a people of unclean lips.* Isaiah 6:5

Isaiah had a vision of God in all His holiness. When he saw God, he saw himself as he really was. This view of God's holiness made him conscious of his own guilt.

A seraphim took a live coal from the altar and laid it on his mouth saying, "Lo, this hath touched thy lips; and thine iniquity is taken away and thy sin purged" (vs. 7). This was a picture of the work of Jesus Christ on the cross to provide cleansing through His precious blood.

Today we need a double vision — to see God in His holiness as did Isaiah, and to see ourselves as we are. If we compare ourselves with others, we may not appear too bad, but when we come face to face with God's holiness our own goodness fades.

We realize then our need for cleansing. Though we may try various ways of earning cleansing, it will be to no avail. Only one cleanser has the power to remove sin. "The blood of Jesus Christ his Son cleanseth us from *all* sin" (I John 1:7).

A jewelry salesman noticed one day how soiled his hands were. He said, "I, of all persons must have soft, clean hands. How can I show diamonds or pearls to a customer with hands that are not clean?"

May our lives be clean that we may show forth our Precious Treasure, Jesus Christ.

Also I heard the voice of the Lord, saying, Whom shall I send, and who will go for us? Then said I, Here am I; send me. Isaiah 6:8

Isaiah had had a vision of the Lord. In the light of the holiness of God, he had a vision of his own self, in his sin and unworthiness.

There were four "C's" in Isaiah's life as a result of his vision of the Lord. 1. Conviction: "I am a man of unclean lips." 2. Cleansing: "this hath touched thy lips; thine iniquity is taken away." 3. Consecration: "Here am I; send me." 4. Commission: "Go and tell."

After he had seen the Lord and experienced His cleansing, he was ready to be called and commissioned for service. Time in God's presence makes you ready to become His messenger. Isaiah gave a simple five word response. He didn't mention to God anything about his ability or lack of it, whether he had training, what connections he had, how much money he had, or who his family was. All he said was, "Here *am* I; send *me*."

He didn't know God's complete purpose for him at first but he answered God's call by faith. Later God gave him his "marching orders." He said, "Go and tell this people."

Isaiah was called to preach to a generation of unbelieving and rebellious people who would hear and refuse to heed God's warning. Yet Isaiah fulfilled his responsibility by going.

The late J. H. Jowett told of seeing seventy Salvation Army men receive their commission for foreign service. No one knew where they were to go. But each one received his commission with a salute.

As Christians we must be ready to answer God's call for service. God is still saying, "*Whom* shall I send, and *who* will go for me?" What is *your* answer?

26   *And Noah builded an altar unto the Lord.* Genesis *8:20a*

In reading this story again not long ago, I was impressed anew with the place God had in Noah's life. I wondered how he felt as he came out of the ark. There was so much work to be done — no home, no crop, nothing. He must have wondered just what to do first. We read that he built an altar to the Lord.

How many times I have looked about and seen so much to do that I have wondered just where to start or what to do first.

We can learn a great lesson from Noah. Before he did anything, before he put up a tent and tried to begin life over again on the earth, he paused, built an altar to God and offered a sacrifice to Him. He paused to worship God, to love Him and thank Him for the safety of the ark.

We read that the sacrifice was a sweet smelling savor and God was pleased. (God is always pleased when He is put in the rightful place in a life — a place of pre-eminence.) Then Noah began to make a new home for himself and his family.

How we need to learn this lesson in our lives. We need to put God first, giving Him the pre-eminent place. Also, we need to take time to pause at our "altar" of worship and praise, communing and fellowshiping with Him.

It is told that one day Abraham Lincoln kept a cabinet member waiting for some time. As he entered the room, the President excused himself for his delay, and then said, "The affairs of state are so grave, I had to spend an extra hour today in prayer."

Is that what we do, or do we cut down on our prayer time when we are busy?

Now the Lord of peace himself give you peace always by all means. The Lord be with you all. II Thessalonians 3:16

27

Several times I have made a tour of some plant or factory. In certain sections where equipment was in operation, the noise was "ear-splitting." One couldn't hear what was being said. He could scarcely even hear himself think. Suddenly one left that part of the plant and went into a room where there was no noise. What a contrast between the two places.

Today we seem to be afraid of silence. In many homes the stereo, radio or television are kept going all the time. Every minute must be filled with some sound.

There is little peace in the turbulent world of today. But there *is* peace for today. There is peace *for you and me,* for the Lord of Peace Himself has promised to *give* it to us. "He is our peace" (Ephesians 2:14).

His peace is available to us at *all* times, in any circumstance or situation, in any need. Why then do we not have this peace? Perhaps it is because we have failed to accept the *"by all means."* We may not like some of the means He uses to deliver His peace to us. It may be through a heartache, an illness or in financial difficulties. We fail to receive His peace, for we are rebelling against His way of giving it to us.

"Now may the Lord of peace Himself grant you His peace [the peace of His kingdom] at all times and in all ways — under all circumstances and conditions, whatever comes. The Lord [be] with you all" (Amplified).

His peace comes to us through His presence. We can be filled with the *peace* of God as we are filled with the *presence* of God.

28 *And the vessel that he made of clay was marred in the hand of the potter: so he made it again another vessel, as seemed good to the potter to make it.*
Jeremiah 18:4

Clay vessels have been formed on a potter's wheel for many centuries. The clay is prepared and put through a number of processes in the making of vessels.

A vessel may be marred in the process of being made. Perhaps all the impurities were not removed or a piece of foreign material in the clay didn't yield to the work being done on the wheel. The potter would not throw it away but would put it back on the wheel to be made again.

In Isaiah 64:8 we are compared to clay. "But now, O Lord — we are the clay and thou art the potter, and we are the work of thy hand." He puts our earthen clay lives on the potter's wheel to make us vessels of purpose for Him. As we yield to His hand, He will fashion us into His chosen vessel. "As the clay is in the potter's hand, so are ye in mine hand" (vs. 6).

Sometimes we spoil His plan. Some bit of a foreign element gets into our clay lives and doesn't yield to His hand. He doesn't despair of us. But because He loves us so dearly, He puts us back on the wheel again. "He made it *again* another vessel."

There was once a beautiful window in a cathedral. Many came to admire its loveliness. One day during a fierce storm it was shattered. Someone carefully gathered together all the broken fragments and put them away. A man offered to take the broken pieces and remake the window. Some time later he returned with a window which, though made out of the broken fragments, was even more beautiful than the former window.

Arise and eat: because the journey is too great for thee. I Kings 19:7b

Elijah had been God's man of the hour. He had been used as a man of prayer. When he prayed for the rain to be stayed, it was. Then he prayed for rain and it came. He prayed at Mt. Carmel and the fire came down. But now he was frightened of Queen Jezebel and fled for his life. "And when he saw *that*, he arose, and went for his life" (vs. 3). He had looked away from God to the circumstances and had become discouraged and depressed. He came and sat under a juniper tree. He wanted to die. "And said, It is enough; now, O Lord, take away my life" (vs. 4).

It is good that God doesn't always answer the way we pray. God did not grant Elijah's request. His physical strength and nervous energy had been overtaxed so He gave him sleep.

God sent a sympathetic, ministering angel who said, "Arise and eat; because the journey is too great for thee." He was refreshed and revived from food and sleep. The strength we get from the food God gives is always enough for our need. Elijah traveled in that strength for forty days.

Into our lives today come times of discouragement. We, too, begin to look out at the circumstances instead of up to God. And we may even despair of life as Elijah did. Also we may feel that we have lost our purpose in life. Nothing seems worthwhile; no one understands.

But even then there is encouragement for us. God will refresh and revive us. We can experience what the Psalmist wrote about, "But thou, O Lord, art a shield for me; my glory, and the *lifter up* of mine head" (Psalm 3:3).

30   *And after the earthquake a fire; but the Lord was not in the fire; and after the fire a still small voice.*
I Kings 19:12

Elijah still had some lessons to learn. He had to learn the importance of being still and quiet that he might hear the voice of God speak to him. Someone has said, "Not in the college or academy but in the silence of the soul do we learn the greater lessons of life; and quiet hearts are rare."

After being nourished and refreshed by God, he went to Mount Horeb. There he lodged in a cave. But God still knew just where he was. He said to Elijah, "What doest thou *here?*" We can go no place where we are hidden from God.

God told him to go and stand on the mount. Then came the roar of the winds; the shaking of the earthquake; the heat of the fire. The wind, the earthquake and the fire revealed the power of God. But He did not reveal Himself to Elijah in these.

Finally it became quiet and in that moment came the still small voice of God. Elijah was in the Holy Presence of God. He covered his head with his mantle and bowed his heart in worship.

As God met Elijah in his hour of need so will He meet us. We, too, must learn to be quiet. Our ears need to be tuned to hear the still, small voice that leads the soul into the quiet presence of God.

Bishop Moule said, "Even if you have not a long time to spend in the morning with your God, hem it with quietness."

"In quietness and confidence shall be your strength, and ye would not" (Isaiah 30:15).

Be strong in the Lord and in the power of his might.
Ephesians 6:10

31

The Christian life is a warfare. We are soldiers in the army of the Lord. We are assured of *power* for the conflict. "Be strong — not in yourselves but in the Lord, in the power of His boundless resource" (Phillips).

"We are to be strong in the Lord to be strong for Him." The word strong here has the meaning of "empowered." We cannot make ourselves strong but God can empower us. Only in the Lord is there strength adequate to meet the demands of the Christian life. Our strength isn't sufficient to fight the enemy. Only God can do this. We are to be strong *in the Lord.*

We are in *peril* of the enemy who is strong. We are not fighting against human strength but against principalities and powers.

God has provided an armor for *protection.* It is strong enough to meet this foe. Christ Himself is our armor and gives complete protection.

We are to take the whole armor and then to stand. Someone has said, "We are to stand in God-reliance but sometimes we are self-reliant instead."

Then we are to be *prayerful* at all times in the battle. This is a spiritual battle and can be won on our knees. God is our Commanding Officer. We must keep in touch with Him for our orders, for briefing, for His battle plan, for strength in prayer. Chrysostom said, "Prayer has bridled the rage of lions, extinguished wars, appeased the elements, expelled demons, burst the chains of death, assuaged disease, rescued cities from destruction, stayed the sun in its course and arrested the progress of the thunderbolt."

"Pray at all times — on every occasion, in every season — in the Spirit, with all [manner of] prayer and entreaty" (vs. 18, Amplified).

1   *Charge them that are rich in this world, that they be not highminded, nor trust in uncertain riches, but in the living God, who giveth us richly all things to enjoy; that they do good, that they be rich in good works, ready to distribute, willing to communicate. I Timothy 6:17, 18*

How transient are the riches of this world! There is no permanence in them. They can be swept away in a moment of time. Even though material things are for this life only, yet we spend much time and energy accumulating them.

Riches in themselves are not evil, but it is exceedingly important that we give them the proper place in our lives. Our trust must not be in riches but in the *living* God. He is the source of all our blessings.

He is a *giving* God, ready and willing to give "us richly all things to enjoy." His giving is specific and personal — He "giveth *us.*" Have you ever paused to consider just how rich you are? Take time to list ALL the blessings God has given you, both material and spiritual. I am sure you will be weary before you have completed the list.

How can we enjoy to the fullest all that God has given us? Does not our greatest joy come from sharing with others? As a little girl I experienced a joy I have never forgotten. One Sunday evening at church a man gave me a nickel. Since our family had very little money, I was delighted. As I walked home with a little friend, something she said caused me to give the nickel to her. I shall never forget the joy in my heart as I shared with her what had been given to me.

Everything we have is a sacred trust from God. We are not to hoard it, but to be "ready to distribute, willing to communicate."

Let us run with patience the race that is set before us, looking unto Jesus the author and finisher of our faith. Hebrews 12:1c, 2a

2

Paul often uses figures borrowed from various Greek games played in the amphitheatre. In the above verse of Scripture, for example, he likens the Christian life to a race. As the race begins, the runner fixes his eyes upon the goal. Then he concentrates on the track and the race to be won. It is not how others run but how he runs that counts. He must put aside anything that might hinder. It is by failing to concentrate on the race before him and losing sight of the goal that he loses the race. It is not the cheering crowd that is important.

Christians, we are in a race — the race of life. The goal of our race is Jesus Christ Himself. The apostle says, "I press toward the mark for the prize of the high calling of God in Christ Jesus." We must keep our eyes fixed on that goal, "simply fixing our gaze upon Jesus, the author and finisher of our faith." The Author is with us at the beginning of the race; the Finisher will be there to greet us at the end of it. The success of our race depends on the direction of our eyes.

The skipper of a yacht was asked if he, an American, thought the scenery of the Bay of Naples was beautiful. "Yes, it's beautiful, but when you're out there to race, you don't have time to admire the scenery," he answered.

There are obstacles along our way. We must lay aside all the weights that may hinder. We must train regularly. We must exercise daily as we read the Word, pray and share Jesus Christ with others.

"So run, that ye may obtain" (I Corinthians 9:24).

3   *He saith to him again . . . Simon, son of Jonas, lovest thou me? John 21:16*

In this Scripture portion we read of the miraculous draught of fishes and Jesus' revelation of Himself to the disciples. After breakfast Jesus said to Peter, "Lovest thou me more than these?" He used the strongest word for "love" — "unselfish love." It is the word used for "God" in the expression "God is love." The Lord was saying to Peter, "Do you have unselfish love?" Peter replied, "Thou knowest that I love thee." He used the word meaning "natural affection." Three times Jesus put this question to Peter. The last time He used the same word that Peter had used. The Lord was asking him, "Do you really love Me with your natural affection? Are you sure of that?" I can see Peter lift his eyes and hear him say tenderly, "Lord, You know all things; You know that I love You. Even though I have failed You, I still love You."

Today the Lord is looking for those who love Him. What would be your answer if the Lord asked you today, "Lovest thou Me? Do you love Me more than anyone or anything?" We need to search our hearts to see how genuinely and deeply we love Him. Is ours a love from the lips or is it a love from our hearts that gives all to Him and is willing to do anything for Him?

A young man once wrote a letter to his sweetheart. In endearing terms he assured her that he would climb the highest mountain, swim the deepest sea, or brave the fiercest storm for her, so deep was his love. At the end of the letter he added, "I'll be over Saturday night if it doesn't rain."

As His love fills your heart and life the things of this world fade into insignificance and you say with Peter, "Lord, Thou knowest that I love *Thee*."

. . . that they may adorn the doctrine of God our Saviour in all things. Titus 2:10

4

"To adorn" means "to add beauty to something." A house may be adorned to make it more attractive. Exactly the right frame is carefully selected to display a beautiful picture to advantage. A diamond may be placed in a lovely setting to enhance its beauty.

We have the privilege and joy of speaking forth the Gospel. But reality and beauty are added to it when people see it set forth in our lives. Henry Drummond said, "The best evidence of Christianity is a Christian."

When one selects a diamond ring the diamond is the most important consideration. Yet one is also careful to select a beautiful setting that will display the stone in all its loveliness. So the Christian's life should be a setting which will display the loveliness of the person of Jesus Christ. In I Peter 3:3 and 4 we read, "Whose adorning . . . let it be . . . the ornament of a meek and quiet spirit, which is in the sight of God of great price." What more precious privilege could we have than to adorn the doctrine of God our Saviour? Our lives can be beautiful settings to show forth the beauty of our lovely Lord.

It is easy to adorn the doctrine on days when everything goes smoothly. It is not difficult on days when we feel well. But what about the days when problems arise, when our lives are shaken by hard blows, or when annoyances distress us? We read in this verse of Scripture that we are to adorn the doctrine *"in all things."*

What kind of "setting" are you for Jesus Christ?

5   *For ever, O Lord, thy word is settled in heaven.*
Psalm 119:89

We live in a changing world. Because of the insecurity all around us we need a strong support. How reassuring it is to know that God's Word is settled, steadfast and unfailing; that it is always fresh, always new, always up-to-date.

David had been in distress and in his discouragement he turned to the Word. In his time of trial he experienced the comfort of the Word that was "settled in heaven."

Our God is unchanging. "Accordingly God also, in His desire to show more convincingly and beyond doubt, to those who were to inherit the promise, the unchangeableness of His purpose and plan, intervened (mediated) with an oath" (Hebrews 6:17, Amplified).

Since God is unchanging, His Word, too, is unchanging. "This was so that by two unchangeable things [His promise and His oath], in which it is impossible for God ever to prove false or deceive us, we who have fled [to Him] for refuge might have mighty indwelling strength and strong encouragement to grasp and hold fast the hope appointed for us and set before [us]" (Hebrews 6:18, Amplified). Our Lord has promised, "Heaven and earth shall pass away, but my words shall not pass away" (Matthew 24:35).

Not one word of the Book has had to be altered; not a prophecy has ever failed. It is the Miracle Book. It is the one and only Word in which we can rest our destiny for time and eternity.

This same unchanging Word is available for us today. God's Word will uphold us day by day in every situation and need. We can claim His promises one by one, day by day, for situation after situation.

It has been said, "We can ease our aching heads on the pillow of God's promises and then rise up stronger."

As for God, his way is perfect. Psalm 18:30a **6**

Today our hearts can be encouraged as we recognize the truth of this comforting verse. We may be wondering about certain things that have happened to us. Our plans may have been completely changed. Sorrow may have clouded our skies. We may be wondering what is best for us. We may not know which way to turn. But we can be sure that whether we experience joy or sorrow, sunshine or clouds, sickness or health, want or plenty, God's way for us *is* perfect. We cannot doubt that. He sees the end from the beginning. He sees the pattern He is working out in us. We may not understand why, but He does. We can know that He makes no mistakes. We can say, not with a sigh but with a song, "God! — perfect is His way" (Berkeley).

Not only is God's way perfect, but He makes our way perfect. "It is God that . . . *maketh my* way perfect" (vs. 32). Our way must be brought into conformity to His. A "making process" is necessary to perfect His way in our lives. It is this "making process" against which we rebel.

A woman was complaining about the many trials and troubles in her life. She said to someone, "I wish I had never been made." "My dear," replied the friend, "you are not yet made. You are only being made and you are quarreling with God's processes."

As we yield ourselves to Him, He will complete the process of making our way perfect. "For my thoughts are not your thoughts, neither are your ways my ways, saith the Lord. For as the heavens are higher than the earth, so are my ways higher than your ways, and my thoughts than your thoughts" (Isaiah 55:8, 9).

7   *For which cause we faint not; but though our outward man perish, yet the inward man is renewed day by day. II Corinthians 4:16*

Today's world has made us extremely age-conscious. As we become older, it becomes increasingly difficult to secure employment. Regardless of the worker's capabilities or training, his age seems to be his primary qualification. Many companies automatically retire their employees when they reach a certain age.

Paul began to feel the increasing weight of his infirmities as he grew older. The beatings and shipwrecks he had endured had taken their toll. He knew his outer man was weakening. Yet he realized that inwardly he was constantly being renewed.

David also experienced this renewal of strength. He said, "For by thee I have run through a troop; and by my God have I leaped over a wall" (Psalm 18:29). This wasn't the kind of strength acquired by eating the proper cereals and vegetables or by taking vitamins. This kind of strength came from God's Word. "Strengthen thou me according unto thy word," was the request of the Psalmist (Psalm 119:28). This kind of strength came through prayer. "My voice shalt thou hear in the morning, O Lord," he said (Psalm 5:3a).

In our own lives we experience the weakening of the outer man. What a comfort to know that we, too, can be renewed inwardly! Dr. Scroggie said, "The body is the tent; the soul the tenant. The tenant continues after the tent has blown down." It is a real and glorious triumph to be spiritually renewed. "Though our outward man perish [is outwardly weakened], yet the inward man is renewed [inwardly strengthened]."

Spiritual renewal comes as we wait on the Lord. We go into His presence weary and tired. We leave it refreshed and strengthened. "They that wait upon the Lord shall renew their strength; they shall mount up with wings as eagles; they shall run, and not be weary; and they shall walk, and not faint" (Isaiah 40:31).

For our light affliction, which is but for a moment,
worketh for us a far more exceeding and eternal
weight of glory. II Corinthians 4:17

8

Christians are not promised ease and comfort; they cannot expect to sail smoothly through life.

Paul wrote from experience when he spoke of affliction. Because the inner man was being renewed daily and because he kept his eye on the final goal, he spoke of his affliction as "light." He said, "We are perplexed because we don't know why things happen as they do, but we don't give up and quit. We are hunted down, but God never abandons us. We get knocked down, but we get up again and keep going" (II Corinthians 4:8, 9, Living Letters).

Our present troubles may seem heavy. We may sometimes wonder why we have so many afflictions. In the light of eternity, however, they are only for a moment. They are *working* for us an eternal weight of glory.

James writes, "Count it all joy when ye fall into divers temptations" or "trials of any sort," as the Amplified translates it (James 1:2). *"Count"* it all joy. You may ask, "Are we to count all of the trials joy?" Yes. Trial itself isn't joy, but it is working eternal glory for us. In heaven we will realize that our light·afflictions were not only preparing glory for us but preparing us for glory. The disappointments and difficulties will all be forgotten when we see Him face to face.

9 *While we look not at the things which are seen, but at the things which are not seen: for the things which are seen are temporal; but the things which are not seen are eternal.* II Corinthians 4:18

Verses 16 through 18 of this chapter have become very real and precious to me. It is the portion of Scripture which the pastor used at the funeral service of my husband.

Since then I have been re-evaluating my life in the light of the seen and the unseen, the temporal and the eternal. I know we were putting emphasis on eternal things in our life together, yet our lives were more deeply rooted in material things than I realized.

Paul had the proper spiritual perspective. In the midst of his light afflictions he looked away from the material world to the eternal. He saw all of his troubles and trials in the light of eternity. This removed the stress and strain from his life.

We are told that after looking at something closely for a long period of time we should rest our eyes by looking away to the far horizon. As Christians we find this is true also with regard to our spiritual eyes. When we look constantly at our afflictions they become magnified. We need to shift our spiritual gaze from the material things which are seen and focus our sight on the eternal things which are not seen. As we view our trials in the light of eternity we realize that all of our problems are working a "weight of glory" for us.

If those who have gone on could speak to us today, I am sure they would say, "It is worth it all." One moment of glory will outweigh a lifetime of suffering. Someone wisely prayed, "Help us to look with eyes of faith at the things which are unseen in order to better evaluate the things which are seen."

When thou goest, thy steps shall not be straitened;
and when thou runnest, thou shalt not stumble.
Proverbs 4:12

10

Before us lies the path of life. God is interested in the walk of His children. He has planned our path from beginning to end, but He doesn't show us all of it at one time. We would like to see it clearly before us to the very end, but this is not God's way. We are to take only a step at a time.

It is well that we cannot see more than a step at a time. If we could, perhaps we would be so filled with fear and dread that we would turn back. We might become discouraged and give up. If we saw something wonderful ahead, we would perhaps hurry to reach it and thus miss the lessons that God intended for us.

All God asks us to do is to take the next step by faith. In the Hebrew this verse can be translated, "As thou goest step by step, the way shall be opened up before thee." As He opens the way, we can move forward with Him step by step. Problems arise when we set off on paths of our own making. But God waits for us to come back into step with Him.

A man once related one of his most rewarding experiences. As he was about to cross a crowded street in a great city, a little child looked up into his face, put her tiny hand in his great one and said, "Take me across the street to the other side." He said, "It was a great honor to take that trusting child through the traffic across the street."

He who goes God's way must keep God's pace. Step by step, moment by moment, our loving God walks with us.

11 *I have told you these things that My joy and delight may be in you, and that your joy and gladness may be full measure and complete and overflowing. John 15:11, Amplified*

As we go about day by day, how much joy do we see on the faces of those around us? Not much, do we?

One day my sister-in-law called me. She said, "As I was riding the bus today, I saw you walking along the street. You looked as though you had lost your last friend. Is something wrong?" I realized then how closely we are observed. Now as I leave home I pray that my face may reflect the joy in my heart. Joy is contagious.

There is one *source* of real joy — one place where we can go for daily joy. It is to the Lord Himself. Scripture says, "*Happy* is that *people,* whose God is the Lord" (Psalm 144:15). Joy — His joy — is available. But we must draw upon it from its source. "In thy presence is *fulness* of *joy,*" the Psalmist declares (Psalm 16:11).

The life of our Lord provides an example of joy. We read in Hebrews, "Looking unto Jesus the author and finisher of our faith; who for the *joy* that was set before *Him* endured the cross, despising the shame, and is set down at the right hand of the throne of God" (Hebrews 12:2).

The *joy* of the Lord brings us *strength*. "The joy of the Lord *is your* strength," Nehemiah 8:10 tells us.

His *presence* gives us a joy beyond words. Peter says, "Without having seen Him you love Him; though you do not [even] now see Him you believe in Him, and exult and thrill with inexpressible and glorious (triumphant, heavenly) *joy*" (I Peter 1:8, Amplified).

The joy of the Lord in our hearts is not to be bottled up but is to overflow into our lives so that others may be blessed.

Ask of me, and I shall give thee the heathen for thine inheritance. Psalm 2:8

12

In this Psalm, God the Father, the Son and the Holy Spirit are speaking together. In verse 8 the Father speaks to the Son, saying, "Ask of me, and I shall give thee the heathen [or the unbelieving] for thine inheritance."

Today we have a share in the work the Father gave to the Son. We read in II Peter 3:9, "The Lord . . . is not willing that any should perish, but that all should come to repentance." We, too, are to come to Him in prayer, asking Him for the unbelieving. We are to ask Him to bring others into a personal relationship with Jesus Christ. This is conditional — "Ask of me [our part], and I shall give thee [God's part]." Are you asking today? How many do you have on your prayer list?

Perhaps you need to ask God to give you a renewed and enlarged vision of those about you who need spiritual help — of the many around the world who do not know Jesus Christ. "Where there is no vision, the people perish" (Proverbs 29:18).

A few years ago several missionaries in Korea decided to meet together at noon each day for prayer, asking God to bless their work. At the end of a month they saw no results, so one of them suggested that they discontinue their prayer meeting and pray at home. Does this sound familiar? However, the others were convinced that they should continue to pray even more faithfully, which they did for several months. Finally, the Spirit of God moved in their midst, and many lives were transformed. One of the missionaries said, "It paid well to spend several months in prayer, for when God began to work, more was accomplished in half a day than all of the missionaries could have accomplished in half a year."

As we pray, asking for the unbelieving, God will work in hearts, drawing them to Himself.

13   *All scripture is given by inspiration of God, and is profitable for doctrine, for reproof, for correction, for instruction in righteousness: that the man of God may be perfect, throughly furnished unto all good works. II Timothy 3:16, 17*

The Bible is given to us by God as His Book of Instructions, showing us His plan for us and how it is to be accomplished in our lives.

Paul writes that the Word is profitable, "teaching us what is true" (Living Letters). Many people today are seeking the truth about God. Only the Bible teaches this truth. Jesus said, "I am the . . . truth" (John 14:6).

It is profitable for reproof or conviction, "to make us realize what is wrong in our lives" (Living Letters). It also corrects us or "straightens us out." Occasionally we hear someone say, "I am going to set him straight." As we meditate in the Word, it will reveal God's way before us and "straighten out" our lives so that they conform to God's will. Phillips says that the Bible is profitable "for re-setting the direction of a man's life."

God's Word gives us our instructions for "living right." Do you desire to know the right way to live? Go to God's Word. Do you want to know how to please Him? Seek the answer in His Word.

His Word also equips us for every good work. "It is God's way of making us well-prepared at every point, fully equipped to do good to everyone" (Living Letters).

We must know God's Word to become spiritually mature. The King James Version reads, "That the man of God be made perfect, throughly furnished." A godly pastor whom I knew used to say, "That we may be furnished through and through." As we saturate ourselves through and through with the Word, we become equipped through and through for every good work.

And a certain woman . . . when she had heard of Jesus, came in the press behind, and touched his garment. Mark 5:25, 27

14

People were crowding around Jesus. In their midst was a woman who had a great physical need. She had suffered many years and was continually growing worse. She had spent all she had in a desperate search for relief; the physicians had done all they could for her. Humanly speaking, all help was gone.

When this suffering woman heard that Jesus was near by, hope welled up in her heart. Here was a new source of help for her. She knew the Master could help. She said, "If I but touch His clothes, I shall be healed." Her faith in Him was great.

There was a great crowd of people thronging about the Saviour. But quietly this woman slipped through the crowd and touched the hem of His garment. To her great joy, she realized that her body had been made well. Suddenly Jesus said, "Who touched my clothes?" Trembling, the woman came and told Him the truth. "He said, Daughter, *thy faith* hath made thee whole." He wanted her to know that the healing power was not in His garments but was the result of *her faith* in *Him*.

The woman did more than exercise her faith; she took action. She reached out in faith and touched the One who could meet her need. There were many people thronging about Jesus. But she was the one who touched Him by faith, and her need was met.

Perhaps you have a desperate need as this woman did. Jesus is willing to meet your need as He met hers. You need such faith in Him as she had. Faith has been defined as "knowing Jesus well enough to trust Him." Then you must add action to your faith. Reach out now and touch the One who can meet *all* your needs.

You're just a touch of faith away from Him.

15

Nay, in all these things we are more than conquerors through him that loved us. Romans 8:37

A conqueror is one who has overcome, one who has triumphed and become a victor. In our Christian lives we can be conquerors, overcomers, victors — nay, we can be more than conquerors.

To conquer is to gain the victory over our foes. To be more than conquerors is to learn from our foes lessons that could not be learned in any other way, lessons so valuable that we are glad the battle came. We become more than conquerors by making the battle serve a good purpose in our lives. Our adversity will then be turned to our advantage.

Day-by-day life brings tribulation, trials, troubles. The sphere of our conquest is stated in the phrase *"all* these things." We get our eyes on "all these things" and begin to go down in defeat. But God has promised a "more than conquering" victory in "all these things" — not in spite of them but in the midst of them. We can rise up victorious and triumphant time after time.

You may conquer as you patiently endure a storm in your life. But you are more than a conqueror as you rise above the storm in radiant victory and triumph. A great sorrow may come into your life. You may accept it as God's will and become a conqueror. Or you may seek to draw closer to God through it and learn to know Him better that your heartache may enable you to be a blessing to someone else. Thus your tears turn to triumph and you are more than a conqueror. The secret of being more than a conqueror is through *Him* — the One who loved us.

"But thanks be to God, which giveth us the victory" (I Corinthians 15:57).

Beloved, think it not strange concerning the fiery trial which is to try you, as though some strange thing happened unto you. I Peter 4:12

16

Many of the early Christians experienced great suffering. Peter reminded them that suffering had a purpose and would eventually end in glory. Therefore, they could rejoice in it.

Down through the years Christians have been beset with trials. We may wonder why; we do not understand the reason. But Peter wrote that trials are not unusual. We are not to think it strange that they come. He says, "Don't be bewildered or surprised when you go through the fiery trials ahead, for this is no strange unusual thing that is going to happen to you" (I Peter 4:12, Living Letters).

Trials are a proving ground for testing us. Therefore it is extremely important how we react to them. It has been said, "The man of God is not perfected except by trial." We may murmur and complain. We may indulge in self-pity. Bitterness may creep in. But if we let God have *His* way in the trial, He will use it for His purpose and His glory.

A story is told of a conversation between the gravel walk and the bed of mignonette. "You smell delightfully fragrant," said the gravel walk to the mignonette one day. "We have been trodden on," said the mignonette. The gravel walk answered, "Treading on me produces no sweetness. I only become harder as I am trodden on." "Oh," said the mignonette, "the secret is that we are crushed and bruised. Thus we give forth the sweet perfume you smell."

Trials sometimes embitter and harden. However, if we allow God to have His way in the trials, we become mellow and sweeter through them. Through the crushing experiences our lives are filled with the fragrance of His presence.

17   *With my whole heart have I sought thee: O let me not wander from thy commandments. Psalm 119:10*

A boy was applying for a job. The employer who was interviewing him said, "I suppose you have many outside interests and hobbies that are even more important to you than your work. You are probably interested in baseball, cars, and other things boys enjoy." "Yes, sir," replied the lad. "I like baseball. When I play it, I play it for all I'm worth. But when I am here, I'll be all here. I'm not big enough to be divided." He was given the position.

If we want to succeed in business we must put our whole heart into it. If we want to achieve top honors in any field it will cost us our time and effort. Our whole life must be dedicated to it.

Isn't it even more necessary to give ourselves wholly to God and His work? The Psalmist says that He gave God his undivided attention: "With my *whole* heart have I sought thee" (Psalm 119:10); "I cried with my *whole* heart" (vs. 145a); "I will keep thy precepts with my *whole* heart" (vs. 69). Whether he was seeking God, crying out for help or keeping God's precepts, he did it with *all* his heart.

Do we seek *Him* in His Word? We need to consider whether we merely read it casually or whether we search it word by word, seeking *Him* in it with our whole heart.

Do we seek *Him* in prayer? Do we pause until our hearts are quieted in His presence? Is our attention given wholeheartedly to Him or are we thinking only of what we are going to ask of Him?

Do we seek *His* will or our own? Someone has said that sometimes by our manner of life we are saying, "*my* will be done."

As we seek *Him* with our *whole* heart in the Word and in prayer, we will truly *love* Him with our whole heart.

Open thou mine eyes, that I may behold wondrous **18**
things out of thy law. Psalm 119:18

As I read God's Word I find in it many precious gems. Each morning it is such a joy to open His Book, read a few verses or a chapter, and ask Him to give me something new, fresh and precious for that very day. Sometimes it is a new thought from some very familiar portion. At other times it is a verse tucked away in a chapter that I have never particularly noticed. But, oh, how it sparkles and shines with new meaning as it opens up to me!

As a miner goes into the mine digging for ore, so we can go to God's Word each day to dig out some precious jewel or gem, some treasure or nugget with which we can enrich our lives that day.

"Uncover mine eyes and I will look — wonders out of thy law," is the literal rendering of this verse. The last phrase is said to be a kind of exclamation made by the Psalmist after the covering had been removed from his eyes. God is ready to give us the treasures of His Word if we but ask Him.

"But as it is written, Eye hath not seen, nor ear heard, neither have entered into the heart of man, the things which God hath prepared for them that love him. But God hath revealed them unto us by his Spirit: for the Spirit searcheth all things, yea, the deep things of God" (I Corinthians 2:9, 10).

19 *Let us make a little chamber, I pray thee, on the wall; and let us set for him there a bed, and a table, and a stool, and a candlestick: and it shall be, when he cometh to us, that he shall turn in thither.*
II Kings 4:10

The above verse was spoken by a Shunammite woman to her husband. We know very little about her. In fact, we do not even know her name. *But* we do know that she made room in her home for the prophet of God, Elisha. Her faith and love for God prompted her to build an extra room where His servant could stay. It was a simple room, but provided with the necessities for his comfort. Someone has said that she was "running a boarding house for God."

What about the "room" of your life? Is it so furnished that God will feel at home in it? Let us consider the importance of the furniture this woman placed in the "prophet's chamber."

First, a bed is mentioned. This speaks to us of rest. How important to have "rest" in our lives! Our rest is "in the Lord." In *Him* we rest for our salvation. In *Him* we rest for our daily living. Is the room of your life furnished with *His rest?*

A table was in the room, indicating the importance of food. God's Word provides food for our lives — bread, milk, meat. This is His way of nourishing us spiritually.

Next a stool is mentioned. This suggests the humble place at His feet, where we learn of Him. Mary found this place, as she sat at His feet, hearing His Word: Have you?

A candlestick is also mentioned. The Light of the World must be kept shining brightly within us that His light may shine *out* to others.

Is your life a chamber furnished for God's use? Are you resting in Him day by day, feeding on His Word daily? Are you sitting at His feet, learning more about Him? Is your life shining for Him where He has placed you? Does He feel at home in your life?

May our lives truly be chambers indwelt by God and furnished for His use.

What is the Almighty, that we should serve him? and what profit should we have, if we pray unto him? Job 21:15

20

All of us are interested in profit or loss, whether it be in the business we own or in our personal affairs. When a business begins to lose money, the owner analyzes it to find the cause. He changes methods; he cuts costs; he does everything possible to remedy the situation. He cannot operate very long if his business continues to suffer financial loss.

Have you ever stopped to consider the profit and loss in your prayer life? Let us consider what God's Word says about loss in prayer. First, we do not profit from prayer because we do not ask. "Ye have not, because ye ask not" (James 4:2). Second, we ask wrongly. "Ye ask, and receive not, because ye ask amiss" (James 4:3). Next, sin in our lives brings loss in prayer. "If I regard iniquity in my heart, the Lord will not hear me" (Psalm 66:18). "Behold, the Lord's hand is not shortened, that it cannot save; neither his ear heavy, that it cannot hear: but your iniquities have separated between you and your God, and your sins have hid his face from you, that he will not hear" (Isaiah 59:1, 2).

We can turn to the Word of God for assurance that there can be profit in our prayer life. "The effectual fervent prayer of a righteous man availeth much" (James 5:16). "If ye shall ask any thing in my name, I will do it" (John 14:14). "Call unto me, and I will answer thee, and shew thee great and mighty things, which thou knowest not" (Jeremiah 33:3). There is great profit in prayer.

"Prayer doesn't need proof; it needs practice."

21   *Yea, the sparrow hath found an house, and the swallow a nest for herself, where she may lay her young, even thine altars, O Lord of hosts, my King, and my God. Psalm 84:3*

Both sparrows and swallows are mentioned in this verse. Usually sparrows are considered of little value. Jesus said, "Are not two sparrows sold for a farthing?" (Matthew 10:29a). But in Luke 12:6a we read, "Are not five sparrows sold for two farthings?" When four sparrows were purchased, an extra one was added without charge.

Without God, we, too, are of no value. "For I know that in me (that is, in my flesh) dwelleth no good thing" (Romans 7:18a). Yet we are valuable to God — so valuable that He provided redemption for us. We may be as poor, worthless sparrows, yet we are the objects of God's love and grace.

We are told that the swallow is one of the most restless birds. It keeps moving most of the time, is never still. So, too, without Christ we are restless. We have no real rest apart from Him.

Altars (plural) are mentioned in this verse. In the Old Testament worship there were two altars. First was the brazen altar, a picture of the work of Christ on the cross. As the little sparrow found "rest" at the altar of God, so we find the "rest of salvation" at God's altar. Our salvation is complete, not in what we do, but in receiving what has been done for us. "While we were yet sinners, Christ died for us" (Romans 5:8b).

There was also the golden altar from which arose the sweet fragrance of incense to God. This altar speaks of Christ and His constant ministry of intercession for us. He who died for me now lives to intercede for me and to present my every need before God. As the swallow found rest at the altar, so we can take our burdens and cares to our great Intercessor and leave them with Him. From Him comes the rest we need for living day by day.

"Be still and rest in the Lord; wait for Him, and patiently stay yourself upon Him" (Psalm 37:7, Amplified).

. . . appoint them every one to his service and to **22**
his burden. Numbers 4:19
. . . to serve, and for burdens. Numbers 4:24

In this chapter we are told that various tribes were assigned certain responsibilities in taking down the tabernacle and setting it up again on their march through the wilderness. Aaron and his sons were to appoint them to their service and to their burden.

Christian service is God-appointed, not man-chosen. God has a place for us to serve, and blessing comes only when we are in that place. Someone has said, "If we are in the wrong place, the right place for us is empty."

It is most important for us to be in God's appointed place of service. This service will not be the same for each of us, and not all of us will serve in the same place. But God will give us our special appointments.

Along with this "God-appointed" service comes a "'God-imposed" burden. This does not mean that we are to be burdened with the cares of service, but there is a burden that comes with God-appointed service: it is the burden we carry on our hearts for a needy world. The Lord gives us compassion for those who are without hope. It has been said, "Intercessory prayer might be defined as 'loving our neighbors on our knees'."

Today there are many who do not want to assume Christian responsibility. They want to serve when it is convenient for them, or when such service can be fitted into their own plans.

There is a God-appointed place of service for you. Are you in it? Are you carrying a heart-burden? Are you an intercessor?

23

I will sing a new song unto thee, O God: upon a psaltery and an instrument of ten strings will I sing praises unto thee. Psalm 144:9

At Thanksgiving time we are especially reminded to take time to praise God. We have ten-stringed instruments with which to do it.

One night at a prayer meeting an old man prayed, "Lord, we will praise Thee with our instruments of ten strings." People in the service wondered what the ten strings were. He prayed on. "We will praise Thee with our eyes by looking only unto Thee. We will praise Thee with our ears by listening only to Thy voice. We will praise Thee with our hands by working in Thy service. We will praise Thee with our feet by running in the way of Thy commandments. We will praise Thee with our tongues by bearing testimony of Thy loving-kindness. We will praise Thee with our hearts by loving only Thee."

We can praise God best by placing our ten-stringed instruments in His hands and allowing Him to play His melody of life. First we are to praise Him with our eyes — we are to look to Him, focusing our eyes upon Him. "Looking unto Jesus the author and finisher of our faith" (Hebrews 12:2). Life has true meaning and purpose when our eyes are filled with the vision of Him. We praise Him with our ears by listening to His voice. Samuel said, "Speak; for thy servant heareth" (I Samuel 3:10). We praise Him with our hands by using them for Him. "Whatsoever thy hand findeth to do, do it with thy might" (Ecclesiastes 9:10a). We praise Him with our feet by walking on errands for Him. "How beautiful upon the mountains are the feet of him that bringeth good tidings, that publisheth peace" (Isaiah 52:7a). We praise Him with our tongues by telling others of Him. "That which we have seen and heard declare we unto you" (I John 1:3a). We praise Him with our hearts by loving Him. "Whom having not seen, ye love" (I Peter 1:8a).

Instruments of ten strings — our lives — in tune with God and available to Him for His use will bring praise to His name.

By him therefore let us offer the sacrifice of praise to **24**
God continually, that is, the fruit of our lips giving
thanks to his name. Hebrews 13:15

Praise is thanking God for all He has done for us and all He gives to us. In this verse we are reminded to bring an offering or sacrifice of praise to God, and to do so *continually*. We glorify God through our praise, for He says, "Whoso offereth praise glorifieth me . . . " (Psalm 50:23).

Praising God in everything is the secret of a joyful life. Praise brings a blessing out of the circumstances that come into our lives. It lifts us above our difficulties. We are to praise God with the fruit of our lips. Our lips produce words. Where do our words originate? Scripture says, ". . . out of the abundance of the heart the mouth speaketh" (Matthew 12:34).

Search your life for reasons to praise God. Is tribulation coming into your life? Praise Him for the patience you are learning through it. Has the heat in your life become more intense? Praise Him that you can come forth from it as pure gold. Are you weak? Praise Him that His strength is made perfect in your weakness. Are you being chastened? Praise Him that He is showing His love to you in this way. Are you having to wait for something? Praise Him that your strength is being renewed as you wait upon Him.

How much time do we actually spend praising the Lord? Instead of counting our blessings and thanking God for them, we murmur and complain. From hearts full of praise comes an overflow of praise in our lives.

Today are you a complaining Christian or a *praiseful* one? May each of us say, "*His praise* shall continually be in my mouth" (Psalm 34:1).

25

I will praise thee with my whole heart: before the gods will I sing praise unto thee. Psalm 138:1

David's praise was not halfhearted. He praised God with his whole heart. Have you ever praised Him for the following blessings as David did in Psalm 138? This Thanksgiving take time to *praise* Him for —

1. His loving-kindness. It has been said that loving-kindness is love in action. God's loving-kindness was expressed by the gift of His Son.

2. His truth. We should praise Him for both the written Word and the Living Word. "Thy Word is truth" (John 17:17). Jesus said, "I am . . . the truth" (John 14:6).

3. Answered prayer. "In the day when I cried thou answeredest me." We bring Him our petitions, but we forget to praise Him for His answers.

4. His strength. "And strengthenedst me with strength in my soul." This is not merely physical strength but inner strength to meet life.

5. Our privilege of hearing the Word. David said, "All the kings of earth shall praise thee, O Lord, when they hear the words of thy mouth."

6. His song. "Yea, they shall sing in the ways of the Lord." Do we sing in His ways, even though they are hard, even though they may not be our ways?

7. His glory. "For great is the glory of the Lord."

8. His respect unto the lowly. "For though the Lord is high, yet He has respect to the lowly [bringing them into fellowship with Him]" (vs. 6, Amplified).

9. His refreshing in times of trouble. "Though I walk in the midst of trouble, thou wilt revive me."

10. His protecting hand. "Thou shalt stretch forth thine hand against the wrath of mine enemies, and thy right hand shall save me."

It has been said, "Praise is our highest exercise." In prayer we approach God for reasons which may be selfish; in praise, we adore Him for what He is in Himself.

Bless the Lord, O my soul: and all that is within me, **26**
bless his holy name. Bless the Lord, O my soul, and
forget not all his benefits. Psalm 103:1, 2

This Psalm is one of the great Praise and Thanksgiving Psalms of the Bible. David had evidently been thinking about God and of the blessings he had received from Him, and his heart overflowed with praise. It has been said that giving praise to God is the highest of all spiritual exercises.

First, God is the object of David's praise. This is not merely lip-praise. Prayer gets things from God; praise gives to Him. From the very depths of his being David lifts his adoration and praise to God for who He is and what He has done. Praise should be personal — "*O my* soul." It should be fervent — "all that is within me" — "my inner life, affections, emotions, intellect and will." This is the outpouring of a heart in grateful praise to the Giver of all. Such praise and thanksgiving lifts one closer to the heart of God.

God is the theme of our song and the goal of our worship. This praise from our hearts will bring joy to the heart of our Heavenly Father.

After the Psalmist has praised God Himself, he praises Him for all His benefits. So often we forget to thank Him for all that we receive from His hand of love. Have you ever made a list of your blessings, not only material, but spiritual? We take many of them for granted and forget that they are really from Him.

Handel said, "When I think of God, the notes seem to come dripping from my finger tips." Is your heart occupied with praising God? Are you remembering to thank Him for all of your blessings?

27

They go from strength to strength, every one of them in Zion appeareth before God. Psalm 84:7

We are fast approaching the close of another year. As you think back on the trials of this past year, are you amazed at the strength with which you met them? Perhaps at the time you were almost overwhelmed. But you learned that His strength was sufficient for you. The Psalmist says, "Blessed is the man whose strength is in thee; in whose heart are the ways of them" (vs. 5).

As the year is nearing its end, remember that God's strength is also available to us for next year. "They go from strength to strength" (vs. 7).

Verse 6 tells us the secret of being able to go from strength to strength. It speaks of passing through the Valley of Baca and making it a well. "Baca" means "weeping." "Passing through the valley of weeping they will make it a place of springs" (Amplified).

Have you been going through the valley of weeping this year? Have you felt the need of His strength? Commit your times of trouble and sorrow to God and let Him make of them a "place of springs."

As we go through the valley of weeping, sustained by the God of all strength, we emerge spiritually stronger. "They go from strength to strength — increasing in victorious power" (vs. 7, Amplified). As we pass through the "valley" experiences and avail ourselves of His strength, we go from the strength of one experience to the strength of the next.

Are you in the "valley of weeping" today? As you turn your face to Him, He will strengthen you as He leads you through it. He will transform your tears into a "spring" flowing out of your life to bless others.

Rejoicing in hope; patient in tribulation; continuing instant in prayer. Romans 12:12

28

Life is not always calm and pleasant. The way ahead may be dark. Problems may arise. We may face troubles and trials. God's Word gives us spiritual exercises to strengthen us at such times.

We are to rejoice in hope because our God is the God of hope. Whatever the situation, we can rejoice because our hope is in Him. Not only do we rejoice in the hope that He will meet our immediate needs but also in the hope of Christ's return for us, which Paul calls "that blessed hope" (Titus 2:13).

We are to be patient in every trying situation. Without patience we "flare up" and "fly off the handle." With patience we have the peace and poise of endurance under pressure.

Our prayer lives are to be "instant" or "steadfast." This is the source of our spiritual strength. As Tennyson said, "More things are wrought by prayer than this world dreams of." We can never overestimate the value of prayer.

A little four-year-old boy had a new sled. After a snowstorm the street in front of his home was roped off so that the children might play on it safely with their sleds. When his mother went out to see if all was well, he called, "Isn't God glad to see me have such a good slide?" God was real to the little lad, and he was happy in the assurance that his Heavenly Father was interested in his life.

God is also interested in our lives. We can rejoice in our hope in a God who is all-powerful. We can be patient in tribulation, knowing that He is near to comfort and encourage. We can be steadfast in prayer, for He has promised to hear and answer.

Hopeful! Peaceful! Prayerful!

29   *Unto thee, O Lord, do I lift up my soul. Psalm 25:1*

David lived in such close fellowship with God that in a moment of need he could instantly lift up his soul to His Heavenly Father. He was on intimate speaking terms with God and kept an open channel between them that his prayers might not be hindered. David approached God in great humility, recognizing the holiness of God and his own unworthiness. Thus he experienced the power of a life of prayer.

As we study the biographies of godly men who through the years have had great influence for God in the world, we discover that their lives have been saturated with prayer. William Hewitson of Dirleton was a great man of God. Dr. Andrew Bonar, who had a very high regard for him, said, "One thing often struck me in Mr. Hewitson. He seemed to have no intervals in communion with God — no gaps. I used to feel, when with him, that it was being with one who was a vine watered every moment. Hewitson could say, 'I am better acquainted with Jesus than with any friend I have on earth.'"

During World War II a British soldier was caught creeping stealthily from a near-by woods to his quarters. He was immediately taken before his commanding officer and charged with communicating with the enemy. His only defense was that he had been praying. The officer demanded, "Are you in the habit of praying?" "Yes, sir," the soldier replied. "Then get down on your knees and pray," his superior ordered. Expecting to be quickly executed, the soldier knelt and poured out his soul in prayer. When he finished the officer said, "You may go. I believe your story. If you hadn't drilled often, you couldn't have done so well in review."

God . . . hath in these last days spoken unto us by   **30**
his Son. Hebrews 1:1, 2

God has chosen to reveal Himself to us in His Son. He is the completion of God's message to mankind.

He is God's appointed. "Heir and lawful Owner of *all* things" (vs. 2, Amplified). Heirship follows sonship. We, as sons of God through faith in Christ, are joint heirs. Do you sometimes feel "poor"? Remember that you are a joint heir with the One who is the Owner of all things. All of His resources are available to you today.

As the Son, He was the great Creator, "by and through Whom He created the worlds and the reaches of space and the ages of time — [that is], He made, produced, built, operated and arranged them in order" (vs. 2, Amplified). In this space age isn't it comforting to know that He made the "reaches of space" and controls them?

God presents His Son as "the brightness of his glory, and the express image of his person" (vs. 3). He is the outshining of God's glory.

He, the Creator, is also the Sustainer of the world, "upholding and maintaining and guiding and propelling the universe by His mighty word of power" (vs. 3, Amplified).

After He had completed His work on earth, our Saviour returned to heaven and "sat down at the right hand of the divine Majesty on high" (vs. 3, Amplified).

Do you have a longing in your heart to know God better? He has revealed Himself to us in His Son. How wonderfully these verses described the Lord Jesus Christ! As we ponder who Christ is and what He does, our hearts are melted before Him and we bow at His feet in worship and adoration. Hallelujah! What a Saviour!

1   *Their strength is to sit still. Isaiah 30:7*

Assyria was threatening the children of Israel. God's people knew their own weakness and need for strength. In desperation they turned to Egypt. But their search for strength was misplaced. The Lord said, "Woe to the rebellious children . . . that take counsel, but not of me . . . that walk to go down into Egypt, and have not asked at my mouth; to strengthen themselves in the strength of Pharaoh, and to trust in the shadow of Egypt! Therefore shall the strength of Pharaoh be your shame, and the trust in the shadow of Egypt your confusion" (vss. 1-3).

Their errand was doomed to failure for they had not consulted the Lord. "For the Egyptians shall help in vain, and to no purpose; therefore have I cried concerning this, Their strength is to sit still" (vs. 7). Scholars say a more correct rendering is "Therefore have I called her Rahab that sitteth still." Egypt made promises but didn't match them with action — she did nothing but sit still. This was all the Israelites could expect from Egypt, for they were going to the wrong source for strength.

The Lord can give us strength when we are sitting still. "In returning and rest shall ye be saved; in quietness and in confidence shall be your strength" (vs. 15). This strength comes quietly and confidently as we sit still in His presence. God reminded the children of Israel, "And ye would not." Sometimes we learned our most fruitful lessons when we "would not." We then had to learn the hard way. God perhaps says of us, "I wanted you to have the strength of My quietness and confidence — and *you would not*. Instead you rebelled at My way of giving it to you."

When I was a child I always disliked having my mother comb my long hair. It would hurt to have the tangles combed out, so I would pull away. This only increased my misery. My mother would say, "Sit still." I discovered that the experience was less trying when I obeyed her instruction.

Today God wants us to experience that *our* "strength is to sit still."

Rejoice in the Lord alway: and again I say, Rejoice.   *2*
Philippians 4:4

"But I can't always have a smile on my face," I hear someone say. The rejoicing of which our verse speaks doesn't always put a smile on the face, but it does give spiritual joy in the heart. From this inner joy comes a glow on the face. This is not joy in our circumstances but joy in the Lord.

In this book Paul makes twelve references to rejoicing and six times he speaks of joy. Doesn't this seem strange when we remember that Paul wrote this book when he was in prison? But he had learned the secret of living in the Lord. Dr. Walter Wilson says, "He was surrounded by the Lord and not interested in prison bars." No matter what the circumstances of his life, he could rejoice, for his entire life was wrapped up in a Person, the Lord Jesus Christ.

We find so many things about which to complain. "If you had to live where I live," "If you had to work with the person I work with," "If you had my job" — these are remarks which we hear frequently. Paul refused to complain and feel sorry for himself. He rejoiced in spite of his trials and testings.

We are not told to rejoice in our circumstances but in the Lord. We can have spiritual joy because of our relationship to Him. For "though now ye see him not, yet believing, ye rejoice with joy unspeakable and full of glory" (I Peter 1:8).

3 *And Jabez called on the God of Israel, saying, Oh that thou wouldest bless me indeed, and enlarge my coast, and that thine hand might be with me, and that thou wouldest keep me from evil, that it may not grieve me! And God granted him that which he requested. I Chronicles 4:10*

In this one verse the character of Jabez is revealed. A life story is given in a few words. He is revealed as a man of prayer. The Word of God records this as his most important characteristic. He was known for his prayer life.

First, he called on God to bless him. From the depths of his heart he desired God's very best for his life. To be a blessing to others, he must first have God's blessing on his own life.

His heart of love for God gave him a vision of an enlarged coast — souls without God. He had a heart of compassion to reach them for Him. Is the prayer of your life, "Enlarge my coast and give me a harvest of souls"?

Jabez prayed for the touch of God's hand on his life to guide and direct him — "Oh . . . that thine hand might be with me." Is the touch of His hand on your life?

He prayed to be kept from evil so that he wouldn't be grieved. The words "not grieve me" mean "that it be not to my sorrow," we are told. Evil in his life would not only bring sorrow to God but also to himself. God honored his humble prayer life and granted him that which he requested.

Great people through the ages have been great pray-ers. William Penn wrote of George Fox, "Above all he excelled in prayer."

What are you known for? If God were to record the most important characteristic of your life, would it be your faithfulness in prayer?

And if children, then heirs; heirs of God, and joint-   **4**
heirs with Christ. Romans 8:17

Have you ever said, "I wish someone would leave me a million dollars"? Not very many of us will ever receive an inheritance of this size. But God has an estate which is available today to His legal heirs. It is the largest one in the world, for He owns everything. When we are born into His family, we immediately become His heirs and are entitled to our share in His great inheritance.

We read that we are "heirs of God, and joint-heirs with Christ." When an estate is left to coheirs, it is divided equally between them. When an estate is left to joint heirs, it belongs to all of them jointly. They all share in the entire estate. In God's estate there is not a *division* of the possessions among the heirs, but there is *equal* possession of *all* of the estate. All that God has belongs to Jesus Christ and to us together.

Can you understand what it means to be a joint heir with Christ? How rich we are! Oh, the marvelous grace of God that has made all of the riches of heaven available to us through our Saviour Jesus Christ!

When someone becomes an heir he is usually eager to receive his inheritance. He makes sure that he receives all that is his. Scripture records all that our inheritance includes. But we must read God's Word to be sure that we do not overlook any part of our possessions.

Today *you* are a joint heir to God's estate. Be sure to collect all that is available for you from it. Don't be a spiritual pauper when you can be a joint heir with Christ to all the riches of glory.

5 *Blessed be God, even the Father of our Lord Jesus Christ, the Father of mercies, and the God of all comfort; who comforteth us in all our tribulation, that we may be able to comfort them which are in any trouble, by the comfort wherewith we ourselves are comforted of God. II Corinthians 1:3, 4*

These verses are often quoted in times of sorrow and heartache. They have been shared over and over in time of need to bring comfort to the heart.

Our God is the God of *all* comfort. He is the One whose loving heart and hand reach out to minister comfort to us today. We read that He, the God of all comfort, comforts us in *all* our tribulation. He understands and sympathizes as no one else can. He pours His "Balm of Gilead" into our troubled hearts, bringing His own peace and quietness within.

The "School of God's Comfort" trains us to be comforters. Have you considered the "ministry of comfort" as a means of blessing those around you? Perhaps God is preparing you for just such a ministry by allowing you to experience sorrow, pain or misunderstanding in your life. You are being prepared to minister to others the comfort with which you have been comforted by God. Perhaps God is trusting you today with a crushing heartache, a deep need or an overwhelming difficulty to prepare you to be a "precious comforter" to someone else going through such an experience. The Indians say, "We cannot really sympathize with anyone until we have walked for two weeks in his moccasins."

We are comforted that we may be able to comfort those who are in *any* trouble. Even though we may not have experienced the particular trouble which is afflicting someone else, pain and heartache prepare us to be more loving and sympathetic toward those in distress of any kind.

You are comforted to be a comforter.

Lo, I am with you alway, even unto the end of the world. Matthew 28:20 **6**

The last words of friends and dear ones are important and very precious. The above words were some of the last which Jesus spoke to His disciples. After His resurrection He appeared to them and commissioned them, *"Go ye* into all the world" (Mark 16:15). This was His *plan* for the work they should do after He returned to heaven.

With His plan for them to go into the world preaching the Gospel came the promise of His *presence.* "Lo, I am with you all the days — perpetually, uniformly and on every occasion" (Matthew 28:20, Amplified). In a short time the world around them was feeling the impact of the Gospel.

Our Lord's last words of commission are for us today also: *"Go ye* therefore . . ." (Matthew 28:19). We are to carry out His plan for reaching the world for Himself.

To some, obedience to the command "Go ye" may mean full-time service, perhaps requiring one to leave home and even country to serve God as a missionary, pastor, teacher, doctor or nurse. It may mean giving up a profession or vocation to preach the Gospel full time. To others, obedience to this command may mean not a "full-time" service but a "lifetime" service — "Go ye into your neighborhood;" "Go ye into your place of business."

To us today also comes His promise, "Lo, I am with you" — "Right there, wherever you are serving, I will be with you today." Weymouth says, "I will be with you day by day." We are told that a literal English translation could read, "I am with you *all* the days." This includes every day. This includes *today.*

Listen for His "Go ye" today. Then *go* in the assurance that His presence is with you. Claim His promise, "Lo, I *am* with *you."*

7   *For a great door and effectual is opened unto me, and there are many adversaries. I Corinthians 16:9*

Paul sent word to the church of Corinth that he was going to remain at Ephesus for awhile. A great opportunity, a great and effectual door had been opened to him and he wanted to take advantage of it.

Ephesus was a place of idolatry and heathen worship. Paul discovered that with the open door there were also adversaries. Before him were opportunities and adversaries, both a part of the open door. Yet this didn't discourage him. He had learned that when God opened a door, He would give him the victory.

God has many open doors of opportunity for service today. In His time He opens them before us. It is our opportunity to enter them. To the church in Philadelphia the Lord gave the message, "Behold, I have set before thee an open door, and no man can shut it" (Revelation 3:8).

We must not try to open the doors by force. Our efforts to do so will only fail. God is working behind closed doors preparing for "Opening Day." He knows all that must be accomplished behind the door and in our lives before He can open it to us.

With our open doors of service also come the adversaries. We can expect opposition to God's work and we must face the fact that there will be adversaries. The adversaries are as real as the opportunities. It is important, however, that we not allow them to become obstacles or hindrances in our lives. We must not become discouraged and quit because of them. We must look to our Victor, the Lord, who gives the victory. "But thanks be to God, which giveth us the victory through our Lord Jesus Christ" (I Corinthians 15:57).

On what are your eyes focused? On the adversaries, or on the Lord and His opened doors?

And when the cloud tarried long upon the tabernacle many days, then the children of Israel kept the charge of the Lord, and journeyed not. Numbers 9:19

The children of Israel had been told to watch the cloud for guidance. With great expectancy they moved forward as it directed. But there were also times when the cloud indicated that they were to wait.

The wilderness was not the most delightful place in which to wait. The barrenness of the desert was not inviting. Waiting in itself is not easy. Regardless of their strength and eagerness to start out again, regardless of their impatience to be on the way, the Israelites did not move until God, by means of the cloud, directed them to do so. It may not have been difficult to wait a short time. But in the above verse of Scripture we read that they had to wait "many" days. This was no doubt difficult. It was a test of their obedience.

Sometimes we are kept waiting, too. We may be in the midst of heartaches, of problems, of trials, of temptations when we see the cloud stop and tarry. If we want what is best for us, we must stop and wait. Sometimes our waiting is for a short period. We may, on the other hand, be kept waiting for a long time. But we dare not move until He moves us.

There are times when we seem settled in a comfortable place. We are happy and contented. Suddenly the cloud begins to move. We may not want to move, yet we will have His blessing only if we willingly move with His cloud.

"The steps of a good man are ordered by the Lord" (Psalm 37:23). Both the steps and the stops of our lives are ordered by the Lord. The important thing is for us to follow where He leads.

9 *I must work the works of him that sent me, while it is day: the night cometh, when no man can work. John 9:4*

Somewhere I saw a little slogan which read, "Today is part of my lifework." Life is important. It has purpose for us.

God brings real purpose into life. He had a great purpose in sending Jesus Christ to earth. "The Father sent the Son to be the Saviour of the world" (I John 4:14). Jesus shared a purpose for living when He said to His followers, "As my Father hath sent me, even so send I you" (John 20:21).

God has a blueprint for our lives: He has planned a lifework for each of us. Each day of our lives fits into His complete plan for us and therefore each day is important. What a value this puts upon our lives!

Today — right now — is very important, for it is the only time of which we can be sure. Jesus said, "I must work the works of Him Who sent Me, and be busy with His business while it is daylight; night is coming on when no man can work" (John 9:4, Amplified). Tomorrow may be the "night" when we cannot work.

Today — right where we are — is part of our life plan. Sometimes we think that to serve God it is necessary to be a pastor, a missionary, a teacher or an evangelist. Not so. Your lifework today may include making a telephone call to someone in need; or baking a cake for a neighbor; or even giving a special smile to someone with a heavy heart. Many times it is through these seemingly insignificant deeds of kindness that God opens opportunities to share Him with others and minister to their spiritual needs.

Work today for tomorrow may be too late.

As I was with Moses, so I will be with thee: I will not fail thee, nor forsake thee. Joshua 1:5

10

Moses had been a great leader. Scripture tells us, "And there arose not a prophet since in Israel like unto Moses" (Deuteronomy 34:10). Moses had led the children of Israel out of Egypt. They were on their way to the Promised Land. But Moses had died.

Even though Moses was dead, God hadn't forgotten His people. God wasn't dead. Joshua was to be the new leader, assuming the responsibility of the march. God said to Joshua, "Arise, go over this Jordan, thou, and all this people, unto the land which I do give to them, even to the children of Israel" (Joshua 1:2). God had previously promised them the land. Now they were to go in and possess it.

God gave Joshua His *promise* that His purpose for the children of Israel would be carried out. He said to Joshua, "Every place that the sole of your feet shall tread upon, that have I given unto you, as I said unto Moses" (Joshua 1:3). God guaranteed that His *presence* would go with Joshua: "As I was with Moses, so I will *be* with thee: I will not *fail* thee, nor *forsake* thee" (Joshua 1:5).

Today we are to move forward, possessing the land for Jesus Christ, claiming it by faith. The Lord has promised that He will go with *us,* never failing us, never forsaking us.

A fine young athlete was planning to do full-time Christian work. He was asked to go to a distant land and open up a new field but he was fearful of going alone. Someone asked, "Would you go with someone like David Livingstone?" "Yes," he replied. Several other great missionaries were mentioned and he agreed that he would not be afraid if he could go with one of them. "Then," someone said to him, "why not go with Jesus Christ?"

11   *And Asa cried unto the Lord his God, and said, Lord,*
it is nothing with thee to help, whether with many,
or with them that have no power: help us, O Lord
our God; for we rest on thee, and in thy name we go
against this multitude. O Lord, thou art our God;
let not man prevail against thee. II Chronicles 14:11

Asa was a good king, one who did right in the sight of the Lord. He kept his eyes on the Lord. He also turned the attention of the people to Him and to His commandments.

One day the rest and peace of the land was broken by an Ethiopian invasion. Knowing that he had an army of only approximately half a million to go against the Ethiopian forces of a million strong, King Asa realized that his people were completely helpless. There was only one place to turn for help. He went to God in prayer. It was a brief prayer, but right to the point. He prayed, "O Lord, there is none beside You to help, and no difference to You whether him You help is mighty or powerless" (Amplified).

To whom else could Asa turn for help? Knowing their power for battle was in God alone, he put his trust completely in God — "We rest on *thee*," he said. The Amplified reads, "For we rely on You." The word "rest" in this verse is the same as "leaned" in II Samuel 1:6. Asa knew that His strength was in leaning wholly on God. "In *thy name* we go against this multitude," he declared. God gave victory to King Asa and his men.

Perhaps today insurmountable difficulties have arisen in your life. All human aid is gone. In your weakness, when you are powerless to do anything, you, too, can cry out to God, "It is nothing for Thee to help." No need is too great for Him to supply. Pray as Asa did, "I rest *myself* on Thee." God can bring all the resources of heaven to your aid, giving victory in your time of deepest need.

For the eyes of the Lord run to and fro throughout the whole earth, to shew himself strong in the behalf of them whose heart is perfect toward him. II Chronicles 16:9

12

At a time of threatened attack by the king of Israel against Judah, King Asa turned to the king of Syria for help. Earlier in his life when the enemy had come against him, he had recognized his need for God's help and had turned to Him in complete trust. But this time he forgot to look up. He began to seek human help. This is a warning for us. We must constantly seek our help from the Lord. Even though we have done so in the past, Satan will do everything possible to keep us from seeking divine aid.

Hanani, the seer, came to Asa with a message: "Because thou hast relied on the king of Syria, and not relied on the Lord thy God, therefore is the host of the king of Syria escaped out of thine hand" (II Chronicles 16:7).

Today the eyes of the Lord are running to and fro in our behalf, seeking hearts which are perfect toward Him. He has perfect vision as His eyes search out the earth in behalf of every one of His own. He not only sees the lives of His children, but He sees their inner motives and attitudes. He sees their temptations, heartaches and needs. He seeks us not as a "policeman" but as a Heavenly Father who loves us. He will show Himself strong in our behalf in time of need, encouraging us and strengthening us.

Someone has said, "Faith brings us to the attention of God."

13

And when the cloud was taken up from the tabernacle, then after that the children of Israel journeyed: and in the place where the cloud abode, there the children of Israel pitched their tents. Numbers 9:17

God called the children of Israel out of Egypt to a new land. The way was unknown to them, taking them through the wilderness. Yet God was unfailing in His provision. They could depend completely on Him for guidance.

While they were still in Egypt, God had promised, "Certainly I will be with thee" (Exodus 3:12). Then as He led them forth He guided them with a cloud by day and a pillar of fire by night. When it moved, they moved; when it stopped, they "rested in their tents." They had to keep their eyes on the cloud and follow its movement. Theirs was a life of daily and hourly dependence on God. "At the commandment of the Lord the children of Israel journeyed, and at the commandment of the Lord they pitched: as long as the cloud abode upon the tabernacle they rested in their tents" (Numbers 9:18).

Today we are on our "march of life." It is God-planned and God-directed. We, too, have the certainty of His guidance for each day. He has promised, "I will never leave thee, nor forsake thee" (Hebrews 13:5). "I will instruct thee and teach thee in the way which thou shalt go: I will guide thee with mine eye" (Psalm 32:8). It is important for us to wait for His "cloud of guidance." We must stand still when "our cloud" stops; we must not move forward until "our cloud" moves.

Moses said, "If thy presence go not with me, carry us not up hence" (Exodus 33:15). Do not run ahead of Him or lag behind, but follow Him step by step.

Search me, O God, and know my heart: try me, and know my thoughts: and see if there be any wicked way in me, and lead me in the way everlasting. Psalm 139:23, 24

14

This is the prayer of the Psalmist David, who desired to please God. He wanted nothing to hinder his fellowship with God. "Search me, thoroughly, O God," he prayed, "and try me; know my heart; know my thoughts." He wanted God to reveal any wicked way in his life that would hinder his fellowship with Him.

Are we, like David, willing for God to search our lives, to try us and prove us? Are we willing for Him to search every corner of our hearts — even the places we have so carefully tried to conceal? What about our thoughts? Can we bear to have God's searchlight turned upon them?

David prayed, "Lead me in the way everlasting." It has been said that this means "Lead me in the way of everlasting things." Life is centered around either the temporal or the eternal things. David wanted to be led in the things that have eternal value.

Are we building our lives around the temporal things or those that have eternal value? Do we desire to be led in the way of everlasting things? As God searches our lives, what does He see? Does He see us reading, studying and meditating on His precious Word? Does He see in our hearts a desire to spend time with Him in prayer? Does He see our willingness for Him to use us in His service? What *does* He see as He searches our lives?

Today can you honestly say to the Lord, "Search me, try me, see me, and then lead *me* in *Thy* way?"

15   *The king's daughter is all glorious within: her clothing is of wrought gold. Psalm 45:13*

A daughter becomes a member of her royal family by birth. So we become a daughter of God's royal family by the new birth. We read in John 3:7, "Marvel not — do not be surprised, astonished — at My telling you, You must all be born anew (from above)" (Amplified). "But as many as received him, to them gave he power to become the sons of God, even to them that believe on his name" (John 1:12).

Today we are all very beauty-conscious. Many beauty contests are held each year to select those who excel in certain types of beauty. The daughters of the King of kings have an inner beauty that does not come from using certain creams or perfumes. Our inner beauty is the presence of the Person of the Lord Jesus Christ Himself in our lives.

Our outer clothing is inwrought with gold. When we become His daughters by the new birth He clothes us in the robes of His own righteousness. Not only do we have His beauty inwardly but also outwardly.

Then we are brought into the presence of our King in raiment of needlework (Psalm 45:14). Needlework puts the finishing touches on a garment to make it complete and give it added beauty. Spiritual needlework is needed to provide the delicate finishing touches which complete the beauty of our lovely Lord in our lives. This is the beautiful fruit of the Spirit which the Holy Spirit perfects in us. Thus the daughters of the King of kings develop more and more of the family likeness.

*I had fainted, unless I had believed to see the good-
ness of the Lord in the land of the living. Wait on
the Lord: be of good courage, and he shall strengthen
thine heart: wait, I say, on the Lord. Psalm 27:13, 14*

16

Today in the "land of the living" we see turmoil and confusion. There is an alarming increase in crime. The cost of living is rising. Men's hearts today are filled with fear.

Even in David's day there was much to cause fear. He said that he would faint unless he had faith to look away from the condition of the world about him and look to God who made the world and was still in control. He saw the "goodness" of the Lord as the sun rose and set faithfully day after day. He saw the "goodness" of the Lord in nature. This was a reminder of the "goodness" and "faithfulness" of God to His own children. It deepened David's trust in his Heavenly Father.

The Psalmist gives the secret of the strength and courage needed to live in such a world — a little four-letter word — *"Wait on the Lord."* The ability to wait is not easily acquired. We are restless and want to be on the move. We do not like to wait in line, or wait in the doctor's office — in fact, most of us just do not like to wait. It is much easier to act than to wait. Someone has said, "Waiting on God is not one of the marks of the average space-age Christian."

Waiting on the Lord is seeking His face for guidance and direction in our lives. It is becoming quiet enough before Him to hear His voice. If we do not take time to wait on Him we may go forth in the energy of the flesh or we may force open a door before His time.

Wait! His clock and His calendar are not always the same as ours, but they are always right on time.

17 *Now no chastening for the present seemeth to be joyous, but grievous: nevertheless afterward it yieldeth the peaceable fruit of righteousness unto them which are exercised thereby. Hebrews 12:11*

Most people have a great desire to be loved and to feel wanted. I have read that Dr. Menninger concluded that many of the patients in his clinic were there because they needed to be loved. He directed his staff to show special love to them in their day-by-day contacts. After a few months he discovered that the average period of hospitalization was reduced by half through a "treatment of love." God so made us that we respond to love.

God loves us — He loves us with an everlasting love. He demonstrated and proved the reality of His love for each of us personally. "But God commendeth his love toward us, in that, while we were yet sinners, Christ died for us" (Romans 5:8).

But perhaps you are saying, "God certainly must not love me. If only I could tell you all of the trials and heartaches I am experiencing!" Have you realized that the trials may be the very proof of His love? "For whom the Lord loveth he chasteneth" (Hebrews 12:6). The present chastening may be part of His discipline in our lives. Someone has said, "A faith which is not tried will never be strong." We cannot always understand God's ways of dealing with us, but if we could, we would not need to exercise faith.

Chastening is not joyous; we do not like it. But there is the "afterward" — the peaceable fruit of righteousness. God knows that through chastening His righteousness, or goodness, is produced in us. "Now, obviously, no chastening seems pleasant at the time: it is in fact most unpleasant. Yet when it is all over we can see that it has quietly produced the fruit of real goodness in the characters of those who have accepted it in the right spirit" (Hebrews 12:11, Phillips).

It may be that the Lord will work for us: for there is no restraint to the Lord to save by many or by few.
I Samuel 14:6

18

Israel was being besieged by the Philistines. Jonathan decided that he and his armor-bearer would survey the strength of the enemy. Believing that God would show him how the enemy could be put to rout, he said to his armor-bearer, "Come, and let us go over unto the garrison of these uncircumcised: it may be that the Lord will work for us: for there is no restraint to the Lord to save by many or by few." Jonathan had implicit trust in God. He knew that numbers were not important with God. His faith in God was so strong that he knew God could reveal His plan of victory.

Today is there an impossible situation in your life, one to which you can see no solution? God is not restrained by your situation or by your resources. He can save by many or by few. We begin to wonder *who* can help us or *what* we should do. We may see no way out — but bringing God into our situation changes everything. Turning it over to Him and taking our hands off gives Him the opportunity to do the impossible. He is not limited to our human resources or our plans.

One day a man brought his son to Jesus for healing. Jesus said to the troubled father, "All things can be — are possible — to him who believes!" He replied, "Lord, I believe! Constantly help my weakness of faith!" (Mark 9:23, 24, Amplified).

There is one thing that restrains Him from working for us — our unbelief. Do not limit Him to *your* vision but know that "with God all things *are* possible" (Matthew 19:26).

19

And now, O Lord my God, thou hast made thy servant king . . . and I am but a little child. . . . Give therefore thy servant an understanding heart to judge thy people, that I may discern between good and bad: for who is able to judge this thy so great a people? I Kings 3:7-9

Solomon was the new king. God said, "Ask what I shall give thee" (vs. 5). What a privilege to be able to ask God for whatever he wanted! Solomon said, "I am but a little child: I know not how to go out or come in." Then he asked God for a discerning heart to judge the people wisely. He was humbled by the great responsibility of ruling this people and he recognized his inability to perform this great task.

God was pleased with his request and granted it. "I have given thee a wise and an understanding heart . . . . And I have also given thee that which thou hast not asked, both riches, and honour" (vss. 12, 13).

God is still ready to give us much more than we request. He not only supplies our needs but much more. Ephesians 3:20 reads, "Now unto him that is able to do exceeding abundantly above all that we ask or think, according to the power that worketh in us, unto him be glory in the church by Christ Jesus throughout all ages."

A mail-order company had this printed at the bottom of their order forms: "If we do not have the article you ordered in stock, may we substitute?" Customers learned that it paid to say "Yes" to this question. Sometimes a customer received a substitute which was worth double the value of what he had ordered. It was the company's policy always to substitute something of much better quality than what was originally ordered.

So it was with Solomon. God not only gave what he requested but more. So it is also with us. God is ready to give us *exceeding abundantly* above what we ask or even think.

No man hath seen God at any time; the only begotten Son, which is in the bosom of the Father, he hath declared him. John 1:18

20

A little boy was drawing a picture. Someone asked him, "What are you drawing?" "A picture of God," he answered. "But," said the person, "no one knows what God looks like." "They will when I get through," was the lad's reply. We may smile at this, but it is an illustration of what Jesus Christ did. He came to reveal God the Father to us.

Man has a desire to know something about God. He goes to the mountains and sees the power of God displayed. He goes to the seashore and sees the majesty of a mighty God. Yet the Word says, "No man hath seen God at any time." However, God did provide a revelation of Himself to man. We read, "In the beginning [before all time] was the Word [Christ], and the Word was with God, and the Word was God Himself" (John 1:1, Amplified). Jesus Christ, the Living Word, is the perfect revelation of God. The Word in flesh is God manifested. Christ was God expressing Himself in a way that man could understand.

There once lived in Persia a monarch who loved his people greatly. In order to know them better he would disguise himself and mingle with them. One day he dressed as a poor man and sat beside the fireman who attended a furnace at a public bath. He shared the coarse food of the fireman and talked with him as a friend. He visited him often until the fireman grew to love him. One day he told him he was the emperor. The fireman replied, "You left your palace to sit here with me and share my fare. You have given yourself for me."

"And this is life eternal, that they might know thee the only true God, and Jesus Christ, whom thou hast sent" (John 17:3).

21   *Trust in him at all times; ye people, pour out your heart before him: God is a refuge for us. Selah.*
Psalm 62:8

This Psalm is often called the "only" Psalm. The word "only" occurs in it eight times. "Truly" here has the meaning of "only." "My soul, wait thou *only* upon God; for my expectation is from him" (Psalm 62:5). "He *only* is my rock and my salvation: he is my defence; I shall not be moved" (vs. 6). Our trust is to be in God and Him *only*.

If you were to count the people in whom you have implicit confidence, those whom you can trust at all times, how many would there be? We can trust God always, at *all* times. He will *never* fail us. We can trust Him when we lose our money, when our health fails, when our families forsake us, when we face trouble and sorrow.

Because we have complete confidence in Him, we can go to Him with every need and pour out our hearts before Him. There are few people with whom we feel free to do this. But He understands as no one else can, and He sympathizes and cares. "It is better to trust in the Lord than to put confidence in man" (Psalm 118:8). How it comforts our hearts to know that we can go to Him and tell Him our innermost needs, knowing that He is a safe refuge for us!

This verse ends with the word "Selah," which means "pause, and think of that; stop, and consider what God is saying."

May Christ through your faith [actually] dwell —   **22**
settle down, abide, make His permanent home — in
your hearts! Ephesians 3:17, Amplified

We are again caught in the rush of the holiday season. We have been preparing Christmas programs. Christmas cards have been addressed and mailed. We are busily engaged in decorating our homes for the festive season. Fruitcakes have been baked and the delicious smell of Christmas cookies and candies fills the air.

We have given much time and thought to selecting Christmas presents. How lovingly we chose gifts for those near and dear to us! Occasionally we found it difficult to reach a decision. Aunt Jane — what could we get her? She has everything. And Bob — what would a ten-year-old boy like? Our minds have been filled with the joys and problems of selecting Christmas gifts.

With the approach of Christmas our hearts are moved as we hear the beautiful Christmas carols. Our minds turn then from "Christmas presents" to "Christmas Presence;" to the One whose "Presence" came into the world when He was born as the tiny Babe of Bethlehem. "And they shall call his name Emmanuel, which being interpreted is, *God with us.*" God had a great purpose in Christ's coming. "The Father sent the Son to be the Saviour of the world" (I John 4:14). He was God's present (His love gift) to the world. "For God so loved the world, that he gave his only begotten Son, that whosoever believeth in him should not perish, but have everlasting life" (John 3:16). More wonderful than the gaiety of the season, more inspiring than the beautful Christmas music, more thrilling than opening Christmas presents, is the reality of *His Presence* within. "Christ in you, the hope of glory" (Colossians 1:27).

In the hustle and bustle of this season may we not forget those in the world who do not know the joy and peace of His Presence. The greatest gift we can give to our Lord is to make known the reality of His Presence to others.

23 *Now thanks be to God for His Gift, [precious] beyond telling — His indescribable, inexpressible, free Gift! II Corinthians 9:15, Amplified*

How exciting these days are as we hurry and scurry to complete the season's tasks! Sometimes the Christ of Christmas is almost forgotten in the feverish preparation for His birthday.

Several years ago I learned a secret that has increased the joy of Christmas. Each year I mail several hundred Christmas cards. This could easily become a burden, but I have recognized it as an opportunity to share God's Christmas message with others. As I address each card, I pray for that person or family. Thus what could be a tedious task becomes a joy.

I have some friends who make an interesting use of the Christmas cards they receive, which in turn has been a blessing to those who sent the greetings. After Christmas they put into a basket all the cards they have received. Each morning after breakfast the husband and wife each draw a card from the basket. They pray for the persons who sent those particular cards. Then they write notes, telling them that they prayed for them. Each year I look forward to the note I receive which assures me that I was remembered in their prayers.

It is also a joy for me to do my Christmas shopping. I ask God to direct me to the right gifts. Then I ask Him to bless those who will receive them. Instead of becoming impatient with the crowds of shoppers, I experience joy in selecting gifts in the true spirit of Christmas. What pleasure enriches my holiday season as I ask God to let me use Christmas as an opportunity to express my thanks to Him by sharing with others the Christ of Christmas.

"For God so greatly loved and dearly prized the world that He [even] gave up His only-begotten (unique) Son, so that whoever believes in (trusts, clings to, relies on) Him shall not perish — come to destruction, be lost — but have eternal (everlasting) life" (John 3:16, Amplified).

Fear not: for, behold, I bring you good tidings of **24**
great joy, which shall be to all people. For unto you
is born this day in the city of David a Saviour, which
is Christ the Lord. Luke 2:10, 11

God's Word tells us to "fear not." I have read that there are 365 promises in the Bible which express the thought of "fear not," one for each day in the year.

On the night of Christ's birth an angel appeared to the shepherds on the hillside. The glory of the Lord shone so brightly that the shepherds were afraid. Quickly the angel said, "Fear not. Do not be afraid. Put away all your fears. I have good news for you!" These words calmed the hearts of the shepherds. Then the angel proclaimed the glorious message of the birth of the Saviour. What greater message of hope and joy could the angel have brought than the good news that God had sent His Son into the world as its Saviour?

Today Christ says to troubled hearts, "Fear not — I have God's message of great joy for you." Instead of fear, we can have joy. His joy is not superficial and transient; it is the deep, abiding joy that comes from a heart at rest in God — a heart that knows the reality of His promises, "Fear not: for I am with thee" (Isaiah 43:5); "Fear not; I will help thee" (Isaiah 41:13).

Freedom from *fear* brings *fulness* of *joy.*

25 *For we have seen his star in the east, and are come to worship him. Matthew 2:2*
And when they were come into the house, they saw the young child with Mary his mother, and fell down, and worshipped him: and when they had opened their treasures, they presented unto him gifts; gold, and frankincense, and myrrh. Matthew 2:11

The Wise men had come to *"worship him"* (vs. 2). This had been their one purpose — all else was secondary. Time, expense, the inconvenience of leaving home, the hardships of travel — these could not hold them back. They had stopped at nothing short of coming to worship Him. When they found Him in Bethlehem, "they fell down, and worshipped him" (vs. 11). Do we take time today to worship Him, or are we so involved in Christmas activities that we neglect this?

Perhaps we should consider what worship is. It has been defined as "the overflow of the love of our hearts for Him." It is a heart-to-heart meeting with God. It is bowing before God in adoration and contemplation of Himself. It is ascribing worship to the One who is worthy. Someone has said, "In prayer we are occupied with our needs; in praise we are occupied with our blessings; in worship we are occupied with *Him*."

We are told that the word "worship" has come down to us from the Anglo-Saxon from which comes our word "worth." When we worship Him, we acknowledge His worth. "Worthship" was difficult to pronounce, so the word was changed to "worship."

The star which the wise men saw in the east brought them to the end of their quest — they saw *Him*, the One for whom they had been searching. They fell down and worshiped Him. Although they saw Him, they didn't say, "We have come to see Him." They said, "We . . . are come to *worship* him." They brought Him gifts, but they didn't say, "We have brought Him gifts." They had come to adore Him.

Someone has said, "Many petition, some intercede, but few worship." Do you?

Where is he that is born king of the Jews? for we **26**
have seen his star in the east, and are come to wor-
ship him. Matthew 2:2

The Magi were on their way from the east in search of the Christ Child. They stopped at Jerusalem and asked, "Where is he that is born king of the Jews?"

Suppose that this question were asked of us today. What would our answer be? He was born in Bethlehem. But what is significant about this? He was born a *Saviour,* the Scripture says. This implies not only His birth in Bethlehem but also His death on the cross and His resurrection from the dead that He might be our living Saviour.

Where is He today in relation to you personally? He is either dwelling in your heart because you have invited Him in or He is still standing outside waiting for you to do so. He will not come in without your personal invitation.

Where is He in relation to those of you who know Him personally? Where is He in relation to your family plans, your neighborhood and business contacts, your career, your daily habits, your pleasures?

Colossians 3:11b reads, "But Christ is all, and in all." This tells us where He should be in our lives today. When He is all and in all, our entire lives will center around Him. Our ambitions, desires and wants will be His.

This Christmas season where is He, the Christ of Christmas? Are you including Him in all your plans, or is He being crowded out? May your answer be, "Christ is all, and in all."

27

Let us now go even unto Bethlehem, and see this thing which is come to pass. Luke 2:15b

Let us go back across the centuries to a hillside near Bethlehem. Can you not see a group of shepherds out on the hillside watching their sheep? In the stillness of the night can you not hear their low voices mingling with the bleating of the sheep?

Suddenly the skies burst into brilliant light and an angel appeared unto them. He gave them the message that the Saviour was born in Bethlehem. Then a heavenly host joined the angel in praising God.

After the angels had disappeared, the shepherds said, "Let us *go* and *see*." When they returned after having gone to see, they *went forth* and *told*. They could share only what was a real experience to them. They had to go and see before they could go and tell.

In God's Word we read of several who had something to tell because they had gone to see Jesus. Because a little boy had gone to see Him, he could go and tell how Jesus had taken his lunch and fed the multitude. Because the disciples had seen Jesus still the angry storm, they could go and tell how He had brought peace to their hearts. Mothers who had brought their children to Jesus could go and tell how He had placed His hands on their heads and blessed them.

Today what can you tell of Him? Can you tell how He took what you placed in His hands and multiplied it to bless others? Can you tell how He quieted the storms in your life? Can you tell how He blessed those near and dear to you as you brought them to Him in prayer?

"Go and see" Him. Then you can "go and tell" what He has done.

Come and dine. John 21:12

28

During the holiday season many of us partake too freely of the delicious "goodies" abundant at this time of year. Perhaps, realizing that you have been overeating, you have said, "As soon as this holiday season is over, I *must* go on a diet."

However, we must continue to nourish our souls with spiritual food. "They received the word with all readiness of mind, and searched the scriptures *daily,* whether those things were so" (Acts 17:11). Do we partake of it joyously? "Thy words were found, and I did eat them; and thy word was unto me the *joy* and *rejoicing* of mine heart" (Jeremiah 15:16).

In John 21 we read that the disciples had been fishing all night and had caught nothing. Jesus appeared and told them to cast their net on the right side of the ship. They obeyed and caught a multitude of fish. As they came to shore with their catch, they discovered that Jesus had built a fire and had provided a meal of fish and bread. "Jesus saith unto them, Come and dine."

Food is necessary to sustain life. We need the Living Bread for eternal life. Today Jesus invites us to "come and dine." He says, "I am the bread of life: he that cometh to me shall never hunger; and he that believeth on me shall never thirst . . . . I am the living bread which came down from heaven: if any man eat of this bread, he shall live for ever" (John 6:35, 51). After we have become Christians, our souls require a properly balanced diet for spiritual growth.

Food will not benefit us unless we eat it; the same is true of spiritual food. "O taste and see that the Lord is good" (Psalm 34:8a).

29

And he led them forth by the right way, that they might go to a city of habitation. Psalm 107:7

The first time we went to New York City the hustle and bustle of the huge metropolis frightened us. We wondered how we would be able to find our way about the city and see the many things that were of special interest to us. A friend introduced us to someone who lived in the city and was very familiar with it. He became our guide and took us on a personally conducted tour which enabled us to see more in two days than we would have discovered in several days of exploring on our own.

This verse tells us that God Himself led the children of Israel on their travels through the wilderness: "And *He* led them forth." The pillar of cloud and the pillar of fire were symbols of His presence. *He* was the One who led their "march" through the wilderness.

We read that some of them wandered in a solitary way, fainting from hunger and thirst. Some were near death. But when they cried to the Lord, *He* delivered them from their troubles (vs. 4-6). When they turned to the Lord, He led them forth by the *right* way. He didn't lead them aimlessly about; He guided them to a specific destination — "a city of habitation."

Today God has the "right way" planned for us, the way which leads us to our destination, the "city of habitation." He is so concerned that we reach our destination that He sent His Son to become *the way* for us. "Jesus saith unto him, I am the way, the truth, and the life: no man cometh unto the Father, but by me" (John 14:6).

We don't know when we will reach our heavenly home. Some will reach it sooner than others. But we can trustingly follow our Guide each day. We may have to stop for a time. An obstacle may have to be removed from our way. The course of our way may be changed completely without our knowing or understanding why. When we reach our destination, however, and know why we were so led, we will rejoice that we did not miss any part of the way *He* led.

If I take the wings of the morning and dwell in the uttermost parts of the sea; even there shall thy hand lead me, and thy right hand shall hold me. Psalm 139:9, 10

30

The dawning light begins in the east and as "wings of the morning" travels to the west. If we travel as does the morning light from the east to the west, God's presence is always with us, for He is the Omnipotent God. He is in all places at all times. No height, nor depth, nor distance, nor place can escape His presence. We cannot get out of His sight. He knows where we are each moment of the day.

This knowledge brings comfort and confidence to our hearts. We may desire to take the wings of the morning and travel to the uttermost part of the sea to get away from the pressures of life. We may wonder if God has forgotten. But *even there* He sees us, His eye is on our way and His ear open to our cry. In time of great need He is present to softly and gently lead us as He holds us by His hand of love.

Our *"even there"* may be in a place out of God's will. Yet in love and patience He is waiting for us to permit Him to lead us back to Himself.

The knowledge that He is an ever-present God brings assurance and confidence to us. One time I was alone in a motel in a strange city. We experienced severe thunderstorms accompanied by heavy rain. A tornado was sighted in the area. I prayed "Lord, I am glad you know that I am 'even here'."

Where are you today? You can be confident of His presence with you *"even there"* today.

31 *Yes, furthermore I count everything as loss compared to the possession of the priceless privilege — the overwhelming preciousness, the surpassing worth and supreme advantage — of knowing Christ Jesus my Lord. Philippians 3:8, Amplified*

At this time of year we are thinking about our accomplishments during the year that has passed. Forms received from the Internal Revenue Department must be filled out. We are trying to determine our profit or loss for the year.

This portion of Scripture has been called "Paul's Balance Sheet." It is the standard by which he balanced his life, determining its profit or loss. In verse 6 he enumerates all the things that were advantageous to him. Yet he says that whatever was gain to him was loss for the Lord Jesus Christ. As we study our profit and loss sheets for the past year, we find that the things which were gain to us were loss for Christ.

What about our time? For whom do we use it? Is it profit or loss for Christ? Who profits from our money? Our talents? Our friendships? Our possessions? Our pleasures? As we balance these things on the profit and loss sheets of our lives, are they profit or loss for Christ?

Paul's supreme goal in life was to know Christ and to make Him known to others. "[For my determined purpose is] that I may know Him — that I may progressively become more deeply and intimately acquainted with Him, perceiving and recognizing and understanding [the wonders of His Person] more strongly and more clearly" (vs. 10, Amplified). All is loss compared to the priceless privilege of knowing Him and making Him known to others. What are the entries on your ledger sheet — profit or loss for Christ?